The right to life in Japan

Noel Williams

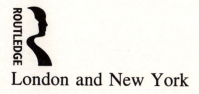

London and New York

First published 1997
by Routledge
11 New Fetter Lane, London EC4P 4EE

Simultaneously published in the USA and Canada
by Routledge
29 West 35th Street, New York, NY 10001

Typeset in Baskerville by
J&L Composition Ltd, Filey, North Yorkshire

Printed and bound in Great Britain by
Redwood Books, Trowbridge, Wiltshire

British Library Cataloguing in Publication Data

A catalogue record for this book is available from the British Library

Library of Congress Cataloging in Publication Data

A catalogue record for this book has been requested

ISBN 0–415–15617–3

Contents

Series editor's preface

we are a people whose glorious history will bear to be held up to the gaze of Western nations. We have learned a great many things from the West, but there are some instances of our having out-stripped our tutors.

So wrote Count Okuma in *Fifty Years of New Japan*, published in 1910, some five years after Japan had emerged victorious in the Russo-Japanese war. Over the 86 years that have elapsed since those words were written, the history of Japan's relations with the rest of the world has passed through phases more turbulent than Okuma could probably have imagined. The tragic and terrible history of the 1930s and 1940s gave way, however, to decades in which the Japanese forged an amazing (and often deserved) reputation for economic development and efficiency. The idea of the Japanese out-stripping their tutors is no longer as exotic as it must have sounded to an English-speaking readership in 1910, but its content has been radically changed with the passage of time. At the same time, Japan's performance and practice continues to attract withering scepticism from some Americans and others. In a recent message on the Internet, Chalmers Johnson attacks 'Chrysanthemum Clubbers' and writes that one of his interlocutors '. . . seems not to know that Japan has basked in the favorable and exceptional treatment of the United States from John Foster Dulles's peace treaty to Mickey Kantor's last minute dive last summer in the auto talks'. How the Japanese seek to resolve the dilemma of how far they can preserve a distinctive Japanese identity and practice in an increasingly globalizing world is fascinating to watch.

The Nissan Institute/Routledge Japanese Studies Series is ten years old in 1996. The Series seeks to foster an informed and balanced, but not uncritical, understanding of Japan. One of its aims is to show the depth and variety of Japanese institutions, practices and ideas. Another is, by using comparison, to see what lessons, positive and negative, can be drawn for other countries. The tendency in commentary on Japan to resort to outdated, ill-informed or sensational stereotypes still remains, and needs to be combated.

In Western countries 'right to life' debates in recent years have focused especially on the difficult moral dilemma presented by legalized abortion, where two separate moral values – the 'right' to life of the unborn, and the 'right' of a woman to control her body – have been pitted against each other. It is no doubt a reflection both of value perceptions particular to Western countries and of the power structures operating in those countries that this is largely how debates about the value attributed to human lives have been conducted. In Japan, with a substantially different set of traditions about moral values, and a power structure which is *sui generis* in certain ways, 'right to life' debates have been more broadly based and cover a wider range of issues. Abortion, though a matter of concern, is seen as less central, and capital punishment, the equality of the right to life, the social value of death (including such phenomena as 'apology suicide'), and the problem of *karōshi* (roughly translated as 'death by hard work') are widely discussed in Japanese society. Dr Noel Williams discusses these issues from a legal and constitutional point of view, bringing to bear also a deep understanding both of the character of Japanese society and of the power structures that inform modern and contemporary Japan. He writes with great subtlety and perceptiveness about questions and issues under discussion in Japan, the understanding of which may help Western societies come to grips more effectively with similar issues at home.

J.A.A. Stockwin

Figures and tables

FIGURES

TABLES

Preface

In the study of Japanese history, legal history plays a significant role. As Ishimoda Shō[1] writes, history involves a search for the historical basis of particular legal concepts in any given period. It is important, he argues, to comprehend the historical necessity for the appearance of specific items of law. A legal approach to the analysis of any society offers an opportunity to gain a unique insight into the nature and socio-political values of that society.

This book concerns itself with the right to life under the present Japanese Constitution. The theme of what life is, and has been, in Japanese society is approached from an essentially legal perspective. This study questions the supremacy of the constitutional provision of the right to life *vis-à-vis* other values in Japanese society, and examines the extent to which traditional Japanese values override the sanctity of the individual's right to life.

In an attempt to assess the degree to which Japanese values clash with the Western value of the right to life, we concentrate our attention on areas where both law and practice conflict with the core fundamental right to life. The legal argument as to what life is, and when it begins and ends, together with the infringements of this right within the modern company organization, and by the state, are examined. There arises the subsidiary, but by no means unimportant, issue of the equality of the right to life, which demands attention. All the questions raised lead us to an understanding of how the concept of life itself is perceived in Japan.

During the course of writing this book, which is based on my University of Oxford doctoral thesis, I received help and encouragement from many people. I wish to thank, in particular, my supervisor, Professor J.A.A. Stockwin, Nissan Professor of Modern Japanese Studies at the University of Oxford, and Fellow of St Antony's College, for his continued guidance and support. I am also grateful to Professor Gordon Daniels of Sheffield University, and Dr Ann Waswo, Fellow of St Antony's College, Oxford, for their wise words of advice. I also wish to thank Dr I.J. McMullen, Fellow of Pembroke College, Oxford, for his interest in my research and his warm encouragement; and to those other Fellows at the University of Oxford involved in Japanese Studies who helped me in various ways. I am also grateful to the Daiwa Anglo-Japanese Foundation, and to the Sasakawa Fund, for their financial support. Finally, I wish to thank all at Routledge involved in bringing this work into print.

Noel Williams,
Daitō Bunka University,
Tokyo

Conventions

The following conventions have been observed:

1 Japanese names are written in the original order, with the surname first and the personal name second.
2 Long vowel sounds in Japanese words and names have been indicated with a macron. I have omitted the macrons in place-names, except where they appear as places of publication in Japanese books.
3 The following abbreviations are used:

(a) *Minshū*: *Daishinin minji hanreishū* (A Collection of the Judgments of Civil Cases of the Great Court of Judicature); *Saikō saibansho minji hanreishū* (A Collection of the Judgments of Civil Cases of the Supreme Court).

(b) *Keishū*: *Daishinin keiji hanreishū* (A Collection of the Judgments of Criminal Cases of the Great Court of Judicature); *Saikō saibansho keiji hanreishū* (A Collection of the Judgments of Criminal Cases of the Supreme Court).

(c) *Gyōreishū*: *Gyōseijiken saiban reishū* (A Collection of the Judgments of Cases on Administrative Law).

(d) *Rōhan*: *Rōdō hanrei* (Judgments of Cases on Labour Law).

1 Introduction

In 1947,[1] the right to life (*seimei*), along with other fundamental rights, was bestowed upon the Japanese people by the Japanese Constitution. Article 13 states:

> All of the people shall be respected as individuals. Their right to life, liberty, and the pursuit of happiness shall, to the extent that it does not interfere with the public welfare, be the supreme consideration in legislation and in other governmental affairs.

The provision confers on the individual for the first time in the history of the Japanese nation the right to life. With the promulgation of the Constitution, the individual became the possessor of a multitude of freedoms and rights,[2] including the right to life, which contemporary Western societies deem an essential building-block of civilized society.

Article 13 identifies three constituent elements of the right to life. First, the Japanese[3] possess this right as individuals. Second, it is limited by the public welfare. Third, where it does not interfere with the public welfare, it attains supremacy over other matters.

Two main questions arise from these elements so identified, and will be the focus of attention in this book. First, has the sanctity of the right to life supremacy over other values? As Japan has the cultural tradition of acknowledging sacrifice as a moral value and of appreciating idealized ways of death, the extent to which the modern Japanese Constitution recognizes the sanctity of the right to life becomes a fundamental question to be answered in this study. How far have the traditional Japanese values given way to the constitutional provision on the right to life? We will see during the course of the study how foreign concepts of the right to life have been received and assimilated into the right to life in Japan.

At the heart of the question of the sanctity of the right to life is the concept of limitation on rights. This is not, of course, a uniquely Japanese phenomenon. This is a common feature of the instruments of international law. In the 1946 United Nations Universal Declaration of Human Rights, for example, we find that, although article 3 provides that 'Everyone has the right to life, liberty and security of persons', the Declaration notes limitations on these and the other fundamental rights listed therein. Article 29 states:

1 Everyone has duties to the community in which alone the free and full development of his personality is possible.
2 In the exercise of his rights and freedoms, everyone shall be subject to such limitations as are determined by law solely for the purpose of securing due recognition and respect for the rights and freedoms of others and of meeting the just requirements of morality, public order and the general welfare in a democratic society.

Likewise, the European Convention on Human Rights of 1950 provides limitations on *inter alia* the right to life. By article 2:

1 Everyone's right to life shall be protected by law. No one shall be deprived of his life intentionally save in the execution of a sentence of a court following his conviction of a crime for which this penalty is provided by law.
2 Deprivation of life shall not be regarded as inflicted in contravention of this Article when it results from the use of force which is no more than absolutely necessary:
    (a) in defence of any person from unlawful violence;
    (b) in order to effect a lawful arrest or to prevent the escape of a person lawfully detained;
    (c) in action lawfully taken for the purpose of quelling a riot or insurrection.

The Japanese Constitution employs the abstract term '*kōkyō no fukushi*' (the public welfare) to denote limitations on fundamental human rights. This has raised the question of what the public welfare is under the Constitution, and in what instances the public welfare denies human rights. In this book we look at instances where the public welfare limitation overrides the constitutional provision on the right to life, and examine the reasons for this.

The second question which the book raises is this: do all individuals possess an equal right to life? On the question of equality under the law, article 14 of the Constitution states:

> All of the people are equal under the law and there shall be no
> discrimination in political, economic or social relations because of
> race, creed, sex, social status or family origin.

Does this principle of equality under the law apply in respect of the
right to life? This question arises from the fact that, previous to the
promulgation of the present Constitution, the idea of individuals
being the recipients of equal rights never existed in Japanese law.

Theories of natural rights, which have as their basis the belief that
people already possess rights equally when they are born, flourished
in the works of such early philosophers as Marcus Tullius Cicero
(106–43 BC), St Augustine (354–430), and Thomas Aquinas (1225–
74), and in the works of the English liberals Thomas Hobbes (1588–
1679) and John Locke (1632–1704), and the French thinker Jean-
Jacques Rousseau (1712–78),[4] but did not find fertile ground in Japan
easily.

Natural rights theories were introduced into Japan at the beginning
of the Meiji period (1868–1912) by liberal thinkers, and the doctrine
was translated into Japanese as '*tenpu jinken setsu*' (theory of hea-
ven-given human rights).[5] In the years 1880 and 1881, with the rise of
the movement for democratic rights, the doctrine was used as a base
for the theory that sovereignty rested with the people. However, with
the promulgation in 1889 of the *Dai Nippon Teikoku Kenpō* (The
Constitution of Great Imperial Japan) – commonly referred to as the
Meiji Constitution[6] – this doctrine was dropped from legal thought.
Against this background, the operation of the principle of equality
under the law enunciated in the present Constitution demands
examination.

Rights of 'living' conferred under the present Constitution have
largely been studied and discussed in relation to article 25. This
article concerns itself with *seizonken* (the right to continue one's
existence). Under this article, in contrast to the right to life found
in article 13, the individual is guaranteed a quality of life. Article 25
notes:

> All people shall have the right to maintain the minimum standards
> of wholesome and cultured living. In all spheres of life, the state
> shall use its endeavours for the promotion and extension of social
> welfare and security, and of public health.

The concept of the quality of life, which is found first in law in the
Weimar Constitution of 1919, became a common principle of
twentieth-century constitutions. Although the idea only appeared in

Japanese law with the promulgation of the present Constitution, it had already been introduced into Japan through the writings of scholars in the 1920s.[7]

Since 1947, two stages in the development of the discussion on *seizonken* in Japan can be identified. The first stage was the immediate post-war discussion which emphasized *seizonken* within the context of the Japanese economy, and was the direct result of the economic crisis which had beset the country in the aftermath of the war. The second, which focused on comfortable living conditions, took place with Japan's recovery from her post-war difficulties and the rebuilding of her economy.[8]

In contrast to *seizonken*, the right to life is the right to live, infringement of which affects the very essence of man's existence, denying him his most priceless and treasured possession – his life. With the inclusion of the right to life in the present Constitution, the guaranteeing of this right in practice has become of primary importance to individuals. We examine the operation of this right, bringing into the discussion the questions posed earlier, and focusing attention on those areas where an individual's right to life has, arguably, been infringed. We concentrate in this book on the individual.

To begin our examination we attempt, in Chapter 2, to understand the historical background to the Constitution. We examine two issues in particular: first, what law has been in Japan; second, how rights have been expressed in the Japanese context.

In order to understand what the right to life in Japan means, we examine, in Chapter 3, the question of what life is in contemporary Japan, and look at several problematic issues which have arisen in respect of the beginning and end of life.

Chapter 4 deals with the essential question raised at the beginning of this chapter; namely, whether the right to life is bestowed equally upon all individuals. We examine whether instances of inequality find expression in law, and ask why this has been made possible.

In Chapter 5 we examine the contemporary phenomenon of the infringement of the right to life within the structure of a 'modern' organization – the company. We examine the conflict between company values and the individual's right to life within the organization.

In the final chapter we bring to the discussion an understanding of the social and cultural significance attached to the issues raised in the body of this book.

2 Law and rights in Japan

The history of the present Constitution begins with Japan's acceptance of the Potsdam Declaration of 26 July 1945, which defined the terms for Japanese surrender to end the Second World War.[1] The present Constitution incorporates the demands of democracy and freedom of the individual contained in the Declaration. Article 10 demanded that:

> The Japanese government shall remove all obstacles to the revival and strengthening of democratic tendencies among the Japanese people. Freedom of speech, of religion, and of thought, as well as respect for the fundamental human rights shall be established.

This was not the first time, however, for the Japanese to have been brought face to face with the Western concepts of freedom and rights, for the early years of the Meiji period had brought with them an increasing recognition of the rights of the Japanese subject. The introduction of the new concept of rights necessitated the invention of a new Japanese term. Mitsukuri Rinshō employed the term *kenri* (comprising the two characters 'might' and 'reasoning') in his translation of the French Penal Code to express the notion of *droit subjectif*. Mitsukuri did not invent the word himself, however, but took it from a Chinese translation of an international law text published in the early 1860s.[2]

In an attempt to explain the term *kenri*,[3] Fukuzawa Yukichi (1834–1901) stressed that, despite the unfortunate connotation of the two characters which made up the settled Japanese translation of rights (they being inappropriate as the character for *ken* implied 'might' and *ri* suggested vulgar 'profit'[4]), the term *kenri* itself stood for a concept which gave to the people – irrespective of their social status – an equal right to the protection of their lives, property and honour. In Fukuzawa's words: 'Men have a right to preserve their property, life and honour – rights which may not be infringed in the least without due reason.'[5]

Rights, in Fukuzawa's mind, were bestowed upon the people and protected by the state against illegitimate infringement, for:

> the individual alone is not strong enough to protect his rights in a society where good and evil are so intermingled in human character and behaviour. It is for this reason that governments are set up to protect people's rights.

Here we find the advanced idea that the purpose of the state is to protect people's rights, a notion he derived from Western liberalism and enlightenment.[6]

The Meiji period was a time which witnessed the assimilation of new, foreign ideas. In order to put these ideas into practice it was necessary to reform the legal system. So as to understand the historical background to the dilemmas concerning the right to life which we examine in this book, let us briefly look at the legal history of Japan prior to the Meiji period.

The history of the Japanese legal system prior to Meiji can be divided into three distinct periods.[7] First, the native law period, which existed before the Chinese legal system had exerted its influence on the early Japanese legal system. Elements of this native legal system can be found in the historical texts of the *Kojiki* (Records of Ancient Matters)[8] and the *Nihon shoki* (Chronicles of Japan),[9] and in the *Norito* (Purification Prayers) section of the *Engishiki* (Procedures of the Engi Era)[10] legal text. The concepts of *amatsutsumi* (heavenly offences)[11] and *kunitsutsumi* (earthly offences)[12] are examples of such elements.

The second period was that of the adoption of the Chinese *lü-ling* (Japanese, *ritsuryō*) legal Codes. This period arguably lasted from the Taika Reform[13] of 645 until the formation of the Kamakura *bakufu* (feudal government) (1192–1333). At the beginning of this period the state adopted the *lü-ling* legal system of China, drew up its own *ritsuryō* Codes,[14] and established a state patterned after this system. The *ritsuryō* functioned as a base upon which to operate the centralized government. Whilst the *ryō* ordinances regulated the administration of the government, the *ritsu* law established the system of criminal law.

The third period, which lasted some seven hundred years, and which was characterized by the rule of the feudal Houses, was one in which various laws coexisted. From a legal point of view, this period can itself be subdivided into three phases.

The first period was that between the formation of the Kamakura *bakufu* in 1192 and Ōnin no ran (The Civil War of Ōnin) (1467–77).[15] By the end of the Heian period (794–1191) – the period of the rule of the Court and the *kuge* (Court nobles) class – members of the warrior class had already been appointed to the position of *kebiishi* (a combination of policeman and judicial officer) due to their skill in apprehending criminals swiftly and for having demonstrated the ability to keep order in society.[16]

Under the *ritsuryō* system, discrepancy between the Chinese-originated *ritsuryō* Codes and the reality of Japanese society brought with it the practice of customary law. This customary law became the primary law when the warrior class came to attain power. The *Jōei shikimoku* (the laws compiled in the first year of the Jōei period),[17] compiled in 1232 at the command of Shōgun Hōjo Yasutoki (1183–1242), is an example of a collection of laws additional to the customary law. Generally speaking, matters were judged in accordance with customary law, and new laws were made when neither the *ritsuryō* nor the customary law could be applied.

The second phase was characterized by the rule of the feudal Houses during the so-called Sengoku period (1467–c.1567).[18] During this period of civil war, the whole of Japan was divided into territories under the rule of regional feudal lords. Laws were made and enforced by the individual feudal rulers of the various regions.[19] These laws, reflecting the period, have as their essence a simple trial and severe punishment, and include provisions relating to spies and cliques.

The third phase was characterized by the laws of the Tokugawa era (1600–1868). Whilst the laws of the first half of this period were modelled on the *Jōei shikimoku*, the law of the second half was case-law.[20]

Rights, prior to Meiji, can be categorized under *mibunhō* ('class' or 'status' law). The legal scholar Takikawa Masajirō[21] has divided *jinkenhō* (the rights of persons) in Japanese legal history into *mibunhō* and *nōryokuhō* ('attribute' law). Whereas the former defined rights attached to status, the latter classed people according to their 'attributes'. People's 'attributes' were determined in the *ritsuryō* according to such factors as sex, age and health, and allowances and duties decided accordingly.[22]

Rights thus corresponded to class. Of the 'right' to life, we can note that the lives of individuals were never treated as having equal value, and the protection of this 'right' differed greatly according to class.

With the downfall of the Tokugawa regime and the restoration of Imperial rule in 1868, Japanese legal history entered a new phase with the introduction of Western legal ideas. From the perspective of legal history, the period following the Meiji Restoration is characterized by a mixture of laws: both the revival of early Japanese law, and the assimilation of the new Western concepts of freedom and rights. Let us look briefly at both of these.

With the restoration of Imperial rule, the Meiji government took as models for its law the early Japanese *ritsuryō* and the more modern Ming (1368–1644) and Ch'ing (1644–1911) Chinese systems. This law remained in force until the government compiled new laws derived from Western legal systems. As the Meiji government sought to model its legal system on the *ritsuryō*, the contemporary legal codes inherited the essence of the *ritsuryō* Codes, particularly those areas concerned with moral values.

The early part of the Meiji period witnessed a reaction against the rulers of the feudal Houses by restoring both the administration system and laws of the *ritsuryō*. In the administrative field, the Meiji government readopted the *dajōkan* system in May 1869, the structure of which consisted of the *jingikan* (Office of Divinities) and *dajōkan* (Great Council of State), under which were six ministries.[23]

In the field of written law, the revival of the *ritsuryō* can be observed in the laws compiled in the early Meiji period. Prior to the compilation of the new laws, the Meiji government had used the *Kujikata osadamegaki* (Provisions Governing Public Matters) from the Tokugawa period for a short while. This changed with the compilation of the *Shinritsu kōryō* (The Essence of the New Code),[24] based on the *ritsuryō*, in 1870, and, together with its amendment, the *Kaitei ritsurei* (The Statutes as Amended) of 1873, it continued in operation for some ten years until the *Kyū keihō* (Old Penal Code)[25] came into effect.

The assimilation of the new concepts of freedom and rights began with the compilation and promulgation of the *Kyū keihō* in 1880, which was drafted by the French jurist, Émile Gustave Boissonade de Fontarbie (1825–1910), and was strongly influenced by the French Penal Code.[26] Such assimilation, in accordance with the disciplines of the legal systems of certain European countries – particularly of France and Germany – is believed to have resulted from the eagerness of the government to amend the unequal treaties between Japan and foreign countries.[27] Showing to the West that Japan had a modern legal system comparable to those of Western countries was crucial to the government's attempts to have Japan recognized as a modern nation. Efforts were thus made to build a modern, Westernized legal system. Various laws, such as the *Minpō* (Civil Code), the

Shōhō (Commercial Code), as well as the *Keihō* (Penal Code) were drafted by Boissonade de Fontarbie and by the German academic Hermann Roesler (1834–94),[28] who also contributed to the drafting of the Meiji Constitution.

The Meiji Constitution, which was greatly influenced by the Prussian Constitution, gave recognition to the rights of the Japanese 'subjects', protected by law, for the first time in their history. According to the Preamble to the Constitution:

> We now declare that We will respect and protect the security of the rights and of the property of Our people, and to secure to them the complete enjoyment of the same.

The rights of the Japanese subject are listed in Chapter 2 of the Constitution, and are listed in Table 2.1.

All these rights so recognized by the Meiji Constitution were granted to Japanese subjects conditional upon their withdrawal by the Emperor's special ordinance powers 'in times of war or cases of national emergency'.[29] The Meiji statesman Itō Hirobumi defended this limitation on rights:

> It must be remembered that the ultimate aim of the State is to maintain its existence . . . in times of danger the State will have to sacrifice, without hesitation, part of the law and of the rights of the subjects, in order to attain its ultimate end.[30]

Although the protection of the subject's right to life appears in the *Nippon kokkenan* (Draft Constitution of Japan),[31] and was one of the principles cherished by Itō,[32] we can observe from reading the list of rights in Table 2.1 that the provision relating specifically to the protection of the life of the Japanese subject is, however, absent from the Constitution.

Rights – excluding the right to life – were bestowed upon the subject at the Emperor's will. It was the ability of the sovereign to ordain the Constitution of his own will which led the legal scholar Hozumi Yatsuka (1860–1912) to classify it as an authorized Constitution, as opposed to a national-contract Constitution.[33]

The Meiji Constitution was still, strictly speaking, in force following Japan's defeat in the Second World War, and there was felt a need by the Allied Powers to maintain continuity between it and the 1947 Constitution. Whilst some academics view the introduction of the latter as an amendment to the Meiji Constitution through the process provided in article 73, others view it, rather, in terms of a 'legal revolution' brought about by Japan's surrender.[34]

Table 2.1 The rights of Japanese subjects under the Meiji Constitution

Article	Right	Limitation
22	Liberty of abode and of changing the same	Within the limits of the law
28	Freedom of religious belief	Within limits not prejudicial to peace and order, and not antagonistic to their duties as subjects
29	Liberty of speech, writing, publication, public meetings and associations	Within the limits of the law
26	The secrecy of the letters of every Japanese subject shall remain inviolate	Except in the cases mentioned in the law
27	The right of property of every Japanese subject shall remain inviolate	Measures necessary to be taken for the public benefit shall be provided for by law
19	Japanese subjects may be appointed to civil or military or any other public offices equally	According to qualifications determined in laws or ordinances
23	No Japanese subject shall be arrested, detained, tried or punished	Unless according to law
24	No Japanese subject shall be deprived of his right of being tried by the judges	Determined by law
30	Japanese subjects may present petitions	(By observing the proper forms of respect, and by complying with the rules specially provided for the same)

The 1947 Constitution can be considered new in the sense that it introduced both Western principles (such as equality under the law) and new rights and freedoms (such as the right to life) to Japan's fundamental law. The rights of the Japanese people are to be found in the thirty-one articles which form Chapter 3 of the Constitution. They can be divided into the broad categories listed in Table 2.2.

Although the term 'rule of law' does not appear in the 1947 Constitution, Japan's fundamental law has, to quote Takayanagi Kenzō, 'very powerfully adopted the principle'.[35] The individual's rights are protected through the rule of law both by guarantees against arbitrary exercise of governmental power and by judicial review of legislation. Thus no law which endangers individual freedoms and rights is to have legal force. It is left to the Supreme Court, in which

Table 2.2 The rights and freedoms of the Japanese people under the 1947 Constitution

Article	Right	Limitation
13	Right to life, liberty, and the pursuit of happiness	Public welfare
14	Equality under the law	
15	Rights regarding elections and voting	
18	Right not to be held in bondage of any kind	Except as punishment for crime

Freedoms of thought and expression:

19	Freedom of thought and conscience	
20	Freedom of religion	
21	Freedom of assembly and association	
	Freedom of speech	
	Freedom of the press	
	Freedom of all other forms of expression	
22(2)	Freedom to move to a foreign country	
	Freedom to divest oneself of Japanese nationality	
23	Academic freedom	
24	Rights relating to marriage	

Socio-economic rights:

22	Freedom to choose and change residence	Public welfare
	Freedom to choose occupation	Public welfare
25	Right to maintain minimum standards of wholesome and cultured living	
26	Right to education	
27	Right to work	
28	Right of workers to organize and bargain and act collectively	
29	Property rights	Public welfare
16–17 31–40	Civil/criminal procedural rights	

judicial power is vested, to determine the constitutionality of any law, order, regulation or official act.[36]

The rule of law protects all the freedoms and rights conferred by the Constitution, and is not restricted to any particular class, or category, of rights. Thus one's right to life, for example, is guaranteed and protected by the very same mechanisms[37] that protect, let us say, one's freedom of expression.[38]

The Japanese Constitution protects those freedoms and rights which are explicitly laid out in Chapter 3. Other rights, in addition, have been added to this list by the courts. Of note is the right to privacy, the constitutional basis for which derives from article 13, whereby 'all the people shall be respected as individuals'.[39]

Japan's acceptance and incorporation of the 'fundamental human rights' in the present Constitution can be understood in terms of duty, or sacrifice – in this case, sacrifice for the good of the nation. Having never fought for such rights as the right to life, the Japanese people's consciousness was – and still remains to a large extent – one of duty consciousness.[40]

Duty plays a conspicuous role in the present Constitution. The inclusion of duties in the 1947 Constitution was instigated at the request of the Japanese themselves.[41] As under the Meiji Constitution,[42] the present Constitution imposes duties on the Japanese people. These are clearly set out in Chapter 3 of the Constitution, and are four in number.[43] The specific duties laid down in the Constitution are the duties to work;[44] to provide education for minors under one's protection;[45] to ensure children are not exploited;[46] and, on spouses, to ensure that 'marriage shall be based only on the mutual consent of both sexes and it shall be maintained through mutual cooperation with the equal rights of husband and wife as a basis'.[47] The Constitution also imposes the duty to pay taxes as provided by law.[48]

In addition to these specific duties, the Constitution imposes the general duty to maintain the freedoms and rights guaranteed by it. These: [49]

> shall be maintained by the constant endeavour of the people, who shall refrain from any abuse of these freedoms and rights and shall always be responsible for utilizing them for the public welfare.

The Japanese attach importance to duties. This can be seen, for example, in the Commission on the Constitution's Final Report, where much discussion is found relating to the 'uneven' emphasis on rights to the detriment of duties. In order to strengthen public duties based on social solidarity, it was suggested by some members that new duties should be created which could be included in the Constitution. These include the duty to observe both the law and the Constitution, the duty to defend the nation, and the duty of faithfulness and loyalty to Japan.[50]

The Chairman of the Commission, Takayanagi Kenzō, on the other hand, along with other members, sought to justify the emphasis on rights over duties on the basis that the Constitution places great stress on the spirit of the rule of law, and that such emphasis was necessary to prevent the abuse of political power by the authorities under liberal democratic constitutions. To introduce additional duties in the Constitution, he argued, would weaken the rule of law, and thus threaten liberal democracy itself.[51]

On a less theoretical level, some members opposed the inclusion of the duty of loyalty to Japan on the grounds that it might not only endanger the guarantee of rights and lead to a weakening of democracy, but also that such a duty might encompass military service. Concerning the demand for specifying the duty to observe both the law and Constitution, some members expressed the opinion that such a duty was prior to the Constitution, and thus did not need to be expressly incorporated into it.[52]

The majority of the members, however, perceived as problematic the present emphasis on rights on the ground that it seemed contrary to the principles of the welfare state, and sought revisions to bring it into line with the contemporary concept of the welfare state concerned with the attainment of the well-being of its people. The concept of the liberal state, with its focus on the rights of the individual, was outdated, and should be replaced by an emphasis on social duties, solidarity, and the co-operation of the people, in addition to the protection of human rights.[53]

The 'fundamental human rights'[54] conferred by the Constitution have relative, not absolute value.[55] They are limited by what the courts deem it appropriate to allow the individual. Rights are limited by what is termed in the Constitution *kōkyō no fukushi* (the 'public welfare'), which is defined by the courts. In the same way as limitations on the exercise of human rights for some larger national or public benefit are common in the instruments of international law, so too limitations exist under the Japanese Constitution, and shelter under the all-embracing umbrella of the 'public welfare'. The concept is one of the fundamental concepts of the Constitution.

Explicit references in the Constitution to the public welfare, as we saw from Table 2.2,[56] are few in number. Article 12 stresses that human rights are to be utilized 'for the public welfare'. The emphasis on the public welfare is again made clear in article 13. Two articles refer to the limitation in relation to specific rights. By article 22, the freedom to choose and change one's residence, and to choose one's occupation, is limited by public welfare considerations. By article 29, similarly, although 'the right to own or to hold property is inviolable', property rights are to be defined by law 'in conformity with the public welfare'.

Thus, at first glance, a seemingly contradictory state of affairs exists between, on the one hand, those references to the public welfare in the Constitution which, reductively, amount to the public welfare being in a position of 'supreme consideration'[57] and, on the other hand, the guarantee that the people are 'not . . . prevented from enjoying any of the fundamental human rights',[58] which places the enjoyment of human rights as the supreme constitutional value. The position would seem to be this: that the state should respect fundamental human rights to the greatest possible extent, except where the exercise of such rights is in some way harmful to the public welfare.[59]

The Constitutional law specialist Ashibe Nobuyoshi has perceived the public welfare doctrine in the following terms:

> I consider 'the public welfare' a principle of restraint of necessity inhering in all human rights in order to fairly guarantee human rights to each person, and maintain the necessity of establishing criteria for concrete standards for restraint, constructing a case law theory based on the 'double standards' theory of the United States.[60]

Following articles 12 and 13, the courts have adopted the view that the fundamental human rights conferred on the individual are subject to the public welfare determined by judicial review.[61] The public welfare has been invoked to restrict not only those human rights where explicit reference to the public welfare is made in the Constitution, but also other areas of rights where no such reference is made. Whether or not the limitation will, or should, be employed to cover all the rights and freedoms conferred by the Constitution is a moot point.[62]

Thus the constitutional basis of the public welfare concept, together with its interpretation by the courts, in effect limits the scope of the fundamental human rights. Although existing under the Constitution, 'rights' so conferred often lack, in practice, a legal basis. Although in the 1947 Constitution the term 'fundamental human rights' is used, these differ sharply from those fundamental human rights which all human beings possess as natural rights by virtue of being human. The legal academic John Finnis observes that the term 'human rights' is a contemporary idiom for 'natural rights', and he uses both synonymously.[63] However, the reality of the situation in Japan is that the appropriate authority can take away such rights from the individual in the name of the public welfare.[64]

Let us now turn our attention to examining specific areas relating to the right to life. The areas chosen illustrate situations where the societal unit one belongs to directly, or indirectly, endangers the life of the individual.

3 Aspects of the boundaries of life

Life is afforded respect by the constitutional provision on the right to life. What constitutes life which is afforded this respect? When does it begin, and when does it end?

The scope of the constitutional provision of article 13 extends from *shussei* (birth) to *shi* (death). Within these two boundaries of life, the individual's right to life is protected by the Constitution.

In Japanese law, individuals acquire private rights at birth. We read in the Civil Code of 1896 that 'the enjoyment of private rights commences at birth'.[1] Similarly, the enjoyment of constitutional rights – including the right to life, as we see in this chapter – arguably commences at birth.[2] Whether the *taiji* ('the child inside the mother's womb') has a right to life can be looked at in our discussion. The term *taiji*, as does the term 'unborn child' in English, includes all the stages of its development from conception to birth.[3]

As the constitutional provision of article 13 arguably only protects the life of the born child, it is necessary to determine what constitutes birth. When does birth take place in law? This problem has been resolved in different ways by different societies. At least four definitions of birth can be identified. These are:

1 Birth takes place with the commencement of labour pains while the foetus is inside the mother's body.
2 Birth takes place with the complete delivery of the baby, involving the whole of the baby's body being outside the mother's womb.[4]
3 Birth is defined as the process involving the emergence of the young from the body of the mother, which is completed only when the baby has become totally independent of the mother for the purpose of breathing, it being able to breathe by means of its own lungs.[5]

4 Birth takes place with the partial delivery of the baby, involving part of the baby's body being outside the mother's body.

When is birth deemed to take place in Japanese law? The Japanese courts have adopted the fourth approach – namely, that partial delivery constitutes birth. In 1919, the *Daishinin* (Great Court of Judicature) was required to decide whether or not the *hikokunin* (accused), who had terminated the life of a partially delivered baby by pressing its face until it died, should be convicted of the crime of *satsujinzai* (murder).[6] The question which confronted the Court was whether the partially delivered baby should be considered a *hito* (human being) or not. The Court held that it should.[7]

As soon as partial delivery has taken place, the newly born baby receives the full protection of the law. It is legally protected in the same way as is any other individual. Thus in a 1989 case, for example, which involved an unsuccessful attempt at aborting a 26-week foetus, the gynaecologist was charged with deserting the baby, causing its death, contrary to article 218[8] of the 1907 Penal Code. He had allowed the newly born baby to die by omitting to give it proper and appropriate medical treatment which would have enabled it to continue living.[9]

This can be understood as reflecting the traditional viewpoint on life in Japan. It is noticeable that there has been a tendency in traditional Japanese society to perceive life as part of a continuous circle. The unborn baby was viewed as one who did not have the destiny to come into the world at that particular moment in time. It was accepted that it was the unborn baby's fate not to be born at that time. Thus the baby who does come into this world is acknowledged as a new life.

In contemporary Japanese law, the position of the *hito* can be contrasted with that of the *taiji*. Whereas the *hito* enjoys the full protection which can be provided by the law, the life-potential of the *taiji* receives much less protection. Unlike the *hito*, the *taiji* enjoys no legal right to life under the Constitution. Let us examine the protection given to the unborn child in Japanese society.

The state has, historically, attempted to protect the life-potential of the *taiji* through the legislative machinery. Continuing the position under the 1880 Penal Code, the Penal Code of 1907 – still in force – laid down provisions relating to *dataizai* (crimes of abortion). These crimes relate to the removal of the *taiji* from the mother's body artificially, and to the 'killing' of the *taiji* inside the mother's body, prior to natural birth. The crimes of *dataizai* thus result in the termination of the life-potential of the unborn child, unrecognized as a *hito* in law. The crime of *satsujinzai*, with which the 1919 case noted above concerned itself, was a more serious crime because it involved the killing of a partially delivered baby – a *hito* in law. Thus in this case, the accused was charged with *satsujinzai*, not *dataizai*.

The crimes of *dataizai* are found in articles 212–16 of the 1907 Penal Code (see Table 3.1). The Penal Code categorizes *dataizai* into four types of crime. These are:

1 Self-induced abortion.
2 Abortion performed by non-professionals.
3 Abortion performed by professionals.
4 Abortion performed without the consent of the woman.

In respect of self-induced abortion, article 212 provides that 'when a pregnant woman causes a miscarriage by the use of drugs or other means' she is to be punished by up to a maximum period of one year's imprisonment.

As regards abortion performed by non-professionals, article 213 provides that 'a person who, at the request of a woman or with her consent, causes her miscarriage' is to be punished by up to a maximum

Table 3.1 The *dataizai* provisions of the 1907 Penal Code

Article	Crime	Who is punished	Maximum punishment
212	Self-induced abortion	Woman	1 year
213	Abortion performed by non-professionals	Person performing the abortion	2 years
	Abortion performed by non-professionals resulting in death or injury	Person performing the abortion	5 years
214	Abortion performed by professionals	Person performing the abortion	5 years
	Abortion performed by professionals resulting in death or injury	Person performing the abortion	7 years
215	Abortion performed without the consent of the woman	Person performing the abortion	7 years
216	Abortion performed without the consent of the woman resulting in bodily injury or death	Person performing the abortion	Life

period of two years' imprisonment. Where death or bodily injury results from the abortion, a maximum penalty of five years' and a minimum penalty of three months' imprisonment are imposed.

Article 214 concerns itself with abortion performed by professionals, with the woman's consent. Where the person who performs the abortion is a professional, being either a 'doctor, midwife, pharmacist, or druggist', more severe punishment is imposed than in the case of abortions performed by non-professionals. A maximum penalty of five years' and a minimum penalty of six months' imprisonment are imposed. Where death or physical injury befalls the woman following her abortion, a maximum penalty of seven years' and a minimum penalty of six months' imprisonment are imposed.

Article 215 concerns itself with abortion performed 'not at the request of a woman or without her consent'. The article imposes a maximum penalty of seven years' and a minimum period of six months' imprisonment for this crime. Where death or physical injury results from an abortion which has not received the woman's consent, the person is to be subjected to the punishment for the crimes of bodily injury laid down in Chapter 27 of the Penal Code, 'if they be graver'.[10]

Despite the aborticide provisions of the 1907 Penal Code, legislation passed subsequently has gradually eaten away at the protection afforded the life-potential of the *taiji*. In doing so, it has allowed various categories of individuals, under given circumstances, to control the fate of the *taiji*.

The year 1948 saw the first move towards loosening the strict protection given to the life-potential of the unborn child. The 1948 *Yūsei hogohō* (Eugenic Protection Law), with its 1949 revision – now the Protection of the Mother Law – introduced provisions allowing for legalized abortion in certain circumstances.

Some authors claim that the introduction of both pieces of legislation was the result of an intention on the part of the government of the day to avoid social disequilibrium by controlling the rate of population growth in the immediate post-war period – the result both of a 'baby boom'[11] and the repatriation of Japanese from territories acquired by Japan during the 1930s.[12] The harsh economic climate, with its scarcity of food and housing, necessitated restriction on population growth.

The 1948 and 1949 legislation permit *jinkō ninshin chūzetsu* (the artificial termination of pregnancy) on one of the following five grounds:

1 physical condition of the child's parent;
2 physical condition of a parent's relatives (to the fourth degree);
3 leprosy;
4 where pregnancy disturbs the mother's health physically or economically;
5 where pregnancy was the result of violence or threat.

The rationale behind permitting abortion on the ground of health
was to protect the life and health of the mother, where the continuation of pregnancy endangers the mother's safety. Here we see the
predominance of the right to life of the mother over the 'right to life'
of the unborn child.

Abortion is permitted on genetic grounds where it has been ascer-
tained that the unborn child carries a genetic disease which will either
mentally or physically affect the child.

Abortion on economic grounds is available where the birth of the child
or the continuation of pregnancy endangers the mother's subsistence.

The rationale behind permitting abortion on the final ground –
moral – is to protect the mother's honour. Thus abortion becomes
available when the mother becomes pregnant as a result of violence
or threat, i.e. rape.

In the 1949 law, no indication is given as to what constitutes
economic grounds for terminating pregnancy. These are to be
found in a 1953 Circular from the Permanent Deputy-Minister.
These are:

1 Where one is eligible to receive welfare benefits.
2 Where the pregnant woman is the main income earner in the
   family.
3 Where 'birth or continuation of the pregnancy would qualify the
   family for welfare status'.[13]

In practice, however, such criteria are not adhered to, and the effect
of the inclusion of the economic aspect in the 1949 legislation has
been to allow the woman easier access to abortion. A 1969 survey, for
example, found that 99 per cent of those surveyed did not qualify
under the criteria laid down in the 1953 Circular.[14]

The available statistics appear to bear out the frequent claims that
Japan has such 'easy' access to abortion, although the number of
those seeking abortions in recent years has decreased since the early
1960s, when demand was greatest.[15]

The argument that boundaries other than birth should be adopted to
denote the beginning of life has been advocated in many quarters,

both in Japan and elsewhere. Thus, for example, in the Glover Report on Reproductive Technologies to the European Commission of 1989, the following five possible boundaries – in addition to birth – were suggested: [16]

1 Conception.
2 Nidation, or implantation (which takes place at about 10 days after conception).
3 The formation of the 'primitive streak'[17] (which takes place at about 15 days after conception).
4 Consciousness.[18]
5 Viability (the point where the unborn child could survive outside the womb).

Those who support the adoption of the first of these boundaries – conception – to denote life base their claim that human beings exist so early in pregnancy on an awareness that that which is developing inside the mother's womb is developing into a fully formed human being.

Much of the advocacy in Japan against abortion is generated from the non-traditional religious sector of society. Japanese Christians, and *Seichō no ie* (the House of Growth)[19] are illustrative of such groups. Whilst the mainstream Protestant traditions show sensitivity to the decision-taking and the circumstances surrounding abortion, the Catholic traditions, whilst placing emphasis on the unborn child, demonstrate an understanding of the difficulties encountered by the woman and her family.

Even when the anti-abortion stance is not generated for religious reasons, the destruction of life is often seen as being morally repugnant, for the life-form existing in the mother's womb is certain to become a human being.

The objection to what the Glover Report terms the 'full strength'[20] right to life argument – that the unborn child acquires this right at conception – has been succinctly put by it. Referring in particular to the embryo, it notes:

> An embryo is in a certain sense a 'human being', but deriving a right to life from this is problematic. The morally relevant features which support a right to life in a developed person (consciousness, the desire not to die) are not present in the embryo ... It is implausible that embryos have a full strength right to life. The convincing and unproblematic arguments which would be needed to support the claim have not yet appeared.[21]

The arguments raised in the Japanese context, as well, have not confronted these questions.

Acknowledging the difficulties which confront the 'full strength' right to life argument, some authors have put forward the suggestion that the boundary of life should be located at a later stage in the development of the unborn child.

Representative of doctors who tend towards this point of view was the gynaecologist Kikuta Noboru.[22] He argued for the criminalization of abortion during the second trimester of pregnancy. This, he argued, would protect not only the life-potential of the developing unborn child but also the mother's health.

Japanese law adheres to the fifth boundary mentioned in the Glover Report, namely viability. It recognizes that the unborn child has a life-potential which should be respected, prohibiting abortion as a general rule once the *taiji* has become viable. Technological developments over the years have resulted in the unborn child attaining viability at increasingly earlier stages in its development. Amendments to the law have been made to keep up with these developments. These are listed in Table 3.2.

The 1990 Order came into effect on 1 January 1991. The reason for lowering the period to the full 22 weeks is noted in section 2(2) of the Order. Given advances in modern technology, the government felt that this was justification in bringing forward by two weeks the point at which the *taiji* becomes viable.

The Order, however, is not without its critics. In an official letter to the Minister of Health and Welfare,[25] the head of *Nihon bosei hogo i kyōkai* (The Japan Gynaecological Association for the Protection of Motherhood), arguing from a practical point of view, drew attention to the fact that, although examples can be found of babies surviving outside the mother's womb at this earlier period, survival is due to the existence of highly advanced facilities, which are limited to some specialized hospitals. He perceives that this lowering of the point of viability would, given the relative scarcity of these facilities, particularly affect minors. Of the 5,778 cases of abortion performed in 1989 on unborn children between 20–23 weeks of development, for example, 1,393 cases involved women under 20 years of age.[26] As there is great social pressure on young unmarried women to have abortions it is wrong, he claims, to reduce the point of viability unless there is a corresponding improvement in the facilities available to help these vulnerable individuals.

In Japan, the legal protection of the life-potential of the unborn child thus commences at the end of the full 22 weeks of pregnancy.

Table 3.2 The viability of the foetus in Japanese law

Date issued	Order	Point at which the taiji becomes viable in law
12 June 1953	The Permanent Deputy-Minister of Health and Welfare, *Yūsei hogohō ni tsuite* (On the Eugenic Protection Law)	8 months
20 January 1976	The Permanent Deputy-Minister of Health and Welfare, *Yūsei hogohō ni yori jinkō ninshin chūzetsu o jisshisuru koto ga dekiru jiki ni tsuite* (On the Time Limits for the Performance of Artificial Termination of Pregnancy in Accordance with the Eugenic Protection Law)	7 months
21 November 1978	The Permanent Deputy-Minister of Health and Welfare, *'Yūsei hogohō no shikkō ni tsuite' no ichibu kaisei ni tsuite* (On the Partial Revisions of the Previous Order, 'On the Implementation of the Eugenic Protection Law')	24 weeks[23]
20 March 1990	The Permanent Deputy-Minister of Health and Welfare, *Yūsei hogohō ni yori jinkō chūzetsu o jitchi suru jiki no kijun ni tsuite* (On the Criterion of Time for the Performance of Artificial Termination of Pregnancy in Accordance with the Eugenic Protection Law)	22 weeks[24]

As a general rule, such legal protection means that the unborn child cannot be harmed after it has become viable. From this point onwards, the life-potential of the unborn child is protected by the state.

So far in this chapter we have concentrated our attention on the pre-birth/birth boundary of life. Let us now look at the other end of the spectrum and examine the life/death boundary. When does life end?

In its report, *Social Concern and Biological Advances*, a study group of the British Association for the Advancement of Science drew attention to the difficulties involved in attempting to determine when life is terminated. 'The moment of death, the end of a human life,' it observes, 'is as difficult to establish as its beginning.'[27] Despite the inherent difficulty, however, attempts have been made to determine the moment of death.

Traditionally, the criteria for the determination of death have been the cessation of respiration, and the stoppage of the heart which invariably follows it.[28] Where the heart stops first, lack of oxygen to the brain causes the brain to cease functioning, leading to the cessation of respiration. These are the conventional signs of death.

While these criteria have traditionally been employed to determine death clinically, advancements in technology and medicine in recent years have brought into question their adequacy in certain circumstances. The problem of brain death is at the heart of the current debate. In the words of a Memorandum issued by the Honorary Secretary of the Conference of Medical Royal Colleges and their Faculties in the United Kingdom on 15 January 1979:

> It is now universally accepted, by the lay public as well as by the medical profession, that it is not possible to equate death itself with the cessation of the heart beat.[29]

Brain death has been perceived as a state of affairs where all brain stem reflexes are absent, and the patient is apnoeic. Brain death represents the state at which, in the words of the Conference, the patient becomes 'truly dead' because, by then, 'all functions of the brain have permanently and irreversibly ceased'.[30] The Conference concluded that:

> the identification of brain death means that the patient is dead, whether or not the function of some organs, such as a heart beat, is still maintained by artificial means.[31]

In contemporary Japan, the following definitions of death are encountered:

1 A person is pronounced dead with the cessation of respiration eternally, the cessation of pulse eternally, and the dilation of the pupils. This is the traditional medical definition of death.
2 *Nōshi* (brain death).[32]
3 Death occurs the moment the last surviving cell in the body dies.[33]
4 Death occurs the moment the soul leaves the body.[34]

Legal definitions of death necessarily follow clinical definitions. As the English judge Lord Justice Edmund Davies observed:

> It is an intensely difficult matter. Somehow a legal definition of death must be devised which is clinically acceptable . . . It is with

the help of the clinician that a legal definition must be formulated which, in turn, both they and the public are prepared to act upon.[35]

In the case of Japan, the lack of a definitive legal definition of the moment of death has led to much discussion in academic legal circles. Jurists have opted for one of the following two general definitions:

1 *The traditional approach*: This approach follows the traditional medical one. Jurists who adopt this approach include Yasuhira Masakichi,[36] Takikawa Haruo and Takeuchi Tadashi,[37] Kagawa Tatsuo,[38] Ōba Shigema,[39] Fukuda Taira,[40] Fujiki Hideo,[41] Ōtani Hiroshi,[42] and Nakatani Kinko.[43]

2 *Nōshi*: Contemporary legal debate has seen the increasing popularity of the *nōshi* theory. Those who take this view include Uematsu Tadashi,[44] Dandō Shigemitsu,[45] Hirano Ryūichi,[46] and Saitō Seiji.[47]

Life is often defined as a state of functional activity and continual change before death. In Japanese law, life relates to the period of existence between birth (defined in terms of partial delivery) and death (there being no consensus as to when death occurs). The period between these two extremes constitutes an individual's lifetime.

Control over entry into the sphere of existence which we call life, however, rests not with the individual himself but with other individuals in society and forces in the universe higher than the human level. One has no control over when, or whether, we are born into the world.

Life can be ended either naturally or prematurely. An individual dies prematurely when his natural lifespan is cut short, and from a variety of reasons. Apart from death caused by disease or natural disasters, premature death can be classified according to one of three broad categories:

1 Termination of life by the individual himself.
2 Illegal termination of life by others.
3 Legal termination of life by others.

Item 1 consists of *jisatsu* (suicide). The killing of oneself takes on various forms. From the perspective of one who gets directly involved in the action, we can divide suicide into two types. The first type is solo-suicide, which involves the suicide of one individual. This act of terminating one's own life is not a criminal offence. Where an individual assists such a suicide, however, the one who assists commits a crime in contravention of article 202 of the Penal Code.[48]

The second type of suicide is that where the killing of oneself involves other people's lives. This type is called *shinjū* (where two or more persons die together in such cases as love suicide, or family suicide).

Love suicide is where two people in love decide to kill themselves together for love or out of sympathy. The idea has existed traditionally in Japan. We find the earliest reference to the practice of love suicide in the text of the *Kojiki*. This is found in the episode which tells of Prince Karu's forbidden love for his sister Princess Karu, who is from the same mother. When their love is revealed to the Emperor, the Prince is exiled to Iyo. Princess Karu follows him, and both die together.[49]

Love suicide plays a prominent part in the works of Chikamatsu Monzaemon (1653–1725) of the Tokugawa period, which are full of such incidents, reflecting a desire on the part of many of his characters to escape from the claustrophobic world of Tokugawa Japan, where the strict hierarchical structure of that society imprisoned them within their own social class. Of Chikamatsu's twenty-four *sewamono* (contemporary-life plays), eleven are plays about love suicide.[50]

Chikamatsu's characters in his *shinjū* plays are cornered into such a position that there is no way out of the situation they find themselves in. The only possible escape for them is to commit love suicide. The lovers clearly know that there is no place left for them in society, and, like Prince Karu and Princess Karu, torn between the moral values of their society and love, choose love.

A more contemporary example of a writer who concerned himself with – and actually committed – *shinjū* was Dazai Osamu (1909–48). His work demonstrates the individual as a sufferer of alienation from society.[51]

Family suicide involves the killing of family members by the parents, who then commit suicide. Family suicide is usually the result of economic hardship, or of parents in despair as a result of them having handicapped children, or problematic children who cause offence to others. In these kinds of cases, the children who are killed do not consent to the killing. The term *muri shinjū* (*shinjū* by force) is used in this context. Where one individual dies and the other survives such *shinjū* attempts the survivor has not committed a criminal offence, unless there was no intention on his part to kill himself at the outset.[52]

Item 2 consists of cases of murder, and other crimes resulting in the death of the individual.[53]

Item 3 includes cases of euthanasia – a term which covers both *anrakushi*[54] (mercy killing) and *songenshi*[55] (letting one die with dignity) – and the execution of prisoners by capital punishment.

At the other end of the spectrum, the family also plays a significant role in controlling the life-potential of the unborn child. There is a marked difference between who 'owns' the life-potential of the unborn child in Japan as compared to Britain, for example.

In Britain, the pregnant woman has the right to the privacy of her body (in the sense that she herself can decide, within the limits of the law, whether or not to have an abortion). In 1978, in the case of *Paton* v. *B.P.A.S. Trustees*,[56] the Queen's Bench Division denied the husband the right to seek an injunction to prevent his wife's abortion, arguing that the man had no legal rights over the unborn child. And in a 1987 case,[57] the Court of Appeal refused the child's father's application for an injunction to stop the unmarried mother aborting their unborn child.

In Japan, on the other hand, the woman usually shares with the husband, or the actual father, the responsibility for the decision to have an abortion. In general, this right vests not with the woman herself, but with the father of the unborn child. The woman cannot generally obtain an abortion unless the father also consents to the abortion. Where an abortion is performed without the husband's consent, the abortion is deemed to be illegal, and the *dataizai* provisions of the Penal Code are applied.[58] Section 14(3) of the 1948 Eugenic Protection Law provides that the father's consent is required, unless 'he is unascertainable, unable to declare his intentions, or has passed away since the pregnancy began'. The father of the child need not, as we noted, be the husband of the unborn child's mother. The actual father's consent is required if the couple are not married.

The legal academic Takikawa Kōtatsu[59] makes the point that the *dataizai* provisions of the Penal Code highlight the importance attached to the right of the father to be provided with a successor.

Japanese law resembles Roman law in this respect, where the consent of the father was required, and for similar reason: it was needed so as not to harm the right of the father to expect, and be provided with, a successor. The Roman law scholar Susan Treggiari suggests that abortion without the consent of the husband was a matrimonial offence in Roman law. 'It is inconceivable', she observes, 'that a husband with *manus* could not divorce his wife for such causes.' Children were considered necessary both to maintain lineage and to support the parents in old age. To quote Treggiari:

> Children protect the parents' old age, are a staff for the aged, act as reinforcements, prop up the house or form its foundation, or are the pole to which the vines may cling.[60]

The requirement of the husband's, or biological father's, consent to abortion reflects the requirement of the consent of the unborn baby's father generally in important matters in Japanese society. This reflects the status and position of the father within the family throughout Japanese history, which has been carried through into contemporary society.

The consent of the father continues to be required in areas which reflect technological development, for example. We have already seen this in respect of abortion. This is also in evidence in the case of artificial insemination.[61]

An important consequence of the presence or absence of the consent of the father to artificial insemination by donor (AID) relates to the status of the child born from such artificial insemination. In civil law, a child conceived by the wife during marriage is presumed to be a legitimate child, the right to rebut the presumption being given only to the husband. A child born through AID, and with the husband's consent, becomes a legitimate child whose legitimacy can never be denied by the husband. If AID is performed without the husband's consent, however, the child is treated as a legitimate child who is not presumed, and application may be made to the courts denying the parent–child relationship, even though the child may have been entered in the *koseki* (family register) as a legitimate child.

The requirement of the consent of the father in such cases involving the continuation of the blood-line reflects not only the status of the father within the family, but also the subordinate position of the individual *vis-à-vis* the family *per se*. The sociologist Susan Long has observed that, in Japan, 'the unit of "privacy" . . . is not the individual, but the nuclear family, especially the conjugal couple', and the family, for some time to come, 'may remain a highly integrated and interdependent unit'.[62]

The opinion exists that the requirement of the consent of family members to abortion amounts to the woman's body being considered an 'object for "families" . . . to manipulate'.[63] It is suggested, however, that underlying the requirement of the consent of family members is not the 'manipulation' of the woman by the husband, partner or parents for some sinister oppression on the part of these members.

Rather, it is to ensure that the life-potential of the unborn child cannot be taken away at the whim of the mother, and that such a decision must be properly reached by the parties directly affected by that decision.

So far in this chapter an attempt has been made to determine the boundaries of life in Japanese society, and we have noted the important role played by the family unit in respect of the beginning and end of life itself.

In addition to the family unit, other societal units can be identified as having claim on the 'ownership' of the lives of certain individuals. One of these is the state, and in the remainder of this chapter we look at the final aspect of the ending of life mentioned under item 3 above – legal termination of life by others; that is, capital punishment.[64]

An important function of criminal law is the protection of the life and liberty of the individual through the maintenance of order in the community. Conflict, however, necessarily exists between the protection of rights in society generally and the rights of criminals in this respect, for society safeguards the rights of the former precisely by limiting the rights of the latter. Thus the criminal is deprived of his right to liberty, for example, when imprisoned for his crime. His right to life, likewise, may be threatened.

The contradiction between the constitutional right to life of the criminal and the function of criminal law is highlighted in the issue of capital punishment, which involves the positive act of terminating life by the state. Capital punishment involves the taking away of the criminal's life, through the machinery of criminal law, for acts perpetrated by that individual which have been judged sufficiently grave by the state to warrant the imposition of the death penalty.

The individual is perceived as having two choices: he may either conduct himself in a manner in keeping with the values, morals and ideals of society, or he may not. If he chooses the former, he may earn the respect of his fellow citizens; if he chooses the latter, he will earn their disrespect, the extent of that disrespect varying with the nature of the act committed. Where the act committed is such as to cause moral outrage, or threaten the social order itself, various sanctions – both legal and social[65] – may be enforced against its perpetrator. The most severe and extreme legal sanction which may be imposed is capital punishment.

Capital punishment finds expression in the 1907 Penal Code. By article 9 of the Code, death is one of the principal penalties which a court may, in cases of capital offences, impose on the offender. The offender is exempt from the possibility of this ultimate sanction in cases of insanity,[66] pregnancy,[67] or on account of age.[68] For other categories of capital offenders, the death penalty may be imposed at the discretion of the judges.[69] This discretionary power is, however, removed in one specific instance: by article 81, the crime of conspiring with a foreign state and causing the use of armed forces against Japan invokes the death penalty. By article 11 of the 1907 Code, 'the death penalty shall be carried out by hanging in the interior of a prison'. Persons sentenced to death 'shall be confined in prison until the penalty is carried out'.[70]

The contradiction between the function of criminal law and the fundamental human rights of the criminal is often perceived to be resolved through the principle of due process of law.[71] According to this principle, only penalties prescribed by law can be imposed, and only in the manner prescribed by law after the person has been duly tried and convicted in accordance with the law.

The due process of law principle in the Japanese context is found in article 31 of the Constitution. Article 31 notes:

> No person shall be deprived of life or liberty, nor shall any other criminal penalty be imposed except according to procedure established by law.

Japanese lawyers generally agree that this article enunciates this principle. It is seen as having been influenced by *inter alia* the Fifth Amendment to the United States Constitution,[72] which states that:

> No person shall be . . . deprived of life, liberty, or property, without due process of law.

The due process of law principle thus attempts to protect the individual's right to life, for example, by ensuring that no arbitrary infringement takes place. The state may not terminate the criminal's life without him having been given an opportunity to properly protect his life in accordance with legal procedure. The legal philosopher Ronald Dworkin[73] interprets the principle to refer to *fair* legal procedure. This approach entails judges exercising sound moral judgement on the fairness of procedures.

The state machinery to protect the right to life of an accused person against improper and unfair infringement can be reduced to certain component parts. Let us examine each in turn.

The first component is the state's adoption of certain legal principles. In addition to the requirements of *actus reus* and *mens rea*, Japanese criminal law has adopted the principle expressed in the maxim, *nullum crimen, nulla poena sine lege*. This states that there can be no crime and no punishment without statutory prescription. Thus no criminal can be deprived of his life unless that crime committed by him (and which he intended to commit) is a specific capital offence prescribed by law. This principle was one of a number of 'revolutionary'[74] principles incorporated by Boissonade in his draft of the Old Penal Code of 1880 as part of an attempt to combine the ideas of justice and utility. The Code, deriving from the 1810 French Penal Code, continued the trend towards absorbing Western legal rules and practices, giving Japan the respectability expected of a 'modern nation'.[75] The legal scholar Ishii Ryōsuke argues that, through the incorporation of such principles into Japanese law, Japan 'emerged from the cramped mold of ancient legal thought'.[76]

Under the Penal Code of 1907, as amended, the death sentence may – and, in one instance, must – be imposed for the commission of certain capital offences; these are listed in Table 3.3.

In addition to the provisions in the Penal Code which appear in Table 3.3, the capital offences listed in Table 3.4 have also been established.

The death penalty may thus be legitimately imposed only on those persons who commit such capital offences. It may not be imposed as punishment for the commission of any other crime.

Second, the state protects the accused's right to life against arbitrary infringement by ensuring him a proper defence of his life through a fair trial. In the words of the Supreme Court in the *Hakata Station Film Case* of 1969:[84]

> the guarantee of a fair trial is one of the fundamental [principles] which our Constitution has established.

It is a basic principle of Japanese criminal law that a person is innocent until proven guilty, the burden of proof resting with the prosecution, and many of the safeguards in the Constitution are geared towards this end. Where a defendant's life is at stake, this right to a fair trial takes on profound significance. The constitutional safeguards which protect the individual faced with criminal prosecution are found in articles 31–40 of the Constitution. Those provisions which aim to ensure fair trial, in its widest sense, are found in articles 32, 37, 38 and 39 of the Constitution.[85] The provisions contained therein, together with comments, are listed in Table 3.5.

The third component of the state machinery to protect the right to life of the accused against improper and unfair infringement is the existence of a system of appeal. The system of appeal acts as a safety net which, in theory, protects the life of the accused from a miscarriage

Table 3.3 Capital offences under the Penal Code

Article	Type of offence	Punishment: Maximum	Minimum
77[77]	Creating disorder for the purpose of overthrowing the government, usurping territorial sovereignty, or otherwise subverting the national constitution		
	Being a ringleader in the commission of the above offences	Death	Life imprisonment
81	Conspiring with a foreign state and causing the use of armed forces against Japan	Death	–
82[78]	Siding with an enemy state, engaging in military service of such state, or otherwise affording military advantage to such states	Death (or 10 years)	2 years' imprisonment
108	Setting fire to, and burning, a building, railroad train, electric car, vessel, or mine serving as a human habitation or in which persons are actually present	Death (or life)	5 years' imprisonment
117[79]	Damaging or destroying structure used for human habitation or in which people are present by causing an explosion of gun powder, steam boiler, or other potentially explosive object	Death (or life)	5 years' imprisonment
119	Causing flood, thereby damaging a structure used as human habitation or in which people are actually present	Death (or life)	3 years' imprisonment
126	Overturning a railroad train or electric car or capsizing a vessel or destroying the same, thereby causing death or injury	Death (or life)	3 years' imprisonment

Table 3.3 Continued

Article	Type of offence	Punishment:	
		Maximum	Minimum
127[80]	Damaging a railroad signal or sign, lighthouse or buoy, or otherwise committing an act of obstructing traffic, thereby overturning or destroying railroad trains, electric cars, or capsizing a vessel	Death	Life imprisonment
146[81]	Causing the death of another by the pollution of drinking water	Death (or life)	5 years' imprisonment
199	Killing another person	Death (or life)	3 years' imprisonment
200[82]	Killing one's own or one's spouse's direct lineal ascendant	Death	Life imprisonment
240	Causing injury to a person while committing the crime of robbery, if death results thereby	Death	Life imprisonment
241[83]	Robbery and rape of a woman, if death results thereby	Death	Life imprisonment

Table 3.4 Capital offences outside the Penal Code

Law	Offence	Punishment:	
		Maximum	Minimum
Kōkūhō (Civil Aviation Law), law no. 231, 15 July 1952, as amended	Causing death by causing an aircraft to fall or become destroyed	Death	7 years' imprisonment
Bakuhatsu butsu torishimarihō (Control of Explosives Law) Cabinet Order no. 32, 27 December 1884, as amended, s.1	Using explosives or letting somebody else use them with the purpose of disturbing the peace or damaging another's person or property	Death	7 years' imprisonment

Table 3.5 Provisions which aim to ensure fair trial

Article	Comments
32[86]	
No person shall be denied the right of access to the courts	Thus in respect of a defendant charged with a capital offence, he has a right to the judicial process. Indeed, as a general principle, the trial may not take place without the accused being present in court
37(1)[87]	
In all criminal cases the accused shall enjoy the right to a speedy and public trial by an impartial tribunal	This provision has been the subject of much judicial review. The right to a speedy trial was held by the Supreme Court in 1972 to refer not only to simply demanding a speedy trial 'in a generally applicable form', but also included authorizing the Court 'to disallow the further continuance of criminal process against a particular defendant' when his right to a speedy trial is infringed following 'extreme delay' in court proceedings. The Court argued that such delays 'make it very difficult for the court to realize the ideals of criminal justice'.[88] When one's very life may depend on ascertaining the facts in any particular case, the provision is of obvious significance in protecting the accused from a miscarriage of justice, as might arise as a result of *inter alia* witnesses forgetting the facts, witnesses and relatives dying, or the loss of key material, through long delay.
	The right to public trial safeguards the defendant from arbitrary proceedings in private. Trials must be public, open to all individuals who wish to attend.
	The provision relating to trial by an impartial tribunal safeguards the defendant from prejudiced judges. The basic concept of the independence of the judges has stood the test of time since the Meiji period, when the concept of the separation of powers was adopted. Whilst the career structure and general conservatism of the judiciary, particularly of the higher appeal courts, have led to criticisms of its often pro-government, non-radical approach to judicial review,[89] no such criticism is made of its capacity to provide an impartial trial on a more day-to-day basis. As a safeguard, however, there is

Table 3.5 Continued

Article	Comments
	built into the system the ability to provide a change of both venue and judge for due cause
37(2) He shall be permitted full opportunity to examine all witnesses, and he shall have the right of compulsory process for obtaining witnesses on his behalf at public expense	As with the previous provision, in cases involving capital offences, the ability to examine prosecution witnesses and to obtain the testimony of defence witnesses is of obvious significance in ensuring fair trial
37(3) At all times the accused shall have the assistance of competent counsel who shall, if the accused is unable to secure the same by his own efforts, be assigned to his use by the state	This provision relating to obtaining the assistance of a state-appointed defence lawyer and legal aid is reflected in article 36 of the Code of Criminal Procedure, which provides that, 'when an accused is unable to obtain counsel because of poverty, or other reason, the court shall assign counsel on behalf of the accused upon his request'. These provisions are seen to be vital to ensure a fair trial for the individual accused of a capital offence, for prohibitive legal costs incurred by such major trials must never prevent the accused from having the benefit of a properly conducted defence of his life. In cases involving the death penalty (or where the punishment is for a minimum of three years) the accused must be represented by a lawyer[90]
38(1)[91] No person shall be compelled to testify against himself	
38(2)[92] Confession made under compulsion, torture or threat, or after prolonged arrest or detention shall not be admitted in evidence	The courts have sought to ensure that evidence presented at trial is both true and not illegally obtained by excluding such confessions from the trial so as not to prejudice the defendant's case. Prior to a Supreme Court judgment of 1966, however, the courts were only prepared to exclude the former. In the 1966 case of *Abe* v. *Japan*, the Supreme Court, for the first time, held that the latter, too, was necessary to protect the defendant's right to a fair trial

Table 3.5 Continued

Article	Comments
38(3)[93] No person shall be convicted or punished in cases where the only proof against him is his own confession	
39[94] No person shall be held criminally liable for an act which was lawful at the time it was committed, or of which he has been acquitted, nor shall he be placed in double jeopardy	Thus, although the prosecution may appeal an acquittal, it may not prosecute after the appeal system has run its course, with no recourse to further process, and the individual has been found innocent – i.e. 'finally acquitted'. Protection against such double jeopardy means that once finally acquitted, the person tried for a capital offence will no longer have his life threatened by further action on that score

of justice. This it does by reversing the decision of the trial judge who initially judged that the innocent person was guilty of committing the crime.

For the reader used to the English legal system, this last sentence may strike one as odd, for in English law the innocence or guilt of the defendant in criminal matters is determined by a jury. Whilst the judge decides on questions of law, questions of fact are left to the jury. This contrasts with the situation in Japan.

For a period, however, Japan did operate a jury system. Between 1928 and 1943 the jury system operated in Japan for cases of a serious nature, including those which carried the death penalty as ultimate punishment. In such cases, law provided trial by jury unless waived by the defendant. Various reasons can be given for the decision to suspend the system, and include the anti-democratic wartime conditions themselves and the need to save on valuable time and human resources; the desire of the Japanese people to be tried by those 'above' them, rather than by their peers – a point which Takikawa Masajirō explains in terms of the Japanese people's desire to subject themselves to absolute authority;[95] and, on a technical note, that by choosing a jury trial there was no possibility of bringing a *kōso*[96] appeal to the High Court on questions of fact. It had become so unpopular that by 1942 only two persons elected to be tried by jury.[97]

Detailed provisions relating to the appeal system are to be found in articles 351–460 of the Code of Criminal Procedure of 1948, as amended. The various elements of the system relevant to the protection of the right to life are illustrated in Figure 3.1. The appeal system consists of two separate components: the 'general' appeal system and the 'special' appeal system.

The 'general' appeal system comprises the *kōso* appeal to the *kōtō saibansho* (High Court), and the *jōkoku* appeal to the Supreme Court.

A motion for *kōso* appeal may be filed to a judgment of the first instance that has been rendered by *inter alia* the District Court or the Summary Court, and such an appeal may be made on several grounds, including improper penalty, error in the application of laws and

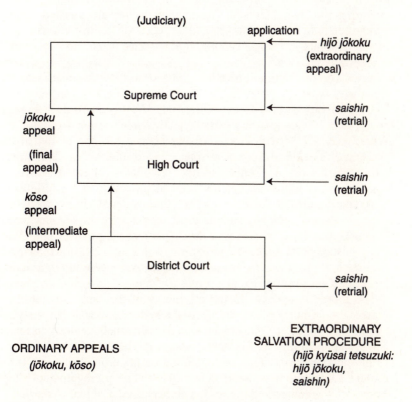

Figure 3.1 The system of appeals in Japanese law

orders, errors in facts, and violation of laws and orders in the proceedings. The appellate court can, under appropriate circumstances, quash the original judgment.

A motion for *jōkoku* appeal[98] may be filed against the judgment rendered by the High Court at first or second instance in cases where the Constitution has been infringed, misinterpreted, or where the judgment was contrary to the precedents of the Supreme Court (or, where no such precedent exists, was contrary to the decision of other courts). The court of last resort is empowered *inter alia* to quash the original sentence.

The seniority of the *jōkoku* appeal over the *kōso* appeal is reflected in the number of judges who sit to listen to the appeals. In the case of *kōso* appeal, as with the *chihō saibansho* (District Court), three judges sit on cases involving capital offences. With the *jōkoku* appeal, however, five judges sit in the case of a Petty Bench sitting, and fifteen judges sit on important cases of constitutional significance involving the Grand Bench. The learned judges are assisted by a number of judicial research officials – judges of inferior courts – to research points of law, enabling the Supreme Court to reach an appropriate decision.

In the law of criminal procedure, the extraordinary appeal system consists of what is termed *hijō kyūsai tetsuzuki* (literally translated as 'special salvation procedure'). This comprises two separate components: *hijō jōkoku* (extraordinary appeal)[99] and *saishin* (retrial).[100] Whereas *hijō jōkoku* is retrial arising from a mistake in the trial procedure, *saishin* is retrial arising from a mistake in fact. The retrial exists for the benefit of the possibly wronged defendant where *inter alia* the documents used as evidence at the original trial were altered or forged, or where the testimony, interpretation, expert testimony, or translation used in evidence in the original judgment was false. A retrial at the bequest of the prisoner must be distinguished from a 'retrial' in the sense of a further trial following *final* acquittal for the same offence, the latter being contrary to article 39 of the Constitution.

The fourth component in the machinery of the Japanese state to protect the criminal's right to life is the system of *onsha* (amnesty). Unlike the first three components already mentioned, amnesty has no general applicability and is only given at the behest of the Cabinet. Unlike the situation which prevailed before the promulgation of the present Constitution – where amnesty was the prerogative of the Emperor[101] – amnesty is the responsibility of the Cabinet. As article 73 of the Constitution notes: 'The Cabinet, in addition to other general

administrative functions, shall perform [certain] . . . functions . . .'
One such function is to: 'decide on general amnesty, special amnesty,
commutation of punishment, reprieve, and restoration of rights'.

The Amnesty Law of 1947 contains provisions relating to these five
types of relief from *inter alia* the death penalty. Two types of *onsha*
exist: *seirei onsha* (amnesty by Cabinet Order); and *kobetsu onsha*
(individual amnesty). *Seirei onsha* is given by the Cabinet on occasions of political change, or at times of national celebration. On such
occasions, the type of amnesty granted is either *taisha* (general
amnesty),[102] *genkei* (commutation of punishment),[103] or *fukken*
(restoration of rights).[104]

Kobetsu onsha, on the other hand, refers to amnesty granted by the
Cabinet to particular individuals at any time. The types of amnesty
which may be granted are *tokusha* (special amnesty),[105] *genkei*
(commutation of punishment), *kei no shikkō no menjo* (reprieve),[106]
or *fukken*, brought about by an appeal from the *Chūō kōsei hogo
shinsakai* (Central Committee for the Welfare and Protection of
Criminals).[107]

The fifth component concerns the period of limitations. By article
32 of the Penal Code:

A period of limitations is completed when punishment has not
been executed within any of the following periods after a sentence
has become final.

Article 32(1) notes the period of '30 years for a death penalty'.

In 1985, the First Petty Bench of the Supreme Court was given the
opportunity to pronounce judgment on the applicability of the period
of limitations to capital offenders who had spent at least thirty years
in prison awaiting the execution of the death penalty.[108] The question
arose in this case as to whether or not execution of the death penalty
was barred at the expiration of the period of limitations. The prisoner
Hirasawa Teichō had been found guilty in 1948 of mass murder by
poisoning, and sentenced to death. He was still awaiting execution.
Hirasawa's lawyers sought his release on the basis of the Habeas
Corpus Act, arguing that the execution of the death penalty was
barred when the period of limitations had expired. As Hirasawa's
sentence had become irrevocable in 1955, his lawyers argued that to
confine him in prison any longer would be contrary to the Habeas
Corpus Act.

The Supreme Court, however, affirming the decision of the Tokyo
District Court, dismissed the petition for *habeas corpus*. The Court
held that, for a person sentenced to capital punishment according to

the provision of article 11 of the Penal Code, no period of limitations operates. Furthermore, as a period of confinement preceding the execution of the death penalty is provided by article 11(2), it should continue until the death penalty is carried out.[109]

The period of limitations does, however, protect the prisoner's right to life where there has been a break in the continuity of prison confinement. Article 32(1) is deemed to apply to protect the right to life of the criminal sentenced to death where he has escaped from prison and evades recapture until the limitations period expires.

It could be argued, however, that this anomaly runs counter to the principles of natural justice. It seems difficult – from the perspective of those who believe in the virtue of capital punishment – to justify a situation which allows a special category of persons to enjoy such protection of their right to life merely because they have literally escaped from the system which originally condemned them to death, whilst denying such a right to those who abide by the 'rules'.

The sixth component which protects the criminal's right to life against arbitrary infringement is the requirement that the Minister of Justice issues the death penalty order. Having exhausted the available appeals procedure, and assuming no amnesty has been granted, the fate of the defendant found guilty of a capital offence and punished by death rests with the Minister of Justice, who makes the final decision as to whether or not the state terminates his life.

Special regulations are laid down in the Code of Criminal Procedure to deal with the execution of the death penalty. By article 475 (incorporated into the Code by Law No. 268, of 31 July 1952), the execution of the death penalty is to be carried out by order of the Minister of Justice. Provided the correct period after the request for reinstatement of the right to appeal, or for retrial, or the petition or application for an extraordinary appeal, or for amnesty, has passed and the procedure has been completed, the order of death penalty must be issued within six months as from the day on which the judgment became 'final and conclusive'. Once such an order has been issued, the execution is to be carried out 'within five days', and in the presence of a public procurator, a secretary of the public procurator's office and the chief of the prison, or his representative. These persons sign and place their seals on the execution statement. The execution then takes place, and the criminal's life is ended.

Article 31 of the Constitution, we remember, introduces the due process of law principle. The implication of article 31 on the right to life has been noted by the Grand Bench of the Supreme Court in the following terms: [110]

even though the life of the individual is precious, it is clear that a punishment that would deprive the individual of life can be inflicted under appropriate procedures established by law.

We have examined what these 'appropriate procedures established by law' are. Let us now turn to examine the issue of the constitutionality of capital punishment.

In a 1948 case, the Grand Bench of the Supreme Court was asked to decide upon the constitutionality of the death penalty. As no specific mention is made of capital punishment in the present Constitution, there was, as a result, a degree of uncertainty as to whether the Constitution permitted or prohibited the death penalty.

At issue in this case was whether *inter alia* the phrase 'cruel punishment' in article 36 of the Constitution included or excluded the death penalty. Article 36 reads as follows: 'The infliction of torture by any public officer and cruel punishments are absolutely forbidden.' If it could be shown that the death penalty *did* constitute a 'cruel punishment' for the purpose of article 36, then it could be argued that capital punishment was itself 'absolutely forbidden' under the Constitution.

The defence lawyer raised this argument as part of his appeal against the imposition of the death penalty on his client, who had murdered his mother and younger sister. He argued that the decision of the lower court was illegal on the ground that it had applied the death penalty, provided by articles 199 and 200 of the Penal Code, 'which is absolutely prohibited by the new Constitution and automatically null and void'. He continued:

Because the death penalty is the cruellest of all punishments, the provisions regarding it in articles 199 and 200 of the Code should properly be interpreted as having been abrogated by the new Constitution.[111]

The Grand Bench, however, dismissed the argument, ruling in favour of the imposition of the death penalty and against the 'cruel punishments' provision of article 36 being applicable to capital punishment. The Court reasoned that:

the death penalty, as a punishment, is not generally regarded as being one of the cruel punishments referred to [in article 36].[112]

The death penalty, notes the formal judgment, would only be considered a form of 'cruel punishment' for the purpose of article 36 when the means of execution is considered barbaric by the standards of the day. Thus, for example, a law would be in contravention of article 36 if it involved such methods as 'burning at the stake, crucifixion, gibbeting, or boiling in a cauldron'.[113] As the method of executing the death penalty in modern Japanese society is not 'cruel' in this sense – it being executed by a method acceptable to a modern, civilized society – the Court ruled against article 36 being interpreted as absolutely prohibiting capital punishment.

The 1948 decision has been followed in subsequent Supreme Court decisions. In 1955, the Supreme Court's Grand Bench again held that the existing method of executing the death penalty did not fall within the 'cruel punishments' category for the purpose of article 36.[114] A similar decision was reached by the Grand Bench in the *Ichikawa Hanging Case* of 1961,[115] which was asked to decide the constitutionality of the method used for carrying out the death penalty. The Court overruled the defendant's counsel's appeal that sentencing his client to death by hanging without specifying the method was an infringement of articles 31 and 36. The Court refused to accept *inter alia* the contention that the present method of killing, based on the 1873 Cabinet Order No. 65 (entitled, 'A Revised Chart of Hanging Equipment'), was contrary to these two articles.

Japan's signing in 1979 of the International Covenant on Civil and Political Rights also acts as a discouragement to those who seek to circumvent the problem of the death penalty by attempting to get it classified as 'cruel' for the purpose of article 36. Although the status of the Japanese Constitution is generally believed to prevail over that of treaties,[116] it seems unlikely that the Japanese government would act in a manner contrary to the provisions of a treaty to which it is a signatory.

The International Covenant on Civil and Political Rights resolves the 'conflict' between the right to life and capital punishment as follows. Although article 6(1) clearly states that 'every human being has the inherent right to life', and that this right 'shall be protected by law', it also states that 'no one shall be arbitrarily deprived of life'. Non-arbitrary deprivation of life is recognized if it is in compliance with paragraphs (2)–(6) of the article. The article also makes it clear that the Covenant neither seeks 'to delay [n]or to prevent the abolition of capital punishment by any State party to the present Covenant'.[117] By article 6(2), the death penalty is to be imposed by member states – including Japan – should they wish to retain capital punishment, only for the 'most serious crimes', and, by article 6(5), those below 18 years of age, and pregnant women, are exempt.[118]

The Covenant makes the clear distinction between capital punishment and 'cruel' punishments. By article 7:

No one shall be subjected to . . . cruel, inhuman or degrading . . . punishment.

Article 7 is a distinct, separate article from article 6 (which contains references to the death penalty). By separating the death penalty as punishment from 'cruel' and 'inhuman' punishments in this way, the Covenant makes it clear that the death penalty is not to be categorized as a 'cruel' or 'inhuman' punishment for the purpose of article 7.

The decisions of the Japanese Supreme Court to uphold the constitutionality of the death penalty are also in keeping with the provisions of the Universal Declaration of Human Rights itself, which does not prohibit capital punishment. Although article 5 prohibits *inter alia* 'cruel' punishment, those states which retain capital punishment[119] rely on article 29(2) as justification for its retention. By article 29(2), limitation on an individual's rights and freedoms can be 'determined by law', and for the purpose *inter alia* of 'public order and the general welfare in a democratic society'. Japan is a signatory to the Declaration.

As with article 29(2) of the Declaration, an individual's right to life under the Japanese Constitution, too, we remember, is subservient to the public welfare. The constitutional provision of article 13 was reiterated by the Supreme Court in the 1948 decision noted above: [120]

It must naturally be presumed that in cases in which the basic principle of the public welfare is violated even the right of the people to life can be legally limited or taken away.

In the words of Justice Inoue:

It must be recognized that the Constitution acknowledges the possibility that for the public welfare human life may be taken as a punishment, according to procedures established by law.[121]

The retention of the death penalty was felt to be necessary as a deterrent to crime, and to protect society. In the words of the formal judgment:

the threat of the death penalty itself may be a general preventive measure, the execution of the death penalty may be a means of cutting off at the root special social evils, and both may be used to protect society.[122]

Despite its acknowledgement that '[o]ne human life is of more importance than the whole earth', the approval of the death penalty:

> must be interpreted as giving supremacy to the concept of humanity as a whole rather than to the concept of humanity as individuals: and continuation of the death penalty must ultimately be recognized as necessary for the public welfare.[123]

Although case-law has left in no doubt the constitutionality of the death penalty in post-1947 Japanese society, such a position is not irrevocable, and in any civilized society there must be room to reconsider the matter.

The ability of a future Japan to reverse the precedents established by the courts in respect of capital punishment was not lost on the judges of the Grand Bench in the 1948 case who were keen to stress the possibility of a reverse course. To quote the opinion of Justices Shima Tamotsu, Fujita Hachirō, Iwamatsu Saburō and Kawamura Matasuke, the Constitution, in providing for the death penalty:

> reflect[s] the people's feelings at the time that the Constitution was enacted; it should not be regarded as eternally approving the death penalty. The judgement of whether certain punishments are cruel is a question that should be decided according to the feelings of the people. However, because the feelings of the people cannot escape changing with the times, what at one time may be regarded as not being a cruel punishment may at a later period be judged the reverse.[124]

The necessary conditions perceived by the learned judges for such a reversal were outlined in the following terms:

> as a nation's culture develops to a high degree, and as a peaceful society is realized on the basis of justice and order, and if a time is reached when it is not felt to be necessary for the public welfare to prevent crime by the menace of the death penalty, then both the death penalty and cruel punishments will certainly be eliminated because of the feelings of the people.[125]

The point has been made that, although the state would, in practice, offer no great resistance to the principle of abolishing the death penalty in Japan, its desire to listen to public opinion makes this prospect remote in the foreseeable future, as public opinion has consistently been pro-capital punishment in nature.[126]

Against this tide of public opinion, however, there have been calls to abolish capital punishment. In 1875, for example, the scholar of

Western law Tsuda Mamichi (1829–1903)[127] criticized the death penalty, arguing that it was contrary to the aim of criminal punishment, which was, he argued, to rehabilitate the offender. Nor, he argued, was it either a practical or socially enlightened form of punishment. Although he was unsuccessful in reforming the practice, he did succeed in stirring up political response, and the next few years saw a discussion on abolishing decapitation and the displaying of the head. Both were, in time, abolished.[128]

A political attempt to abolish capital punishment was again made in the first years of the twentieth century. In 1902, following the presentation of a bill revising the old criminal law system to the Imperial Diet, Ogawa Shigejirō, Hanai Takuzo and others began advocating the complete abolition of the death penalty, again without success.

More recently, in academic circles, a vocal minority have come to support the cause of abolition. There are those, for example, who point to the contradiction between the general pacifist purpose of the Constitution and the right to deprive an individual of his life through capital punishment.[129]

Calls for the abolition of capital punishment are also made by religious groups such as the *Sōka gakkai* (Association for the Creation of Values).[130] Ikeda Daisaku's views on the death penalty are found, for example, in dialogues between him and the historian Arnold Toynbee. Ikeda opposes the death penalty on the ground of the 'Buddhist respect for the dignity of life'. The killing of an individual in retaliation for killing, he argues, 'sets in motion a course of wicked acts'. For him:

> Life, as an absolute entity [is] worthy of the profoundest respect, [and] must never be treated as a means of achieving anything other than life itself.[131]

The imposition of capital punishment, he argues, undervalues life.

Historically, the Buddhist idea of disallowing the killing of any creature led to a 247-year period when capital punishment was abolished.[132] The legal historian Ishio Yoshihisa[133] notes that it was abolished to avoid the act of killing, it being replaced by banishment. The legal scholar Hirano Ryūichi[134] has observed that the period of abolition 'is a symbolic manifestation' of the non-retributive nature of Buddhist- and Confucian-inspired traditional Japanese society.

Despite recent calls to abolish the death penalty, Japan's stance has been – and is – one of retention. This contrasts somewhat with the pro-abolition movement that has emerged amongst a large section of the world community. Since the early 1950s, the death penalty has, to quote the international human rights lawyer Paul Sieghart, 'begun to go out of fashion'.[135] Nevertheless, the pro-capital punishment stance of such countries as Japan, the United States and China is perceived as hindering the emergence of the abolition of capital punishment as a general rule with the character of *jus cogens*, a peremptory norm of international law from which no deviation is allowed.[136]

As current Japanese law upholds capital punishment – which can, and does, take away the right to life of certain criminals – there arises a matter of profound significance: assuming, as many commentators do, that law is morally fallible, such legal use of coercion needs justification. In the context of a discussion on legal coercion and moral principle, the legal philosopher David Lyons observed:

> Coercion deprives us of the freedom to choose by our own lights. Its legal use deprives people of . . . even life. No wonder it seems to require justification.[137]

How, if at all, can capital punishment in Japan be justified?

Alfred Oppler, in his reminiscences on the immediate post-war period in Japan, identifies the two major justifications offered – both then and now – for capital punishment. 'In light of my abomination of the death penalty', he writes, 'the question will be asked why I did not endeavor to bring about abolition in the Criminal Code of Japan.' He replies thus:

> I raised, indeed, no objection to its retention because I had arrived at the conclusion that the overwhelming majority of the Japanese were still convinced of the deterring effect of capital punishment, which some of them also regarded necessary for the retributory satisfaction of the victim or his relative.[138]

The two justifications offered for the retention of capital punishment are thus retribution and utility. Let us examine each argument briefly.

Theories of retribution have as their basis the idea of just deserts – of 'doing and deserving'.[139] One traditional theory of *lex talionis* (law of retaliation) demands 'an eye for an eye'. In the context of capital punishment, it argues that one who deprives another of his life should himself be deprived of life. Immanuel Kant[140] argued that, being 'rational agents' who act for particular reasons, we seek to 'universalize' the 'maxims' of our actions. This brings with it the notion of 'doing unto others as you would have them do unto you'. If

I treat others badly, for example, I will my own punishment for my conduct.

The absence of any sustained argument from a retributory perspective is a prominent feature of the capital punishment debate in Japan, although this is sometimes pointed to as justification for retaining the death penalty.[141] This can be explained in terms of the relative absence of the notion of retribution in Japanese society generally, and the idea of retribution has not rooted itself in Japanese law.[142]

Utilitarianism attempts to lay down an objective principle for determining when a given action is right or wrong. This principle of utility states that an action is right in so far as it tends to produce the greatest happiness for the greatest number of people. Stressing the effects which an action has (rather than the motive), an act is right if it produces more beneficial than harmful effects; it is wrong if the reverse is the case. Utilitarianism thus stresses the rightness or wrongness of an action, and not the goodness or badness of the person committing the act.

Traditionally, the Utilitarian view of punishment sees its function in terms of deterring crime. The deterrent principle has two components. First, general deterrence, where the threat of punishment itself acts as a deterrent to crime. Second, specific deterrence, where the actual punishment of the offender deters him from committing further crimes.[143]

The general deterrence argument is prevalent in Japan. We have already seen this argument being employed by the courts to justify the constitutionality of capital punishment. For the courts, nothing is allowed to interfere with what Oppler[144] refers to as the 'magic formula' of public welfare.

Outside the courtroom, similar sentiments are frequently expressed in both academic and political circles.

The retention of capital punishment is generally advocated in academic circles on the ground that it helps maintain social order, and that without it more harm would befall society. The legal scholar Uematsu Tadashi's views are representative of this way of thinking. Uematsu strongly stresses the social necessity of retaining capital punishment, and perceives the pro-abolition arguments which stress its inhuman aspect to be sentimental and dangerous to the citizens of society. He observes: [145]

The idea that capital punishment is opposed to humanism not only arises from the dogmatism that states we should not take a companion's life without asking why the criminal committed the crime, but also promotes humanism aimed only towards criminals.

Such sentimental arguments, he notes, fail to protect the lives of ordinary citizens from those who seek to do harm. He continues:

> If the lives of atrocious criminals are secured, they will stride along the street fearlessly. The more free a criminal is, the more danger a policeman and a prison officer assuming charge will be exposed to. What's worse, good citizens will have to hide from a dangerous man walking around whose life is guaranteed by the government.

The opinions of academic anti-abolitionists and of the judiciary were echoed by the members of the Commission on the Constitution, all of whom opposed the complete abolition of capital punishment. One view prevailing amongst many of the members was that to abolish it would result in an increase in serious crimes against the person, which might threaten public order. Commissioner Mizuno argued that the death penalty should not be abolished:

> because our country has not yet seen the effective stabilization of order and our general level of culture has not yet attained a sufficiently high plane.[146]

Commissioner Kamikawa, similarly, stressed the public welfare:

> Because man is not by nature a moral creature, if the warning of punishment is lacking, there is the danger that crimes will be committed. When, as in our country today, the inhuman act of murder is so widespread as to be a common occurrence, to revise the Constitution so as to abolish capital punishment would contain the danger of promoting that evil.[147]

The Utilitarian perspective on capital punishment views it as an effective means of social control in that it deters the commission of capital offences. An obvious criticism of the theory is that the threat of the imposition of the death penalty does not effectively deter criminals from committing capital offences. Evidence from research conducted outside Japan tends to reaffirm this claim.[148] This argument is also recognized within the academic community in Japan. Ōno, for example,[149] observes: 'The main negative reason for the abolition of capital punishment is that it is not a deterrent to crime.' Ōno suggests that capital offenders commit crimes for a variety of reasons. Whilst some commit crimes on emotional impulse, others commit crimes due to their own conditions of insanity. Some even commit crimes without fearing the consequences of their acts, no more respecting their own lives than they did the lives of those they murdered. The list may be added to. Thus groups such as terrorists may actively seek the death penalty to be martyrs to their cause and to publicize their cause. In all such cases, the threat of the death penalty will not deter those offenders from committing capital offences (and, in the case of terrorists, it may even promote the commission of capital offences).

The practice now common in Japan of rarely executing the death penalty[150] where offenders are sentenced to death adds to the problem of its efficiency in deterring other criminals. Here, specific deterrence works against the general deterrence to limit its effectiveness.

A major difficulty of the Utilitarian approach to legal coercion is the necessary conflict which arises between it and considerations of individual justice. As it is concerned with serving the interests of the general population, the interests of particular individuals may suffer as a consequence in any conflict between the two, and innocent persons may be tried and convicted of offences they did not commit.[151]

Takikawa Masajirō[152] suggests that we ought to assume that one or two in every several hundred persons in prison in Japan are innocent of the crimes for which they were tried and convicted. They are there, he suggests, to maintain order in society. Those innocently convicted must accept their 'punishment' as a sacrifice on their part for the sake of the criminal system generally. Although the contemporary trial system claims to be scientific in nature, it being based on substantive evidence, the evidence collected, he argues, does not represent total evidence since evidence can only be collected by chance. However much one tries to judge rationally from the evidence gathered, one cannot ascertain absolute truth. In courts higher than, and including, the District Court, judgment is arrived at by several judges, and in many cases persons are found guilty by a majority of one. It is beyond our human capacity to conduct an absolutely correct trial. Acknowledging the inability of human beings to give perfect judgments, Takikawa points to the existence of the amnesty system as providing one final chance to save a life which might have been endangered by imperfect judgment.

Jeremy Bentham,[153] as part of his concept of the 'frugality' of punishment, argued that the criminal system should cause the minimum of suffering to the offender or to others. Whilst it is clear that a proper balance needs to be struck between society's demands for an adequate level of protection from criminal acts and individual justice, determining such a balance in theory, and maintaining it in practice, is indeed a formidable task. Continued discussion on, and clarification of, the role of capital punishment is essential to further efforts to formulate the true nature of this balance.

In this chapter, we have examined some problematic areas relating to the beginning and end of life in Japan. We now turn our attention to look at the question of the equality of the right to life in the sphere of existence between the boundaries of birth and death.

4 The equality of the right to life

In this chapter we examine the question of the equality of the right to life conferred on all individuals by the present Japanese Constitution.

The principle of an equality under the law is enshrined in article 14 of the Constitution. By article 14(1):

All of the people are equal under the law and there shall be no discrimination in political, economic or social relations because of race, creed, sex, social status or family origin.

Article 14 also abolishes the aristocracy, and provides that no privilege accompanies any award of honour, decoration or any other distinction granted to an individual.

The principle of equality under the law found in the United Nations Declaration of Human Rights[1] is reiterated in the International Covenant on Civil and Political Rights of 1966, which grew out of the Declaration. Japan, which added its signature to the Covenant in 1979, is bound by its terms. By article 26:

All persons are equal before the law and are entitled without any discrimination to the equal protection of the law. In this respect, the law shall prohibit any discrimination and guarantee to all persons equal and effective protection against discrimination on any ground such as race, colour, sex, language, religion, political or other opinion, national or social origin, property, birth or other status.

The legal mechanism plays an essential role in the protection of the individual's right to life. This it does by maintaining social order. Under certain political systems in which they are made and applied, laws guide people in defining what kind of behaviour is orderly and what kind is disorderly. Although laws are not essential to the existence of order in society, they do, in practice, form the important means of creating and maintaining such order. The political scientist Hedley Bull observes that:

> Order in social life can exist in principle without rules, and . . . it is best to treat rules as a widespread, and nearly ubiquitous, means of creating order in human society, rather than as part of the definition of order itself.[2]

In Japan, the state proclaimed its intention of adhering to the principle of the separation of powers – namely, the legislature (which formulates policy and enacts it as law), the executive (which puts policy into practice), and the judiciary (which applies the law according to the rules of procedural justice and resolves disputes) – following the downfall of the Tokugawa regime. In article 1 of the *seitaisho* (The Statement of the Form of Government) of 11 June 1868 we read:

> The authority of the *dajōkan* (Great Council of State) shall be divided into three powers: legislative, judicial and executive.[3]

In contemporary Japanese society, the state protects the right to life of individuals against infringement by other individuals through these three separable powers. Legislation to protect the individual's right to life is enacted by the Diet; it is operated by the executive, which ensures *inter alia* the existence of an efficient and effective police force; and it is interpreted and applied by the judiciary through the courts, which mete out appropriate punishment on offenders.

The task of the legislature is thus to draft and enact laws which *inter alia* protect the right to life. This it does in a relative, rather than an absolute, manner. The legislature, whilst physically unable to prevent any particular offender from killing another individual, can protect individuals in a general sense by establishing a framework of criminal law, with its in-built system of punishment, to deter individuals from taking away the lives of other individuals.[4] Criminal law also reflects society's moral values.

The general provisions of, and specific crimes comprising, present-day Japanese criminal law are found in the 1907 Penal Code.[5] The Penal Code criminalizes *inter alia* those acts which result in the unnatural and untimely death of an individual,[6] as well as acts which, although not having resulted in death, do endanger human life.[7] A wide range of punishments are laid down in the Code, reflecting the seriousness (or otherwise) in which those acts are perceived by society.

Two types of inequality under the law exist in the Penal Code.

First, certain categories of persons receive special privilege and protection under the law to their benefit, there being a less severe penalty – or no penalty at all in certain cases – provided in the Code. Second, certain persons are treated in a way detrimental to their interests, there being provided in the Code a more severe penalty for certain acts committed by them. Only the latter has been perceived as problematic *vis-à-vis* article 14(1) of the Constitution. This chapter concentrates on this second type of inequality under the law.

The first type of inequality is to be found in Chapter 7 of the Code, entitled 'Non-Constitution of a Crime and Reduction or Remission of Penalty'. This chapter lists such categories of persons as follows:

1 Those persons who have committed an act 'under law or ordinance or in the course of legitimate business'; that is, those who commit what is termed *seitō kōi* (justified acts).[8]
2 Persons who commit 'unavoidable acts . . . in order to defend the rights of oneself or another person against imminent and unjust violation'.[9]
3 Persons who commit acts in self-defence. These include such 'unavoidable acts done in order to avert a present danger to the life, person, liberty or property of oneself or another person', but excludes persons 'under special obligation because of their profession or occupation'.[10]
4 Persons who commit acts 'done without criminal intent', provided no provision to the contrary exists in law.[11]
5 Persons of 'unsound mind', and of 'weak-minded' persons.[12]
6 Deaf-mutes.[13]
7 Persons under 14 years of age.[14]
8 Persons who have committed a crime but denounce themselves to the authorities before its discovery by officials.[15]

The privileges afforded these categories of persons under the law are listed in Table 4.1, and involve either immunity from punishment or a reduction in punishment. The ordinary criminal is given the normal penalty.

In all the cases in Table 4.1 where unequal treatment results in a decrease in penalty, those individuals in such a privileged position benefit from their special position under the law. Those who, through their actions, terminate the lives of other individuals are shielded from the full might and force of the law, and receive special protection to their advantage.

Let us turn our attention to the second type of inequality under the law identified above. Two cases initially existed under the 1907 Penal

Table 4.1 Non-constitution of a crime and reduction or remission of penalty under the Penal Code

Type of act/state	Privilege	Proviso
Justified acts	No punishment	–
Self-defence	No punishment	If act exceeds limits of defence penalty may be reduced or remitted
Averting imminent danger	No punishment	If act exceeds injury to be averted penalty may be reduced or remitted
Absence of intent	No punishment	Unless specifically provided in law
Mental derangement	No punishment	–
Minors	No punishment	–
Deaf-mute	Either no punishment or, if punished, punishment reduced	–
Weak-mindedness	Penalty may be reduced	–
Self-denunciation	Penalty may be reduced	–

Code where more severe penalties were provided in law for certain individuals: *fukeizai* (crimes against the Imperial Family); and crimes committed by direct lineal descendants against their lineal ascendants.

The question of whether or not to retain *fukeizai* in the present Constitution preoccupied both the Americans and Japanese involved in the process of legal reform. Having failed to retain the principle of *lèse-majesté* in the Constitution, Prime Minister Yoshida Shigeru sought to retain articles 73–76 of the Penal Code (which regulated offences committed against the Imperial Family). In a letter to General MacArthur, dated 27 December 1946, Yoshida tried to persuade the Supreme Command for the Allied Powers not to abolish *lèse-majesté*, arguing that the position of members of the Imperial Family demanded they receive special protection, in the form of more severe punishment for offenders, against acts of violence. In his defence, he cited as an example the act of treason in English law, which carries with it the death penalty. His argument, however, proved unsuccessful.[16]

Thus, the 1947 Constitution and the revised Penal Code, in line with the 'new' policy of ensuring equality under the law, make no special provision for offences against the Imperial Family. For the purpose of punishment there is technically no difference between crimes against a member of the Imperial Family and crimes against any other individual in society. No member of the Imperial Family receives special protection of his right to life in law.

The second case relates to the equality – or, rather, inequality – of the right to life of *chokkei sonzoku* (direct lineal ascendants). Before we examine the fate of the provisions in the Penal Code which gave special protection to direct lineal ascendants in respect of the right to life, let us examine the basis for the creation of this inequality in the law.

Historically, no such principle as the equality under the law provision of article 14(1) can be said to have operated in Japanese society. In law, there existed a series of special categories – both of victim and assailant – and the punishment of offenders differed according to who *inter alia* killed and was killed.

Japanese law has been greatly influenced by both the Chinese and, more recently, Western legal systems. In the *ritsuryō* Codes we see how Japan assimilated much from the Chinese codes of the T'ang dynasty (618–907). Although these Codes are the earliest extant codes in Japan, they are based on earlier versions of the Codes which no longer exist.[17]

In the *ritsuryō*, Japan applied the Chinese legal system, although tailoring certain elements to suit its own taste. This is particularly in evidence as regards the harsh punishments imposed under the Chinese Codes. In the *ritsuryō*, Japan moderated this harshness in keeping with its more delicate sensibilities. Thus, in the *T'ang li* Chinese Code, for example, the crime of committing adultery with the father's, or grandfather's, concubine was punished by hanging;[18] in the *ritsuryō* this is reduced to a two-and-a-half-year term of forced labour.[19] Five types of penalty were provided in the *ritsuryō*, and were, in increasing order of severity: [20]

1 *chi* (beating with a thin stick);
2 *jō* (beating with a thick stick);
3 *zu* (forced labour);
4 *ru* (exile);
5 *shi* (death).

An understanding of the moral values held by the Japanese people of this period can be gained by examining the *hachigyaku* provisions of the *ritsuryō*.[21] The *hachigyaku* were the eight most serious, or abominable, crimes which could be committed, and were considered the most morally detestable deeds by the community. These were considered to be so serious that even those individuals normally immune from punishment for crimes were not excluded. Those ordinarily immune included *rokugi* (six considerations)[22] and lineal descendants who, but for the fact that they had to look after lineal ascendants, would have faced death or exile.[23]

The *ritsuryō* lists the items of *hachigyaku* as follows:

1 *mu hen*;
2 *mu daigyaku*;
3 *mu hon*;
4 *akugyaku*;
5 *fudō*;
6 *daifukei*;
7 *fukō*;
8 *fugi*.

The items are listed as they appear in the text.

The items of *hachigyaku*, together with explanations and details of penalties imposed, are listed in Table 4.2. Of these eight items, six are of interest to us in the present context. *Mu hen*, *mu daigyaku* and *mu hon* demonstrate the supreme position of the ruler, acts against whom

Table 4.2 The eight most serious crimes (*hachigyaku*)

Crime	Explanation	Punishment
1 *Mu hen*	Plotting to endanger the *kokka* (state)	Death by cutting
2 *Mu daigyaku*	Plotting to damage the Emperor's grave or palace	Death by hanging[24]
3 *Mu hon*	Plotting to betray the country and obey a false ruler, rebels or foreign countries	Death by hanging
4 *Akugyaku*	Violence against, and murder of, family members	Death by cutting
5 *Fudō*	Crimes against humanity:	
	e.g. massacre	Death by cutting
	cruel murder	Death by cutting
	murder through satanic ritual	Death by cutting
6 *Daifukei*	Impolite acts against the Emperor: e.g. to damage the *taisha* (shrine),[25] or steal from the shrine	Banishment
7 *Fukō*	Filial impiety	Death by cutting
8 *Fugi*	Crimes against courtesy and manner:	
	e.g. murder of a master	Death by cutting
	murder of a governor	Death by cutting

were not taken lightly. *Akugyaku, fukō* and *fudō*, on the other hand, demonstrate the respect to be afforded lineal ascendants. As we are concerned in the remainder of this chapter with the special position afforded lineal ascendants in law, let us examine more closely the items of *akugyaku, fukō* and *fudō* in the *ritsuryō*.

Akugyaku was committed by the performance of one of the six acts listed in Table 4.3.[26] Here we can note that even causing physical injury to, or plotting to murder, one's own grandparents or parents was punishable by death by cutting. In the other cases listed, the actual death of the persons noted had to have occurred before invoking the death penalty.

Fukō was committed in the ways indicated in Table 4.4, which are itemized according to the penalties imposed.[29]

The items of *fudō* relevant to our present discussion are listed in Table 4.5.[30]

Two points can be made regarding the items of *hachigyaku* in the *ritsuryō* which relate to lineal ascendants. First, the penalty provided becomes more severe the more intimate the relationship betweeen assailant and victim. Second, the items of *hachigyaku* are confined exclusively to acts perpetrated by descendants and inferiors on ascendants and superiors; they do not contain any reference to acts committed by ascendants and superiors against descendants and inferiors. In all instances, it is the descendant or inferior who is the 'guilty' party 'deserving' of blame and punishment, and never vice versa.

Whilst a discussion of provisions relating to lineal ascendants in the *ritsuryō* is in itself interesting, the provisions listed have been brought into the discussion in order to gain a greater understanding of the special and privileged position in which lineal ascendants found themselves until recently in Japan. The spirit of the *ritsuryō* provisions has survived into modern society, and the provisions

Table 4.3 Types of *akugyaku* (crimes of violence against, and murder of, family members)

Type	Punishment
1 Hitting grandparents or parents	Death by cutting
2 Plotting to kill grandparents or parents	Death by cutting
3 Killing an uncle, father's sister, or grandparent-in-law	Death by cutting
4 Killing one's own elder brother or sister	Death by cutting
5 Killing the husband	Possibly death by cutting [27]
6 Killing the husband's parents	Possibly death by cutting [28]

Table 4.4 Types of *fukō* (filial impiety)

Type	Punishment
1 Reporting grandparents or parents to the authorities	Death by hanging
2 Putting a curse on grandparents or parents	2 years' forced labour
3 Saying bad words to grandparents or parents	3 years' forced labour
4 Having a different registration from grandparents or parents, and keeping money separate from them, while they are still alive	2 years' forced labour
5 The son marries of his own free will while mourning the death of his parents	2 years' forced labour
6 During the period of mourning following his parent's death, the son listens to music and changes out of his mourning clothes and into ordinary clothes	1½ years' forced labour
7 Not crying on the death of his grandparents	1 year's forced labour
8 Not showing grief on the death of a parent	2 years' forced labour
9 Telling the lie that grandparents or parents have died	1½ years' forced labour
10 Committing adultery with either the father's or grandfather's concubine	2½ years' forced labour

Table 4.5 Items of *fudō* (crimes against humanity)

Item	Punishment
1 Hitting an uncle, father's sister, or grandparents-in-law	2 years' forced labour
2 Hitting an elder brother or sister	1½ years' forced labour
3 Hitting the husband	Whip 100 times
4 Hitting the husband's parents	3 years' forced labour
5 Reporting an uncle, father's sister, elder brother or sister, grandparents-in-law, husband or husband's parents to the authorities	1 year's forced labour
6 Plotting to kill an uncle, father's sister, or elder brother or sister	Exile
7 Plotting to kill grandparents-in-law, husband or husband's parents	Death by cutting
8 Killing elder members within the fourth degree of relationship	Death by cutting

themselves have formed an important core of Japanese legal thought throughout history.

Disdain for crimes against lineal ascendants was particularly in evidence in Tokugawa Japan, where the strict hierarchical structure of society was predisposed to maintaining the concept of filial piety, and of a basic inequality between ascendants and descendants. Filial impiety was a grave offence, and infringements of filial piety were punished severely. In the *Kujikata osadamegaki* Code of 1742[31] – which brought with it milder punishments generally – we read that the crime of killing lineal ascendants was punished by public display followed by crucifixion.[32]

However strongly filial piety was approved of in Tokugawa Japan, when the issue of loyalty to one's lord came to confront the issue of filial piety, the question arose as to which took priority. The conflict between loyalty to one's lineal ascendant and loyalty to one's ruler, or state, was a dilemma discussed in Tokugawa Japan.[33] The case of Japan differed from that of China in the resolution of this dilemma. In China, the family is seen by many authors as taking precedence over the state. This view corresponded to the reality of the situation.[34] In Japan, on the other hand, loyalty to the state was paramount.[35]

The Meiji period saw a revival of interest in the *ritsuryō* provisions. Indeed, there is a marked similarity between many of the *ritsuryō* provisions and the provisions of the codes of the early Meiji period. Thus, under the *Kari keiritsu* (Provisional Penal Code) of 1868,[36] certain high officials and court personages – *rokugi* – were granted special privileges unless the acts committed were *hachigyaku*. This was, however, abolished by the *Shinritsu kōryō* (Essence of the New Penal Code) of 1871,[37] and replaced by a system which limited criminal liability, extending special privilege to young persons, old people, and persons suffering from physical incapacity and infirmity. Here we see the beginnings of what developed into Chapter 7 of the 1907 Penal Code. As with the *ritsuryō* Codes, the *Shinritsu kōryō* Code contained provisions relating to *inter alia* the murder of lineal ascendants.[38] Those committing this crime were very severely punished.

The principle of punishing lineal descendants more severely than non-lineal descendants is not, however, an exclusively Chinese or Japanese phenomenon. Examples of this practice are also to be found in the Western world. In its majority verdict in the *Fukuoka Patricide Case*,[39] which we shall examine more fully on pp. 61–3, the Supreme Court acknowledged that this principle is but an example of a 'universal moral principle' which has been 'recognized by mankind without regard to past or present or to East or West'.[40] We see examples of its operation in the concept of *parricidium* in Roman law,[41] as well as its modern manifestation in the French[42] and Italian[43] Penal Codes.

An important consequence of post-war legal reforms in Japan was the legal abolition of the *ie* (household) system, formally incorporated as a legal institution in the 1898 Civil Code.[44] The *ie* existed under this Code as a unit for registration. The *ie* comprised the *koshu* (head of the family) and the rest of the family. The *koshu* possessed *koshuken* (the rights of the head of the *ie*), which included the right to hold all of the family property; the right to determine succession; the right to approve or disapprove the marriages of family members; and the right to have a member removed from the *koseki*. According to this law, only the eldest son could inherit the family property and continue the *ie* line.[45]

Filial piety, as we have seen, was an intrinsic component of the traditional family system. Although this system was transformed dramatically and fundamentally by the post-war legal reforms, remnants of such a system can be detected in post-1947 Japanese society. Filial piety, the system's 'ideological pillar', to quote Justice Irokawa,[46] is a particularly visible remnant of the system.

Filial piety is of direct concern to our discussion in that its senior members – lineal ascendants – were granted a privileged position in respect of the value and protection of life even after the 1947 reforms. The dilemma between filial piety and an equal right to life for all individuals under the Constitution can be discussed from the perspective of the punishment, or penalty, aspect of crimes involving the taking away of life. At issue here were the discrepancies in sentences which could be meted out on lineal descendants who commit bodily injury resulting in the death of lineal ascendants, or who murder such ascendants,[47] and which existed to the detriment of lineal descendants.

In the Penal Code we find the term *chokkei sonzoku* (direct lineal ascendants), although no mention is made of *hizoku* (lineal descendants).[48] The term *chokkei sonzoku* excludes both uncles and aunts. It also excludes the step-parent/step-child relationship. It includes, however, the adopting parent/adopted child relationship.[49]

At the centre of the dilemma between the concept of filial piety and an equal right to life for all individuals has been the constitutionality of articles 200 and 205(2) of the 1907 Penal Code – both recently abolished – in light of article 14(1) of the Constitution. Let us first examine how article 205 was interpreted by the courts.

By article 205(1) of the Code:

A person who inflicts bodily injury upon another and thereby causes his death shall be punished with imprisonment at forced labour for a fixed term of not less than two years.

By article 205(2):

When committed against a direct lineal ascendant of the offender or of his or her spouse, imprisonment at forced labour for life or for not less than three years shall be imposed.

The penalties for the crimes of injury resulting in the death of both lineal and non-lineal ascendants under articles 205(1) and 205(2) are listed in Table 4.6. The penalties for the crimes of murder of lineal and non-lineal ascendants laid down in articles 199 and 200 are listed in Table 4.7 (see p. 64).

From Table 4.6 we see that the provisions established differences in both the maximum and minimum penalties for the crime of injury resulting in death, depending on whether the victim is a lineal or non-lineal ascendant.

Alfred Oppler, an American who played an important role in the immediate post-war legal reforms, provides us with an insight into why such discrepancies were allowed in the Penal Code. It was left untouched out of:

> consideration for the sensitive area of family relations that underlay our self-restraint in the revision of the Civil Code.[51]

Discrepancy in sentences under articles 205(1) and 205(2) reflects the different value placed on the lives of individuals belonging to the different categories of persons. The state has a duty to operate an effective law against murder and behaviour likely to endanger life; but does it also have the right, in the process, to discriminate between different categories of persons in respect of the right to life? Based on the deterrence theory, and on the adverse feelings of the Japanese themselves towards crimes and actions which run counter to the concept of filial piety, added protection is afforded the lives of lineal ascendants. Given that the potential offender is well aware of the antisocial nature of his intended deed, and the fact that punishment for harming lineal ascendants is more severe than for harming non-lineal ascendants, lineal descendants are, so the argument goes, less likely to harm lineal ascendants.

An incident of 31 October 1949 brought the apparent conflict

Table 4.6 Crime of injury resulting in death

Item	Article 205(1)	Article 205(2)
Victim	Non-lineal ascendant	Lineal ascendant
Maximum penalty	15 years' imprisonment[50]	Life imprisonment
Minimum penalty	2(+) years' imprisonment	3(+) years' imprisonment

between what Justice Hozumi Shigeto termed the 'old custom' of filial piety[52] and the 'new' equality under the law provision of the Constitution into the legal arena.[53] On that day, a son, provoked by his father, physically assaulted him during a family quarrel. The father died the next day from his injuries. The son was brought before the Fukuoka District Court, found guilty of the offence of bodily injury resulting in death, and sentenced to three years' imprisonment, suspended for three years.

Of relevance in the present context was the court at first instance's insistence that article 205(2) was unconstitutional on the ground that it infringed the equality under the law provision of article 14(1). The Fukuoka District Court argued that the 'so-called beautiful custom' of filial piety was a product of 'quite feudalistic, anti-democratic, and anti-libertarian ideas', and running 'counter to the grand spirit of the Constitution, which stresses the legal equality of all human beings'.[54] It held that the provision of article 205(2), summarized in the words of the Grand Bench of the Supreme Court, was:

> tantamount to establishing, in regard to both the protection of human life and to punishment, a distinction among the people between those who are 'special' and those who are 'ordinary' and that, therefore, giving special protection to lineal ascendants as compared with ordinary people results in an inequality under law.[55]

Similar views were taken by Justice Hozumi Shigeto and Justice Mano Tsuyoshi in their minority dissenting opinions of the Grand Bench of the Supreme Court, to which the prosecution appealed the decision of the lower court. To quote Justice Hozumi, the discrepancy in the severity of punishment suggested that 'we cannot say that the main object of the legislation is not the legal benefit of protection for lineal ascendants'.[56] As it may result in greater protection, it violates the principle of equality under the law. Viewed in such terms, a consequence of such unequal treatment is thus the undermining of one of the fundamental bases upon which stands the concept of democracy – the equality of fundamental human rights for all individuals.

Applied to the right to life, we see that both Justices Hozumi and Mano, and the court at first instance, believed that, as a result of such discrimination, equal protection of human life is not afforded to all individuals. No differential in penalty is reasonable when it is based on concepts which the Constitution specifically aims to correct, or which run counter to the spirit of the Constitution.

The majority of the Grand Bench, however, neither considered article 205(2) to run counter to the spirit of the Constitution, nor did they see article 14(1) as an attempt to correct the Penal Code provision. Instead, the majority verdict stressed that law should not exclude provisions which created inequality if required by morality, justice, or the specific purposes to be served by the law, and having taken into consideration matters such as age, natural qualities, occupation, or special relations with others. The formal judgment stressed that, if it was constitutional for family relations to be considered in weighing penalties, it was equally constitutional to formalize them in law.

The majority verdict emphasized that morality, controlling the relationship between, for example, parent and child, was 'the great fountainhead of human ethics'.[57] Justifying the constitutionality of article 205(2), the Court observed that the Code seeks, through the law, to stress the importance which society attaches to the moral duties of the descendant towards ascendants. The majority found it reasonable to interpret the main object of the legal provision not so much in terms of the protection of the lineal ascendant – the victim of the crime – but rather 'on a special consideration of the anti-moral character' of the descendant – the assailant.[58] The added protection given to the victim simply reflects this.

Justice Saitō Yūsuke, in particular, was incensed by the lower court ruling and of the opinions of the minority on the Grand Bench. In strong language, Justice Saitō lambasted such opinions. To think in such a way, he noted, was 'democratic infantilism, which cannot but be surprising, and a deplorable idea of civil liberties'.[59] He continued:

> We must reject completely such ideas . . . which must be called conceited notions of ingratitude, lacking in understanding of . . . morality, and aimlessly chasing after innovations.[60]

In 1964, the Supreme Court declared its 'ground-rules' for determining the constitutionality of matters falling within the ambit of article 14(1) of the Constitution in the following terms:

> Article 14, paragraph 1 does not guarantee absolute equality to all of the people. It is to be construed as prohibiting differentiation without reasonable ground thereof. It does not prohibit some differential treatment being regarded as reasonable in view of the nature of the matter.[61]

The question of the constitutionality of article 205(2) reappeared on the legal stage in 1974, when the First Petty Bench of the Supreme

Court again held the provision constitutional. Following the guidelines established in the 1964 case, the provision was held constitutional on the ground that the discrepancy between the penalties provided under articles 205(1) and 205(2) was not unreasonably large. The decision was reached by a majority of four to one, with Justice Ōsumi dissenting.

There was, however, a body of academic opinion which favoured the view that article 205(2) should be held unconstitutional as against article 14(1).[62]

The special protection given to direct lineal ascendants was found not only in the offence of injury resulting in death, but also in the offence of murder itself. According to article 199 of the Penal Code:

A person who kills another shall be punished with death or by imprisonment at forced labour for life or for a term of not less than three years.

By article 200:

A person who kills one of his or her own or his or her spouse's direct lineal ascendants shall be punished with death or imprisonment at forced labour for life.

The penalties for the crimes of the murder of lineal and non-lineal ascendants are listed in Table 4.7. In the case of murder, discrepancy thus existed in relation to the minimum penalty which could be imposed in cases of the murder of lineal and non-lineal ascendants.

The practical implication of this discrepancy in the Code was succinctly put by Justice Hozumi in his minority opinion.[63] Whereas in the case of 'ordinary' murder the sentence may be reduced to a three-year term of imprisonment, with a stay of execution granted, in the case of 'special' murder the death penalty could only be commuted to life imprisonment. Even if the sentence was reduced by law and further reduced by extenuating circumstances, sentence could be reduced no lower than a term of three-and-a-half-years' imprisonment, no stay of execution being allowed, for by article 25 of the

Table 4.7 Crime of murder

Item	Article 199	Article 200
Victim	Non-lineal ascendant	Lineal ascendant
Maximum penalty	Death	Death
Minimum penalty	3(+) years' imprisonment	Life imprisonment

Penal Code only a person sentenced to imprisonment for not more than three years may receive a suspension of execution of sentence.[64] The three-and-a-half-year term of imprisonment was thus the minimum penalty which could be handed down under the provision, no matter how justified the killing.[65]

In the early 1970s, the Supreme Court had the opportunity to reconsider the question of heavier penalties for patricide. In the case of *Aizawa* v. *Japan*[66] the accused had strangled her father, who had, over a long period of time, repeatedly committed incest with her. The court at first instance held article 200 to be unconstitutional, applying article 199 to the case instead. The decision was reversed by the High Court, which held article 200 constitutional.

The case came before the Supreme Court for judgment in 1973. It reversed the earlier judgment and held article 200 unconstitutional. The majority opinion of the Court stated in no unclear terms that the legislative purpose of article 200 was to afford 'special' protection to lineal ascendants against loss of life through murder committed by lineal descendants. It noted:

> The legislative policy behind article 200 of the Penal Code is to deter people very strictly from murdering his own or his spouse's lineal ascendants by inflicting a heavier penalty upon such an act than in the case of ordinary murder, thereby making it clear that such an act is highly blameworthy.[67]

The question to be considered in the 1973 case was whether or not article 200 unreasonably discriminated between the murder of lineal and non-lineal ascendants. The majority opinion stated that it was void as against article 14(1) in making 'a clearly unreasonable discrimination' between ordinary murder and the murder of one's lineal ascendants.[68]

Article 200 was held unconstitutional, however, not on the ground that the legislature was prohibited under the Constitution from differentiating between the murder of lineal and non-lineal ascendants *ipso facto*, but on the ground that the *extent* of the discrepancy of the penalty was unconstitutional for unreasonableness. Unconstitutionality arises where 'the extent of the penalty is augmented to such an extent . . . that it loses sight of the legislative purpose'.[69] Article 200 provided a penalty which 'is too heavy in that it provides only for the death penalty or life imprisonment', a penalty 'much heavier' than that prescribed for murder.[70]

The 'legislative purpose' in this instance was held to be that of:

honour[ing] natural affection for one's lineal ascendants, and to preserve the universal principle of ethics. The maintenance of [such] natural feelings and universal ethics is appropriately to be regarded as one of the legitimate objectives of penal law. That descendants pay respect to, and feel obliged to requite *on* [moral indebtedness] to, their lineal ascendants is indeed a fundamental principle of morals in our social life.[71]

Some of the judges, however, took the view that such discrimination – no matter how little – was in itself unconstitutional. In his concurring opinion, Justice Irokawa argued that the majority opinion's strong advocacy of heavy legal sanctions for such violation, in his view,

> just shows that the justices in the majority are still haunted by the conventional concept of filial piety. It is not a principle of natural law applicable to all ages and countries . . . The concept of filial piety which demands blind, absolute subordination to parents is clearly incompatible with democratic ethics based upon the principle of individual dignity and equality.[72]

Justices Tanaka[73] and Ōsumi[74] argued in similar vein.

The difference in emphasis between the majority opinion and the concurring opinions of Justices Irokawa, Tanaka and Ōsumi is thus one between a policy that would allow a reasonable degree of discrepancy in the treatment of the murderers of lineal and non-lineal ascendants, and a policy where no such discrimination whatsoever could be entertained.

Justice Shimoda's dissenting opinion, however, reveals the pro-filial piety stance which still existed amongst certain members of the judiciary. In Justice Shimoda's mind, the term 'social status' appearing in article 14(1) was meant to exclude status within the family. Article 200, therefore, raised 'no constitutional problem'. 'It is within the discretion of the Diet', he argued, 'to decide what kind of penalties are to be inflicted upon each type of offence.'[75]

In this chapter we have seen how one element of the traditional moral value of filial piety – the respect and obedience owed by lineal descendants to their ascendants – has conflicted with the equality under the law provision of the Constitution, and we have noted how the courts have dealt with this perceived inequality. At issue has been the question of whether the provisions under discussion have as their base a type of morality which conflicts with the general purpose of the Constitution. Whereas some judges have seen as problematic the intermingling of law and morality – filial piety not being considered an appropriate subject of legislation – others see no such problem, and fully accept a law based on the demands of morality.

Thus, whilst the discussion above has centred on various aspects of filial piety, the issue can be viewed within the more general question of the relationship between law and morality. As Justice Hozumi succinctly put it, the issue is ultimately not filial piety *per se*; rather:

> the issue is to what extent a moral principle should be enacted into law and whether it is proper to do so from the viewpoint of the essential limitations of morality and law.[76]

The question of the separation (or otherwise) of law and morality raises its head from time to time in both academic and political circles in Japan. In respect of the former, we can, for example, point to the debate between Kawashima Takeyoshi and Makino Eiichi.[77]

In the political arena, this issue could be found raised in the deliberations of the Commission on the Constitution (whose reports, it should be remembered, did not always represent the views held generally in the late 1950s and early 1960s as those with opposing opinions declined to participate in its deliberations). Commissioner Nakagawa, arguing against the revision of article 24,[78] observed:

> it is best to leave [moral problems] to morality, education, and social policy; they should not be brought into the world of law. If the attempt is made to do so, they will be adjudicated according to the values of the old traditional family system and the ideal form of modern family life will be lost.[79]

This perspective contrasts markedly with the more 'traditional' view expressed by the academic Hozumi Yatsuka (1860–1912), for example. Whilst deeply influenced by such legal positivists as Paul Laband (1838–1918)[80] and John Austin (1790–1859),[81] he denied completely their thesis that the legal and moral worlds were separate. Hozumi wrote:

> Law expresses the basic ethical principles of a given society. Law is the publicly acknowledged morality of society. The view that among men ethics and law are different things is a stupid misunderstanding . . . Anyone who has read even a little history can have no doubt that the evidence shows that ethics and law normally advance hand in hand. Law being the right road of social existence, the legal ideal is for ethics and law to form the same body.[82]

Whilst for Laband and Austin there was an equation of law with sovereign command,[83] for Hozumi 'the definition of law as command is the last word of legal theory'.[84] Whereas Hozumi perceived their scientific legal approach, allied with the concept of state as legal person, as separating monarch from law – bringing with it a separation of law from social reality – his own approach entertained no such separation. What united law and morality for Hozumi was reverence for ancestors. This it does

> by making sacred the word of the emperor. Law and ethics thus become parallel and complementary means to the same end: the preservation of society.[85]

The examples of morality in law noted in this chapter can be discussed in the light of the legal philosopher David Lyons' contention of some systematic connections between law and 'moral ideas'.[86] In his discussion of morality and law, he attempts to analyse the special protection afforded certain categories of individuals in society:

> All systems of social organization seem to have some prohibitions on the use of force against individuals. It has been argued (by H.L.A. Hart: *The Concept of Law* (1961) pp. 181–95) that social systems cannot survive unless they incorporate some protections for persons, property, and premises. But these restrictions are quite variable, and some favored groups within a society may enjoy protections that are not enjoyed by all. So, while law may reflect prevailing moral opinion, its restrictions do not necessarily correspond to sound moral principles.[87]

Lyons thus distinguishes between 'moral opinions' and 'sound moral principles' (or 'moral truth'). By 'moral opinions' Lyons means 'the values that people have', including their views on such matters as 'sexual conduct, the use of narcotic substances, property, contracts, and a host of other matters . . . ' They include 'ideas about moral rights and responsibilities'. 'There seems little doubt', he argues, 'that law interacts with moral opinions.'[88] For there to be connection between law and 'moral truth', on the other hand, 'law must meet sound moral tests'.[89]

It is suggested here that, whereas the provision of articles 200 and 205(2) of the Penal Code clearly reflect connection between law and 'moral opinions', the claim that connection similarly exists between law and 'moral truth' is more difficult to justify. This contention is made on three grounds.

First, the type of filial piety which underlay the legal prescription – the duty of descendants to their ascendants – is not a universally accepted moral. Thus, in English law, for example, there is no such itemization of the murder of lineal ascendants, or of injury resulting in the death of lineal ascendants. This is because the concept of filial piety itself has never been at the centre of moral value. In countries such as Italy[90] and Argentina,[91] which distinguish patricide from ordinary murder, law provides not only concrete provisions regarding the duty of lineal descendants to lineal ascendants, but also makes provision to adequately reflect the responsibilities owed by those ascendants towards the descendants, thus balancing the inequality perceived to have existed in Japanese law. These countries reject the one-sided approach adopted by Japan and China.

Second, the situation in reality in Japan casts doubt on the contention that the type of filial piety reflected in articles 200 and 205(2) constitutes 'moral truth'. The basic inequality which existed in the Penal Code in the protection and value of the lives of direct lineal ascendants is derived from a perception that this type of filial piety is a moral value. In practice, however, it is often its antithesis. As Ōtsuka Hitoshi[92] has observed, the incidents involving the murder of lineal ascendants, and physical assault upon them by lineal descendants, are often the result of immense provocation on the part of the ascendants, so much so that the descendants feel they have no alternative but to take action to protect their own person (and, often, sanity).

The traditional social environment in which these assailants find themselves is often the cause for the ensuing unexpected outbreak of violence against the ascendant. The traditional family system – which still survives to a large extent in practice – carries with it the implied expectation that the descendant looks after the ascendant whatever the circumstance. The ascendant comes to rely on the descendant, and the unseen family bond is such as to instil in the descendant a feeling that no 'escaping' the system is permitted or tolerated. The ensuing outbreak of violence can be viewed as a counteraction to a variety of social and parental pressure exerted on the descendant over a long period of time.

The third ground relates to the relationship between law and justice. If the purpose of law in adopting such 'moral principles' as filial piety is to bring about justice, any resulting injustice brought through such adoption necessarily relegates it to something less than 'moral truth'. In the preceding discussion we have seen, from a Western perspective, filial piety appearing to be a tool for operating a legal inequality in respect of the right to life. When law uses filial piety to infringe upon the equality of the right to life, filial piety, viewed from this perspective, cannot avoid acting as moral prejudice against the constitutional provision.

5 The social value of death

Karōshi (death from overwork) and suicide from psychological and physical pressures are current problems inside direct profit-making organizations (such as the company), as well as in organizations and institutions which are not directly profit-making but which serve the community (such as schools and local government). We can, however, recognize in these phenomena, which arise within modern organizations, problems which embrace traditional moral values and dilemmas.

In this chapter we present the ambivalence between the traditional moral values, which tend to act against the individual's right to life inside organizations, and the structure and purpose of modern organizations. We focus our attention on the mechanisms of *karōshi* and suicide within the company in our attempt at understanding what lies behind death in Japanese society.

Derived from the unitary model[1] of the structure of the company organization, the Japanese company – like its Western counterparts – is a mechanism for increasing wealth and, in the process, for generating benefits in the form of profits for its shareholders, the 'owners' of the company.[2]

In Japan, as in Britain, for example, a distinction exists between the company, in a strictly legal sense, and those individual members who make up the company. Upon formation, a Japanese company becomes a separate being with a legal personality having its own legal rights and duties.[3] A company is often referred to as *kaisha hōjin* (an artificial legal person) since it is created by a process other than birth. It is an organization which has a separate legal existence from its shareholders. It is treated as a juristic person in its own right, rather than a collective name for its shareholders.

As a company is an artificial person its activities must be carried on by its human members. Those individual members of a company consist of shareholders, directors and employees. Both Japanese and English company law make a clear distinction between the roles of shareholders of the company and its directors. If the shareholders are the 'owners' of the company, directors are its 'managers'. In a company, ownership and management are separated, with the owners delegating the running of the company to its directors. This is an important consequence of the corporate form, which has created the possibility of a greater or lesser degree of dissociation between shareholders and the agents of effective possession. Recent years have confirmed this inherent separation found in the formal structure of company law, and there has been a growing tendency for strategic control of a company to become increasingly separated from capital ownership.

In law, the company's activities are carried out by, and responsibility for the company's actions rests with, those individuals in managerial roles – the directors of the company. The duties of Japanese directors are found in the Commercial Code.[4] Directors are elected at the shareholders' meeting.[5] The Board of Directors 'determine the administration of the affairs of the company and shall supervise the directors' performance of their duties'.[6] The appointed *daihyō torishimariyaku*, as the term suggests, is the representative director.[7] The Board of Directors appoint 'officers' from among the directors to implement the resolutions of the Board and the shareholders' meetings.

The third group of individuals to be found within the company's internal environment are the workers, or employees. They implement on a day-to-day basis policies formulated, and decisions made, by management.

The distinction made in Japanese law between directors and employees is, however, often blurred in practice. It has been observed[8] that no clear distinction can be made in practice between the director in charge of operations and the employee who assumes the duties of a director, for example. Neither is the legal distinction of profound significance in the minds of those working in the company. Rodney Clark,[9] based on his research into the workings of the Japanese company, has observed that neither directors nor employees pay much attention to the legal distinction. Rather, directors were perceived as being the occupants of the most senior ranks in the company, who for the most part had worked their way up to the top from lower ranks. When appointed directors they resigned as employees. Nevertheless, they continued to do the same work as they had done before being promoted to the Board, and they also held that rank in addition to the new rank of director.

In our present examination of the ambivalence between company values and the member's constitutional right to life, those members so affected are identified as being either members of the Board of Directors or employees. Shareholders, however, are excluded, for they cannot be considered to be working in the company in the same sense as do directors and employees. When used in the Japanese context, the term 'salary man' – the subjects of our discussion – conveys the subservient position of both directors and employees *vis-à-vis* the owners of the company.

The relationship between employer and employee in a Japanese company can be understood in terms of the theory of social exchange.[10] Essentially, the theory is based on the idea that individuals possess certain resources, and act as members of society by exchanging these resources. Such resources are not confined to material resources, but also include such virtues as respect, the taking on of responsibility, loyalty,[11] and sacrifice.[12]

Within the organizational sphere, both company director and employee are, to a significant degree, bound to the organization. The contractual relationship between employer and employee (tilted in favour of the employer), together with the Japanese people's reluctance to break contracts and cause disharmony, has led to a situation where, to a large extent, employees (particularly those in large, economically stable, companies) feel reluctant to change companies, although this has begun to erode given recent developments in the Japanese economy. There is a tendency for employees to remain as committed members of the corporate unit for lengthy periods of time. In certain instances, this commitment – as we shall see – takes on the extreme form of individual members sacrificing their lives for the sake of the company.

In return for an employee's commitment, he is provided with employment, consisting of a good salary, job security,[13] possible job satisfaction, and such benefits as subsidized accommodation, health care insurance, pensions, the use of holiday resorts and frequent company outings. Such employment also brings with it social status and position.[14]

Let us turn our attention to *karōshi*. Whilst not a new phenomenon, the term *karōshi* was first introduced into the Japanese language only in 1982, when it formed part of the title of a book by Hosokawa Migiwa, Uehata Tetsunojō and Tajiri Shunichirō.[15] Okamura Chikanobu[16] defines *karōshi* as a phenomenon which arises from fatigue, involving the destruction of bodily rhythm and the breaking down of the mechanism for the continuation of life, thereby bringing the human body to its utmost limit.

Karōshi is a socio-medical term which refers both to physical death – particularly of illnesses relating to cerebral blood vessels (such as cerebral haemorrhage, cerebral thrombosis, and the effusion of blood inside the arachnoid) and illnesses of the heart (such as myocarditis and cardiac insufficiency, heart diseases which result from a lack of blood to the heart) – and social death brought on by overwork. Examples of social death are insanity, physical handicap and senility arising from severe and continuous fatigue. *Karōshi* itself is thus not a term which denotes one disease, but is a term which covers both socio-pathological death and near-death phenomena in contemporary Japanese society.

Karōshi can be distinguished from *totsuzenshi* (sudden death). *Totsuzenshi* refers to the phenomenon of *sudden* death, where the duration between the appearance of the first signs of symptoms and the occurrence of death is a maximum of 24 hours. *Karōshi*, on the other hand, has no such limit, and the time between the appearance of symptoms and death itself may be many years apart.

Triggered by a growing number of reported *karōshi* cases, worries have generated both public debate and action, neither of which show signs of receding into the background. To give an idea of the scale of the problem, statistics for 1987, for example, can be cited which show that 499 claims for compensation were received by the Labour Ministry on the grounds of *karōshi*, 21 of which were successful.[17] The remainder failed to prove that death was caused by overwork. This reflects the practical difficulties involved in proving causation.[18] It is arguable, however, that the statistics merely represent the tip of the iceberg.[19]

Concern about *karōshi* has been expressed not only in the mass media but also by those working in companies themselves. A recent survey by the Fukoku Mutual Life Insurance Company[20] clearly demonstrates unease amongst members. The survey showed that almost a half of those salaried workers interviewed feared they would fall victim to *karōshi*. Amongst those of senior rank – section chiefs and above – the percentage rose markedly, with two-thirds of those surveyed expressing worries that they would work themselves to death.

Karōshi – which befalls both directors and employees alike[21] – arises from the fact that the individual member is often expected to place the interests of the company above his own interests. In such instances, his first loyalty and responsibility is to the welfare of his company; loyalty to himself and to his family takes second place.

What specific factors contribute to *karōshi*? Uehata Tetsunojō has identified a number of pertinent factors which break the natural rhythm of the body, causing the deterioration of the circulatory organs.[22] Let us examine some of these contributory factors.

A central contributory factor to *karōshi* is sheer hard work over a prolonged period of time. Statistics show that the Japanese work longer hours than their counterparts in the Western world. Statistics released by the Ministry of Labour for 1987,[23] for example, show that the full-time employee working in a company with more than thirty employees worked an average of 2,111 hours. This compares with the United States and British average of some 200 hours a year less, and a West German and French average of some 500 hours less. While public employees have seen a reduction in hours worked since April 1988,[24] this has not necessarily been the case in the private sector,[25] although the recent downturn in the Japanese economy has necessitated, at least temporarily, a reduction in the total amount of overtime worked by employees. Working hours in practice often exceed the legal limit of 40 hours per week.

The question of an unreasonable amount of *zangyō* (overtime) has recently been the subject of much discussion, and the concept as an absolute value has been brought into question. In part, the companies themselves have speeded up the process of reducing the number of hours of overtime worked, for, given the recent severe economic difficulties faced by companies, many see reducing overtime as a cost-effective method of reducing labour costs. We can thus note that this state of affairs has been brought about by action initiated by employers countering economic hardship, and not by pressure or resistance from workers themselves. When economic conditions improve, workers may well see themselves yet again subjected to much overtime.

Case-law on this point does not fare well for the employee. In the legal arena, an important debate has been initiated as to the legality of *zangyō* when it is forced on the employee without his consent. The *Tanaka Case* is central to the debate. On 30 October 1967, Tanaka Hideyuki, an employee of the Hitachi company, was dismissed by the company for continuously refusing to work overtime. Demanding reinstatement subsequent to his dismissal, Tanaka took his case to the courts, and in 1978 the District Court found in his favour, and for his reinstatement.[26]

Hitachi appealed the decision, and on 27 March 1986 the Tokyo

High Court[27] overturned the lower court's ruling, deciding in favour of the company. It upheld the legality of Hitachi's claim that its work rules and collective agreements with employees provided it with the right to order overtime work if necessary. Despite Tanaka's claim that consent was required each time the company asked an employee to work overtime, the Court held that individual consent by workers is not required for each individual request to undertake such work.[28] In December 1991, the Supreme Court upheld this decision.[29]

Not only does the Japanese worker undertake a great deal of overtime, he is also expected to maintain a low rate of absenteeism.[30] The recent survey by the Fukoku Mutual Life Insurance Company highlights this aspect of the employee's duty consciousness. More than 80 per cent of the 500 workers surveyed said that they would not absent themselves from work, even if ill.[31] Such an attitude is instilled in the Japanese people from a young age, and is particularly in evidence in the school and university context.[32] The work context, being a continuation of these earlier social phases, is no different, and the company expects the same – and often more – from its members as does society of its individuals generally in social situations.

There is, in addition, the expectation that a member takes as little in the way of holidays as possible. In 1986, according to statistics compiled by the Ministry of Labour,[33] the average length of annual paid holiday leave in both companies (with at least thirty full-time employees) and the government sector was 14.9 days. In practice, however, as Sengoku Tamotsu[34] notes, employees make use of less than half the holidays they are legally entitled to. Several authors,[35] however, perceive a slight change in attitude amongst the younger generation towards taking full advantage of their holiday entitlement.

A further contributory factor to mounting stress, leading to *karōshi*, for the company member is the Japanese system of *tanshinfunin*. The *tanshinfunin* is a director or employee, usually of middle rank or higher in the corporate hierarchy, who is sent by the company to work either at a branch office in another part of Japan or, as is increasingly common, abroad. He may be sent for a few months, or the duration of his stay may be many years.

Such stays may have detrimental effect on both the worker and his family.[36] The *tanshinfunin* himself may suffer in at least three ways from his posting abroad, or to another part of Japan. First, alone and separated from his family, he is in a position to work even longer hours than would have been the case at home. Second, psychologically, his remoteness from the home environment, with its comforts and stability, may well add to the overall stress. Third, economically, the need to maintain two homes may be a drain on his financial resources. Even given the fact that his new accommodation will be paid for by the company, more frequent visits to places of relaxation[37] necessarily involve considerable financial expenditure.

The system of *tanshinfunin* is supported by the courts. A recent 1986 decision of the Second Petty Bench of the Supreme Court[38] leaves in no doubt the legality of an employer's action in ordering an employee to work away when provision to that effect is laid down in the work rules, even if such a move means leaving his family behind. In this case, the employee, working at the company's Kobe branch, was asked to move to its Hiroshima branch. When he refused, he was ordered instead to the Nagoya office. When he refused again, he was dismissed. The employee refused on the ground that, to comply with the order, he would have had to leave his family behind. Although the courts in the first and second instances considered his refusal to be reasonable, and nullified the dismissal, the Supreme Court reversed the decision. Only when the move was not deemed necessary for the company, or where illegal motives were involved, or when such a move would result in severe hardship, may the employee refuse such a move.[39]

Once the worker has settled in to his new environment, he may legally be ordered to return home at any time. In a decision of the Second Petty Bench of the Supreme Court in 1985,[40] the Court held that the employer need not obtain the consent of the worker when ordering the transferred *tanshinfunin* to return home, unless there were special circumstances requiring such consent. The result of this may be to compound both his, and his family's, feelings of insecurity and uncertainty.

Both Supreme Court decisions have come in for criticism. Nakamura Kazuhisa and Saitō Madoka,[41] legal scholars at Waseda University, have argued that the employee should be able in law to refuse being temporarily transferred unless such transfer is essential to the company and also the employee has agreed with the company on the necessity of future transfers. They argue that the Supreme Court has 'underestimated' the effects of such transfers on the life of the employee. The decisions reveal that, as far as the Court is concerned, the effects of transfer on an employee's life are less important than the benefits which accrue to the company from the transfers.

The changing corporate environment of the last decade has also directly contributed to the increase in the cases of *karōshi*, particularly in its social death aspect. In many instances, unbearable mounting stress leads not to physical death but to mental illness. The journalist Ishikawa Takaaki[42] draws attention to an increase in the trend in 'smiling depression' amongst workers in their forties and fifties, so much so that one psychiatrist has estimated that as many as one in ten workers in their middle years suffer from it. These individuals – overachievers – carefully conceal their inner turmoil with a permanent smile, and signs of severe depression often go undetected until it is too late.

Ishikawa reports the case of a 53-year-old employee of a large bank who, having been denied promotion following a merger with a larger institution, was put in charge of a smaller subsidiary. Loss of promotion prospects, coupled with a need to adapt quickly to his new situation and a rapidly advancing technological environment, led to a deterioration in his mental health.

Ishikawa argues that the rapidly changing environment has influenced the mental health of many of today's middle-aged employees. In the period immediately following the Second World War, those entering companies (as well as other institutions and the civil service) were, given Japan's high growth rate, ensured advancement and promotion in return for loyalty and dedication. Recent years, however, have witnessed a change in this respect, so that now 'keeping one's nose to the grindstone no longer ensures promotion'.[43] An increasing rationalization and streamlining of companies has resulted in a corporate environment which has come to value creativity and leadership. This tends to work to the benefit of younger employees, and to the detriment of older employees – particularly those unable to keep up with the new technology. All these factors can be seen as contributing to an increase in the incidence of mental illness amongst company members.

Let us now turn our attention to apology suicide. The demand that someone takes personal responsibility for mistakes made by institutions is, as Michael Reich has pointed out, a 'longstanding Japanese cultural pattern'.[44] Responsibility can be expressed in a multitude of ways, and in different circumstances.[45] Frank Gibney[46] has gone so far as to refer to apology in Japanese society as a 'rite'.

For the individual, the most extreme act of public apology for company error is apology suicide. Robert Lifton, Katō Shūichi and Michael Reich have termed the act 'apologize by dying', and refer in their work to the Japanese phrase *shinde owabi o suru*. Motivation for such an act, they argue, is 'group-centered', allowing the overcoming of 'otherwise unmanageable resentments of company authority (which might well have been a factor in causing the error)'.[47]

Lifton *et al.* cite as an example of apology suicide an incident of food poisoning involving Japan Air Lines. The outbreak of food poisoning amongst the passengers was traced back to the contaminated hangnail of an employee under the supervision of the director of the food-supply section of the company. The director committed suicide as an act of apology. Commenting on the incident, Lifton *et al.* stress the reasons for the suicide as including the restoration of group harmony between company and passengers, and the perpetuation of the good name of the company. By such an act was resolved an otherwise unresolvable situation for the group, it having removed the cause of social animosity.[48]

The 'involuntary' nature of the act of apology suicide should be emphasized. The legal scholar John Haley[49] has argued that the public apology serves as a form of social control. Lack of formal sanctions in the legal system to compel certain behaviour, he argues, may lead to extra-legal substitutes, and to a reinforcement of the feasibility of existing methods of coercing behaviour. Reich, however, criticizes Haley on the ground that he 'understates' the involuntary nature of public apology, and of the 'enormous pressure' on individuals to make public apologies in Japanese society. The public apology, he argues, becomes 'a nearly institutionalized "informal" sanction'.[50]

The question arises, however, as to whether public apology, even if it were to serve as a form of social control, as Haley argues, should be so extreme as to involve the taking of one's life to apologize for some act. Here we see that apology suicide serves not only to appease pressure originating outside the organization but also to counteract pressure emanating from within the organization itself, to take responsibility for the wrongdoing. In a sense, the person committing such suicide takes on himself the role of scapegoat inside the company structure, and/or against society, on behalf of the company.

Acting in this extreme manner follows the traditional pattern of taking responsibility. The background to this form of behaviour can be found, on the one hand, in the practice of imposed vicarious liability of the *renza*[51] and *enza*[52] systems, and, on the other hand, in the sympathetic attitude to the act of suicide in Japanese society.

In contemporary Japanese society, vicarious liability, although not legally imposed, nevertheless operates in practice. The voluntary resignation of one's position to take responsibility for wrongdoing by other members of the same section in a company, or of individuals under one's direction, is most common.

Suicide was condoned in traditional Japanese society.[53] This tradition has made the act of apology suicide more available psychologically to Japanese company employees. The institutionalizing of apology suicide for the sake of the larger group is an extension of this, rendering such suicide acceptable and plausible – both for the individual concerned, the company, and society generally.

Whilst the life of one individual is expendable to the company, for the individual this is his extreme sacrifice. His act of apology is 'involuntary' in the sense that, had not the incident giving rise to social animosity occurred, the individual would not have contemplated the taking away of his life.[54] This contrasts markedly with situations of nihilistic suicide, for example, where the individual, for whatever personal reason that existed, takes his own life in the absence of external pressure of the kind that exists in the case of apology suicide. Whereas nihilistic suicide is internally motivated, the result of conflict within the *psyche* of that individual, apology suicide is externally motivated, it being the product of conflict existing outside of his personal self, but which, nevertheless, impinges on his ability to choose between the various options open to him.

We have, in this chapter, illustrated two situations of death arising inside the company structure. Our discussion can be extended to include company arrangements after death. As an example, the social anthropologist Nakamaki Hirochika[55] has pointed to a resemblance in after-death arrangements between the corporate structure and relationships in the structure of the warrior class. Nakamaki notes the formal positioning of the gravestones in the *kigyōbaka* (company graves), which have become a popular practice. Commenting on the *kigyōbaka* on Mount Kōya,[56] outside Kyoto, he observes that those buried there include *junshoku* (employees who die whilst on duty), those dying through *karōshi*, and those company members dying through natural causes. Nakamaki draws attention to the similarity between the arrangement of the gravestones on Mount Kōya with the positioning of the *daimyō* (feudal lords) and the *kashin* (vassals of the *daimyō*) – see Figure 5.1.

Nakamaki's observation of the arrangement of the gravestones confirms the existence of the following three phenomena. First, although the legal position asserts that it is the shareholders, not the founder, who own the company, and that the founder does not possess total power in law, it, nevertheless, reflects the moral relationship which exists within the company in practice. Second, the company sphere often takes priority over the family sphere in the employee's life. Third, the death of an individual member is perceived as the death of a particular member occupying a specific position within a given company, rather than as the death of an individual *per se*.

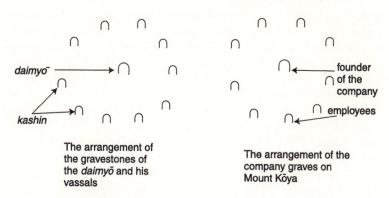

Figure 5.1 The resemblance in the formal positioning of the graves of warriors and company employees

This kind of control over both the individual and his family by the company makes it psychologically difficult for an employee's family to complain to, or make complaint about, the company, even if the family feels the company to be responsible for an employee's death.

The question which arises from this discussion – one which the courts have not yet had occasion to deliberate – is whether or not the actions of the persons acting for the company (which caused and contributed to the individual member's stress and consequent *karōshi*, and the encouraging of a corporate environment in which it becomes 'natural' to commit apology suicide) should be unconstitutional as infringing the right to life of the individual.

Central to the discussion is the concept of corporate social responsibility[57] (in Japanese, *kigyō aruiwa kaisha no shakai sekinin*). Corporate social responsibility is a fashionable concept, both in Japan and the West, and in its 'new', fashionable guise implies that there are social norms and values intended as guides to behaviour by those in managerial roles.[58] This contrasts with the 'old' traditional conception which assumes that, in line with the general position in company law in respect of social responsibility, responsibility concentrates on the company's shareholders (although, of course, there also exist legal duties in relation to employees, citizens and the state, duties which go beyond those under present discussion).

The reality of the position of the company in Japan can be understood in terms of the 'old' unitary perspective of corporate social responsibility. Crucial to the stability and prosperity of Japan is its economic base. A prosperous corporate sector is necessary to achieve an economically prosperous society. Ensuring a financially healthy corporate sector is thus in the public interest. The efforts of workers contribute not only to the profitability of individual companies, but also, following the arguments of economists such as Milton Friedman[59] and F.A. Hayek,[60] benefit society as a whole. This, they argue, constitutes the company's social responsibility.

According to this 'old' view, the company is a mechanism for increasing wealth and, in the process, for generating benefits in the form of profits for its shareholders, providing behaviour is kept within the limits of the law. This, they argue, ensures the well-being not only of the company but also of society, for companies are thus able to make best use of the resources at their disposal and devote their energy to providing the goods and services required by society. Such an 'organic' view of responsibility sees as unproblematic the relationship between the traditional economic role of industry and its duties to other beneficiaries, including employees (which we are presently concerned with), consumers, and society itself. By carrying out its traditional economic responsibility of ensuring an adequate level of profit, the company is seen as fulfilling its social responsibility to all in its internal and external environments.

Thus, when viewed from such an 'organic' perspective, the individual director's and employee's right to life becomes of secondary importance when compared to the public welfare, for working hard is seen as a requirement of the company becoming a socially responsible organization. Indeed, such hard work on their part is – the argument goes – indirectly beneficial to the individual member, he being a member of society.

If, viewed from this perspective, actions on the part of members which give rise to incidents of *karōshi* are not at present unconstitutional infringements of the right to life provision, apology suicide, likewise, is constitutional. Such sacrifice is necessary to appease potentially harmful social forces likely to damage the company financially. Removing the source of this social animosity is thus beneficial to the financial stability and prosperity of the company.

It can be argued, however, that – from the point of view of individual company employees or social units having relationship with the company – the corporate social responsibility model adopted by Friedman and Hayek is not the preferred model to be adopted in Japan (or other countries, for that matter). What other models exist which may better protect the individual member's right to life in corporate situations?

According to one 'new' conception of social responsibility derived from a pluralistic model[61] of the structure of the organization, provided the company's total prospective profit does not fall below the minimum needed to continue in business, some profit should be sacrificed for the wider 'social' purpose, allowing groups in the company's external environment to be considered in the decision-making process while at the same time not prejudicing unduly the interests of the shareholders. Groups which are generally considered to fall into this category include the local community, suppliers, consumers, as well as society itself.

It can be argued, however, that this 'new' conception does not go far enough. Whilst including the interests of groups in the company's external environment in the decision-making process, directors often fail to consider the interests of groups in the company's internal environment – employees and the directors themselves. As they are members of society, to exclude them from such consideration is, in a sense, unnatural.[62]

Viewed from this perspective, some profit should be sacrificed for the well-being of employees and directors alike so as to redress the balance between the member's sacrifice and an insufficient protection and concern for his life within the corporate environment. There is a need for more to be done to protect life if members are to enjoy the protection which the right to life provision theoretically gives them. There must be a reduction in the psychological stress and physical hardship which many members find themselves subjected to. Furthermore, there is a need to establish a corporate environment in which members are actively discouraged from committing suicide to apologize for corporate mistakes, or – as is sometimes the case – to prevent suicide brought on by overwork itself.[63]

An important question arises from this discussion. Who should take on the responsibility of ensuring a socially responsible company (in the sense suggested above) in practice? Two theories may be identified in this connection. First, that this is the responsibility of the company itself. This theory is termed *hōjin jitsuzai setsu* (the theory of the existence of legal personality). Second, that persons within the company organization should bear such responsibility. This is termed *hōjin hinin setsu* (the theory of the denial of legal personality), or *hōjin gisei setsu* (the theory of legal personality as fiction).

The first theory holds that the legal person is treated the same as a natural person. Those who view social responsibility from this point of view suggest that the company itself should bear such responsibility. One Japanese scholar,[64] for example, has argued that:

Up to a point social responsibility through the action of the directors has been recognized, but now, even if theoretically, the company must bear its own responsibility as an 'enterprise entity'.

Such an argument, however, has serious limitations. As the company *per se* has neither body nor soul,[65] those authors who, both in
Japan and the West, support the second theory reject the notion of the
company as a corporate body being socially responsible. Friedman,
for example, observes:

> What does it mean to say that 'business' has responsibilities? Only
> people can have responsibilities. A corporation is an artificial
> person and in this sense may have artificial responsibilities, but
> 'business' as a whole cannot be said to have responsibilities, even
> in this vague sense.[66]

The corporate form presents difficulties for control and for securing
responsibility. A company is an artificial person whose activities must
be carried on by its human members. As the company's activities are
performed by, and responsibility generally rests with, those in managerial roles, it is suggested that these very same individuals should
bear responsibility for the company's social responsibility – or lack of
it – in relation to both directors and employees alike. Those in
managerial roles – its directors – should be held responsible for
ensuring that no infringement of the right to life of either director
or employee occurs.

In this chapter we have seen how, in respect of the phenomena
under discussion, corporate values can, and do, impinge on the lives
of individual members. For many in the corporate environment,
responsibility to, and sacrifice for, a social organization is valued
more than life itself. As a result of unity between the new capitalist
mechanism of the corporate form (motivated by profit) and the traditional Japanese ideals of responsibility and loyalty inside the hierarchical structure of the organization, infringement of the individual
members's constitutional right to life has become possible.

6 Moral value and Japanese law

This study has addressed certain aspects of the right to life under the Japanese Constitution. We are now in a position to conclude our discussion.

We begin by asking whether the right to life, both in international law and under the Japanese Constitution, is, to use Joel Feinberg's terminology, an 'absolute' or 'categorically exceptionless' right,[1] subject to no exception whatsoever, or is relative in nature.

The argument that absolute rights exist in international law is one advanced by such legal scholars as John Finnis and Paul Sieghart. It is noted that freedom from torture and other ill-treatment, and the freedom from slavery and servitude, can be categorized as absolute rights.[2]

The right not to be tortured is found *inter alia* in article 5 of the United Nations Declaration of Human Rights.[3] We read that, 'No one shall be subjected to torture . . .' Although, as we noted earlier in this study,[4] limitations are placed on 'the exercise of [one's] rights and freedoms' by article 29, article 5, argues Finnis, is outside the scope of these limitations for it does not purport to define a right but, rather, imposes a negative requirement. Such a right, rather than being 'inalienable' (but subject to limitations), is absolute.[5]

Under the Japanese Constitution, similarly, it can be argued that certain absolute rights exist. The right not to be tortured can be considered an absolute right under the Constitution. Article 36 provides that:

> The infliction of torture by any public officer . . . [is] absolutely forbidden.

It has been suggested that the public welfare doctrine possibly extends to cover all rights and freedoms listed in the Constitution.[6] Whilst the courts have decided that the public welfare doctrine applies as a limitation to many rights contained in the Constitution, even though no explicit reference is made to such limitation in respect of those rights in the Constitution, it does not necessarily follow, however, that the courts would, or should, interpret the public welfare limitation as applying to all the rights listed in Chapter 3 of the Constitution. Does not the inclusion of the word 'absolutely' in article 36 suggest that the draftsmen wished to emphasize that this particular right should not be limited in any way?

Similarly, the right not to have 'cruel punishments' inflicted upon oneself can be viewed as an absolute right, and for the same reason as the right not to be tortured can, for both are 'absolutely forbidden' under the Constitution.[7] The constitutionality of the death penalty is perceived not to affect the validity of this argument for, we remember, capital punishment has been held by the courts not to constitute 'cruel punishment' for the purpose of article 36.[8] Only when the method of executing capital punishment is inhumane might capital punishment be perceived as 'cruel' for this purpose.

Can the right to life, similarly, be defined, both in international law and under the Japanese Constitution, as an absolute right?

In the international arena, the right to life is perceived by certain academic human rights lawyers to be the most basic of the fundamental human rights possessed by individuals. Menghistu defines the right to life as 'the most basic, the most fundamental, the most primordial and supreme right', without which the protection of all other rights becomes 'meaningless'.[9]

This perception of the right to life is also found amongst organizations involved in the field of the international law of human rights. Following the examination of reports submitted by the parties to the International Covenant on Civil and Political Rights, the Human Rights Committee of the United Nations, in general comments adopted in 1982, described the right to life provided in article 6 of the Covenant as 'the supreme right'.[10] In the drafting of an article on the right to life, it was maintained by the Secretary-General of the United Nations at the Tenth Session of the General Assembly that the right to life was 'the most fundamental of all rights'.[11] The Commission on Human Rights, in a 1983 resolution, similarly observed that the right was 'a cardinal right of every human being', and should be safeguarded to ensure the enjoyment of economic, social, cultural, civil and political rights.[12]

Similar views can be found if we examine the legislative history of the right to life provision in the Inter-American legal system. Thus in the first draft of the American Declaration on the Rights and Duties of Man of 1948, we read that:

The first of the fundamental rights of man, by order of logic and of importance is, without doubt, the right to his own life.[13]

The Inter-American Commission on Human Rights of 1987, similarly, observed:

The right to life remits a special consideration because it is, without a doubt, the foundation and sustenance of all the other rights.[14]

If such perception is quite common, it does not accurately reflect the position of the right to life in the international law of human rights. The right to life is not accorded status commensurate with its perceived primary position in any list of freedoms and rights. Rather, in such international instruments as the International Covenant on Civil and Political Rights,[15] the Council of Europe's Convention for the Protection of Human Rights and Fundamental Freedoms of 1953,[16] and the American Convention on Human Rights of 1978,[17] the right to life can legitimately be limited in certain instances.

And so it is with the status of the right to life under the Japanese Constitution. Although article 11 of the Constitution expressly states that all fundamental human rights guaranteed by the Constitution are conferred on the people as 'inviolate' rights, it is clear that the right to life *inter alia* is subject to the limitation of the public welfare, a limitation provided in articles 12 and 13.

Article 31, likewise, trades away an individual's right to life in the name of the public order, an aspect of the public welfare. In terms of 'ownership' of life, it has been seen that the Japanese state has the power of life and death over its citizens in respect of capital punishment. The life of the individual convicted of a capital offence – and, indeed, even one who might be innocent in reality, despite a trial intended to give fair justice or judgment – thus rests with the state machinery of justice, and with the Minister of Justice as the final, or ultimate, 'owner'.

The Utilitarian doctrine of the public welfare (which, arguably, began in Japan from a need on the part of the Meiji leadership, following the overthrow of the Tokugawa regime, to legitimize modern political norms) aims towards the common good of the mass of the population. This replaced the *Kōgi*, the Tokugawa regime itself, towards which everything was directed.

According to the Utilitarian concept, rights – even such a primary right as the right to life – may justifiably be limited where it is believed that the net benefit of imposing restraint is likely to be greater than the net benefit derived from protecting that right against limitation. By performing a balancing act between existing interests and rights and the common good, certain interests and rights are subordinated to others. In respect of the right to life, there has been, as is inevitable with Utilitarianism, the sacrifice of certain individuals' lives for the well-being of the mass of the population.

It is thus the case that, in terms of absolute human rights, both international law and the Japanese Constitution ascribe to the right to life a status lower than that given to the right not be be tortured, or the right not to be enslaved. Whereas the latter rights can be classified as absolute, the former cannot, and this on the basis of the presence or absence of limitations on the exercise of those rights.

The existence of limitations in legal instruments on human rights for the sake of the common good has been criticized by some academics. Thus, for John Finnis, rights contained in the Universal Declaration of Human Rights are an expression of what is implicit in the term 'common good'; namely, that everyone's well-being must always be considered and favoured by the political mechanism. As a consequence, no appeal can be made to the 'general welfare' which infringes upon the exercise of individual rights. If the general welfare is a reference to a Utilitarian aggregation, then, he argues, it is 'merely illusory', for the common good of a human community cannot be measured, as Utilitarians assume, as an aggregate.[18]

The validity of the inclusion of the public welfare limitation in the Japanese Constitution has itself been brought into question. Members of the Human Rights Committee of the United Nations have questioned the inclusion of the public welfare concept on the ground that such a constitutional restriction was not in accordance with the International Covenant on Civil and Political Rights, to which Japan is a signatory. They questioned its legality as the 'public welfare' was not one of the grounds of limitation specified in the Covenant.[19]

In defence of the inclusion of the public welfare in the Constitution, a representative of the Japanese government argued in front of the Committee that the 'public welfare' was essentially the same as those limitations specified in the Covenant (public safety, order, health and morals), and that it was strictly interpreted.[20]

In its Report submitted to the Human Rights Committee, the Japanese government stressed that the public welfare:

> serves to harmonize conflicting fundamental rights so that the individual's rights will be equally respected and it is not a concept to place unreasonable limits upon human rights.[21]

The claim that the public welfare harmonizes conflicting rights to ensure that individual rights are equally respected is open to debate. For the convicted capital offender, for example, the denial of his right to life through the execution of the death penalty in the name of public order cannot be said to be an attempt to ensure that his rights are equally respected. It is also arguable that the death penalty itself constitutes an 'unreasonable limit' upon his rights, for if this does not constitute an unreasonable limit, from his perspective, then what does?

Rights, including the right to life, thus subordinate to the general welfare of society in both theory and practice. Beside the public welfare, we found that there exists in practice the disturbance of rights in the context of social institutions and organizations. It is the case that the rights of individuals are subordinate to the common good or interests of the social entity to which they belong. Two such groups in particular have been the focus of attention in this book: the family and the company.

When we consider the life of an individual in the family context, we must remember that the individual forms merely one part – often an unequal part in Japan – of the whole unit. The individual within the family group tends to be viewed not as an individual *qua* individual, but according to his position in relation to other members of the family.

This also seems to be the position of the individual member of institutional organizations such as the Japanese company. The individual member and the company are interdependent units. Such interdependency, however, is not equal in degree, and the balance is tilted against the individual member, who is tied to the company for his economic and social needs. The theologian John Macquarrie, discussing the polarities of the individual and the community, notes:

> If individuals tend to disrupt community by self-seeking, societies tend to oppress individuals through collective egoism and institutional injustices.[22]

This conflict can also be observed in the Japanese context. Oppression and institutional injustice operates in the corporate arena. Rather than the corporate community being the frustration of the member's life, such oppression actually results in both the physical and social death of company members.

We thus see that, particularly in relation to collective and institutional injustice in the family and company groups in Japan, the right to life of the individual members of these groups not infrequently has a lesser value than familial and corporate interests.

From the point of view of a rights-centred observer, the source of the 'problem' of the subordination of the right to life of an individual existing within such groups lies in the hierarchical structure which has been built into the traditional Japanese family system. The company resembles the hierarchical structure of the family institution. We find in these groups that there always exists an in-built imbalance of 'rights' already incorporated into each position and role within these groups.

In the family institution, as we have seen in our discussion on equality under the law, law regulated the superior position of the parents *vis-à-vis* their lineal descendants. In the case of the married couple, although in law the wife and husband inside the family unit are equal, in practice the wife is often under psychological pressure from both the husband and parents-in-law. In terms of the hierarchical structure, the wife is often to be found at its bottom, below that of the husband and parents-in-law. This imbalance of power, depending on position inside the family, is reflected in the matter of the right to life of individuals which we found inside the family institution. This is seen in particular in the phenomena of *oyako shinjū* (parent–child suicide) and of the sacrifice of the family for the sake of the company.

In company law, the company exists as a legal person separate from its human members. For many members of Japanese companies, the company is more than a mere legal person. It is something one belongs to until the end of one's life, which must be protected, and to which one devotes one's life, and even sacrifices that life for. Therefore, the bond inside the company is very strong and tight, and loyalty towards the company bears resemblance to the loyalty found within the social structure.

Thus, on the question of the equality of the right to life posed at the beginning of this study, obstacles to individuals obtaining an equal right can be analysed as follows.

The status of the right to life of individuals is a reflection of the fact that, in practice, the individual sometimes counts for less than the interests of the group as a whole in Japanese society. The ethical thinker Watsuji Tetsurō (1889–1960) has pointed out that the Japanese term for person, *ningen*, literally meaning 'between people', expresses the importance attached by the Japanese to relationship between people over that of the existence of the individual *per se* existing outside of human relationship. A person, *ningen*, is thus not only a *hito*, existing only as an independent entity, but also participates in relationships.[23]

A similar theme was taken up by the philosopher Nishida Kitarō

(1870–1945), who developed the argument that people do not exist in an absolute sense. In the case of objects, such as human beings, they exist in relation to others. Human beings have meaningful existence only when they interact with others in relationships.[24]

This perception of the individual permeates through to the perception of rights themselves by the Japanese, who tend to view rights, in practice, not as being possessed by individuals *qua* individuals, but by individuals within the context of social relationships. Such rights are thus not absolute, but may be taken away within, and for the sake of, social or group relationships.

These ideas which can be seen rooted in Japanese society prevented the concept of natural rights (which are in-born in every individual) from prospering in Japan. Thus, even after the individual came to possess equal rights under the law, the perception of rights in Japan, in practice, still contrasts with its theoretical concept. The Western concept, transplanted into the 'revolutionary' 1947 Constitution, has as its base the idea that rights are endowed on an individual *qua* individual. Here, the individual possesses rights without recourse to – and prior to – any relationship which he/she may enter into. Thus, the individual possesses rights irrespective of any group to which he/she belongs. He/she is shielded from the influence exerted by others in the group in his/her legitimate claim to uphold rights against others, either within or outside the group.[25]

Thus, in theory, individuals can make legitimate claims against other individuals to protect threatened or actual infringement of their rights. They are able to do so not because they belong to a particular group, or have particular privileges to pursue the claim, but because they themselves possess rights as individuals. The rights of the individual, and the corresponding obligations owed to him/her by others, exist independent of social relationships.

In practice in Japan, the application of rights varies not only to the extent to which the courts, in given instances, deem it legitimate to interfere with the individual's rights for the sake of the public welfare, but also with the position of individuals within groups. The philosopher Alasdair MacIntyre[26] argues that the Japanese understand rights as being 'secondary aspects' of more fundamental norms and relationships, which belong, in practice, to an individual's role and relationships with others. In this study we have seen how the right to life is taken away within corporate and familial hierarchical group structures.

Conflict thus exists between relationships within such group structures and individual rights such as the right to life. Victor Koschmann[27] remarks on the Japanese failure to replace 'power' with individual rights as the central principle of hierarchical relationships. 'Power' is an incorrect interpretation of the phenomenon, however. His analysis fails to grasp the significance of the ethical features attached to roles within groups. Each member identifies himself with a certain role. Thus, it is not that the Japanese have failed to obtain rights as a result of their having been oppressed by power within the group. Rather, each member's role and duty within the group is considered and perceived to be superior to his/her own rights.

The strength of ethical features attached to roles is particularly in evidence in respect of the vertical relationship, with its inequalities, beween lineal ascendants and their descendants within the family structure, which has survived the post-war changes in traditional Japanese values. This relationship survived not only in practice, but also in law. Whilst the courts limited the scope of the inequality in the relationship between lineal ascendant and descendant to what is reasonable in the light of the equality under the law principle established by article 14 of the Constitution, recent legislation has abolished the legal status of the unequal relationship and of the unequal value in law of the lives of lineal ascendants *vis-à-vis* lineal descendants, where the wrongness of the act was still judged from the perspective of the relationship between offender and victim, a historical remnant of the way in which the criminal law perceived that acts committed against other people had different degrees of moral blameworthiness attached to them depending on the relationship between the people concerned.

The subordination of an individual's right to life to ideals attached to the group hierarchical structure has also been seen in respect of the employer–employee relationship. This fundamental relationship can deprive the individual worker of his/her life and/or sanity. Here, the individual may be deprived of the constitutional right to life for the larger interest of the group, and, ultimately, of the interest of society itself.

In answer to the question raised at the beginning of the book on the equality of the right to life, we see a clear difference beween theory and reality in Japan. Unlike the concept of natural rights, we have seen that, historically in Japan, rights – even the primary 'right' to life – were, both in theory and practice, dependent on one's status. In post-war Japan, in theory, all individuals possess a right to life equally. In practice, however, the right to life provision in the Constitution does not mean that every individual possesses this right in equal measure. Rather, the right to life is possessed relatively, according to the individual's position and role within particular groups.

This answer leads us to identify how this disregard of the equal right to life has been made possible.

The subordinate position of the right to life *vis-à-vis* both the general welfare and the interest of the group is a reflection of, and is made possible by, the general perception of the relative (rather than absolute) value of life itself in Japan. Thus, we can bring the question of the value of life itself into our consideration.

For many Westerners, life is often perceived, in Armando Martins Janeira's description, as:

> the ultimate value, the only true possession of man, before he disappears into the infinite silence.[28]

Life has paramount value, because death is the 'tragic limit'. Man lives but one life on this earth, and there is no opportunity for redemption in future reincarnations. As death is the absolute, ultimate measure, whatever awaits each of us in the next world cannot undo the reality that man's destiny is forever changed by death.

This perspective has repercussions for the value of life itself, and is often considered to be the most basic of the fundamental human values, taking priority over all other values. As we see in the writing of the human rights scholar Christian Bay, human life is placed foremost in the core principles of humanistic politics as:

> the highest value, which politics and government must serve to protect, ahead of all other values.[29]

To understand the Japanese perception of life, it is necessary to bring the Japanese attitude to death into our discussion. We are able to identify two elements contained among the Japanese aspects of death which help our understanding of the matter under discussion. First, we can observe the tendency that the Japanese do not perceive death as the end of everything but as merely the beginning of a new (and, possibly, better) phase of being. Although Buddhism has a teaching of Hell and punishment after death, the idea has not penetrated deeply the Japanese individual's conception of the next world.[30] Death is not the 'tragic end', but merely one stage of being.[31]

Second, from the aesthetic perspective, the Japanese have traditionally considered that death itself should be connected with beauty, and *how* a person dies is considered important. Thus, from this point of view, whereas the sacrifice of one's life in a beautiful way is honourable, the mere clinging on to life for its own sake is considered ugly and vulgar.

These two aspects of death in Japan are particularly in evidence in cases of *shinjū* (love suicide). In the idea of *shinjū* we see the trust in a better life in the next world, or the world after death, which contrasts with the Christian idea of punishment following the Day of Judgement, based on one's conduct in this life.

In contrast to those Western scholars, such as Bay, who place an absolute value on life, there exists a school of thought in the West, as well, which does not give paramount value to life. An exponent of this latter view is John Finnis. He argues that while all the basic values identified by him[32] are equally fundamental, when one focuses on a particular basic value it may attain an unequal importance for particular individuals *vis-à-vis* other basic values. Thus, whilst all of his basic values are equal, one, or some, may be more important in certain circumstances. Values considered primary when viewed from one perspective may seem relatively less important when viewed from another. An individual is in a position to choose which values he/she personally will treat as being more, or less, important than other values in life. Each individual possesses a 'subjective order of priority' of the basic values, and these will change and evolve constantly with the changing circumstances of life.

The individual in Japan, like the individual portrayed by Finnis, possesses a set of basic values, the importance of which may vary depending on both circumstance and the character of the individual. As with Finnis's individual, the Japanese individual, too, possesses an 'order of priority' of basic values. In contrast to his individual, however, choice for the Japanese individual is not based on subjectivity. Rather, choice is limited by the expectations of society and groups which, as we have seen, pressurize his choice silently or expressively.

Finnis's assumption that free choice can be exercised by the individual *per se* as between various values holds good only to a certain extent in relation to life. Generally speaking, individuals may make a choice between committing suicide and not committing suicide, for example. They can, all else being equal, choose between upholding or relinquishing, through their own actions, their own right to life. In the case of *anrakushi*, similarly, they are free to give or withhold their consent to the taking of their own lives by others, provided this is done within the limits of the law. Again, they can choose whether to take advantage of their right to life or not.

Finnis's assumption of the free choice of the individual, however, represents only part of the picture. This needs to be balanced against the taking away of one's right to life by others without consent. Thus, while it is legally allowed to take one's own life from free choice, it is a completely different matter to impose the choice on another, or to take away his/her life without the individual's consent. There is a world of difference between the right to take one's own life and the right to decide the fate of the lives of others. The cases of *karōshi*, apology suicide, *ikka shinjū* and *oyako shinjū* (in contrast to love suicide), for example, should thus be considered within the sphere of the infringement of the constitutional right to life.

In our study we have examined instances where other values have taken precedence over the right to life. So far in this chapter we have glanced at elements in the Japanese view on death which allow the common practice of *shinjū* to take place. We now turn our attention to the conflict between moral values and the individual's right to life.

The idea of dying in Japanese society is commonly connected with concrete purpose, rather than abstract ideal. In essence, as the Catholic thinker Onodera Isao[33] argues, the Japanese sacrifice their lives for the praxis of *ba*, not for some abstract ideal. *Ba* derives from *basho*.[34] The term '*basho*' denotes not only physical location, but also 'place' in the sense found in the phrase, 'one's place (or position) in the company', and in the phrase, 'one's place of work' (*hataraku basho*). The concept of *basho* thus contains numerous separate elements, referring not only to geographical location but also to artificial social spheres.

The significance of *basho* in Japanese thought, in the sense of physical location, has long been recognized. Yamaori Tetsuo[35] draws attention to the Japanese *kami* (gods) having the tendency of residing at certain specified places, such as mountains or rocks. This contrasts with the concept of God found in other societies. God, to the Western Christian thinker, is not located regionally in any one particular place; rather, he is the Supreme Being beyond place.

In Nishida Kitarō's philosophy, *basho* is the place where one reflects upon oneself, observes and knows by intuition. *Basho* is somewhere one can be as one is. And in Onodera's theory, *ba* always means something eternal for the Japanese, for which people are ready to die.[36]

Onodera's argument contributes to the understanding of death taking place inside the company and family units. In the cases of *karōshi* and apology suicide, employees die in the company as *basho*. In the cases of *ikka shinjū* and *oyako shinjū* we can note that, in a sense, the family itself is *seikatsu no ba* (the place of everyday life), where the family is united as a social institution.

However, even in these cases, death cannot be understood simply as dying for the *basho*, this being due to the emergence of the following two problems. First, each *basho* has its own structure, and each element has a position, role and morality attached to it. This means that not all members of the same *basho* are to die for an identical reason: that of dying for the company. Rather, in the company context, the moral value demanded of the employee is complete loyalty to the company – a loyalty which, if need be, extends to death itself. In the family context, the morality demanded is obedience of children to their parents, and the sacrifice of the family – particularly the wife (who is in an unequal and unfavourable position) – for the benefit of the husband and his career. Thus, inside one *basho* there exists a complexity of moral ethics, which compete with each other.

Second, we can note that one belongs to more than one *basho*. Whilst having considered matters from the perspective of single groups, such as the company or family, so far we have not dealt with the fact that individuals belong to more than one group concurrently. We must bear in mind that the individual who works in a company, for example, is also a member of a family. In the cases examined earlier, such as a male employee committing apology suicide, or dying through *karōshi*, not only has his loyalty and sacrifice superseded the value of that individual's life in these situations, it has also taken precedence over any duties and responsibilities he has inside the family institution of which he is a member. Here, the ethics of loyalty to the company or the social organization take precedence over the interests which both the individual and his family have in respect of that individual's life and the welfare of the rest of the family. In such cases, one is exposed both to the interests and responsibilities which accompany membership of the institution one belongs to, and to the social organization one works for.

This kind of dilemma existing in contemporary Japanese society, which even involves one's life, has brought with it an added dimension – the concept of 'inviolate' rights – to the moral dilemma between family and company in post-war Japan. If, in Tokugawa Japan, individuals' loyalty to their lord took precedence over their loyalty to their fathers, so too many employees' primary loyalty seems to be to their companies, their families' and their own personal welfare being (at best) secondary considerations in cases of conflict. Whilst it clearly exaggerates the position to claim that the employer enjoys primacy of loyalty over the family, or the self, in all companies, and at all times, such a state of affairs is not uncommon in many companies.

How this fact of self-sacrifice for the company is allowed to involve the sacrifice of the family, as well, when the interests of the two conflict can be looked at from two perspectives. The first relates to economic grounds. Just as individual family members, particularly descendants and wives, coexist within the group in unequal and subservient positions *vis-à-vis* the group as a whole in Japan, so we can also note the relatively weak position of the family group as a unit *vis-à-vis* other social groups such as the company. Those families who send their members to work for companies demonstrate their weakness as an economic unit to subsist independently. In exchange for assistance in supporting the financial needs of the family, both the family and the individual employee, in effect, relinquish, in varying degrees, their claim to certain rights (including the employee's right to life), and with it risk subsequent loss of happiness for the family.

The second aspect relates to the morals of Japanese society, and groups within that society. In the case where the husband is an employee in a company, the family, in many respects, is viewed as belonging to that company. In such cases, the smallest unit of privacy is not the employee as individual, but the family unit. Thus, conflict arises between the family and the company. Next to the individual, the family unit is to be sacrificed. As the term '*miuchi*' (inside body) refers to the related family, the family is viewed as part of the self, and is supposed to act as one body. In the case where there is the sacrifice of one's welfare, the legal position at present supports this idea as well.

From the legal perspective, we see that law gives preference to the sacrifice of the family, and to the elements we examined which contribute to the causes of *karōshi* or apology suicide inside the corporate structure (such as *zangyō* and the *tanshinfunin* system). Law supports this ethical position.

Recently, however, the dilemma faced between family and company has been brought more to the fore. This contrasts with the position previously when this dilemma did not occur to the Japanese (or, at least, opposition was not voiced openly). They accepted without protest this position, based on the willingness of the family to sacrifice itself for the sake of the husband's, or father's, position in society.

We can attempt to identify what has contributed to the growing awareness of this problem in contemporary Japanese society. Up to the present time, the traditional moral values have not been over-turned by the constitutional provision of the right to life. However, we see in the case of the company, in particular, that the irritation of workers, and their wives and families, with the intrusion of company values on the individual's right to life has begun to be voiced. This tendency is backed by constitutional provisions (including that of the right to life) and, encouraged by the prosperous economic climate, it has been possible to demand individual welfare. An increase in the power of women[37] (the result of the increasing trend to educate women to a higher level, and of their being in possession of money), combined with an awareness of current social trends, has made it possible to raise the issue of the welfare of the husband and his family. This consciousness of rights under the Constitution is likely to continue to increase in areas such as *karōshi*, where the right to life provision has not yet been able to command enforcement.

We can now bring together the various strands of thought already noted in this book. The legal position regarding life does not exist in a vacuum, independent of Japanese cultural norms and values, but rather, in part, reflects them. Although rights have been conferred on the Japanese people by two Constitutions, these were not won through the bitter struggle of the people. Although the foreignness of individual legal rights in contemporary Japan should not be exaggerated, it can be noted that the Japanese still experience difficulty in digesting the concept of rights itself, which is sometimes perceived as being in conflict with Japanese moral values.

Whether it is possible for one country to adopt a foreign law was the subject matter of a debate in nineteenth century Germany. The debate took place between Anton Friedrich Justus Thibaut (1772–1840), Professor of Roman Law at the University of Heidelberg, and Friedrich Karl von Savigny (1779–1861), Professor of Law at Berlin University and Minister of Law in Germany. Savigny argued that Roman law should be brought into the German legal system. As the Germany of his time was too immature to clarify the guiding truth which a legal system should aim towards, so, he argued, the German legal system should be built on the basis of the Roman law system, where this guiding principle could be found. The value of law for Savigny was that, like language, it was formed naturally through an awareness of race and developed naturally. Being a product of a unique social environment, law developed within the context of that society cannot be expected to serve a people in a different social context.

Thibaut argued against this school of thought, and believed that a foreign law *could* serve the people of a different culture. He argued that Germany should take as its model the French Civil Code (which Napoleon had enforced in Germany) to unify legal systems which varied from region to region.[38]

The Japanese have attempted to incorporate foreign law into the Japanese legal system three times in its history. First, there was an attempt to introduce the Chinese *lü-ling* system, both from a need to secure international recognition at this time and in order to build the foundations of a centralized state. The attempt resulted in many discrepancies between the foreign codes and Japanese social reality, and led to modifications being made to the strict Chinese models to appease Japanese taste. Even so, there emerged a customary law which suited Japanese society, and which existed side by side with the *ritsuryō*.

The second attempt was the introduction of the Roman law system during the Meiji period[39] by Boissonade de Fontarbie and Hermann Roesler. The *Minpōten* and *Shōhōten*, drawn up by these French and German jurists, were criticized by academics of the British School of Law from Tokyo University and the *Hōgakushi kai* (LL.B. Association),[40] which were under the influence of the English common law tradition. They argued that Japanese traditional customs and culture were not incorporated in their work, and that an essentially foreign code should not be superimposed on Japan. Rather, codes should be devised which would be largely Japanese in character, whilst at the same time incorporating the better aspects of Western law and legal principles.[41] As a result, amendments were made.[42]

The promulgation of the 1947 Constitution marks the third chapter in attempts to introduce foreign law. As with the earlier attempts, difficulties are encountered when implanting in undiluted form law operating within one particular social environment into a quite separate and distinct context.

In the field of law in Japan, there have thus been attempts to adopt foreign models, to a greater or lesser extent, and for varying reasons and under varying circumstances. Each time Japan tried to incorporate the structure of foreign legal systems there was a corresponding effort on the part of the state to adopt more modern forms. Each time, Japan has employed the formation of the new legal system as the foundation of the new form of the state. Thus, the function of law in such contexts was to support the existing functions of the state. The concept of the public welfare in Japan, consequently, could not avoid being used as a tool of the state to prevent individual 'rights' from overriding the interests of the state.

In these attempts to receive foreign law, we see as a characteristic of the Japanese way of incorporating it the layering of the new system on top of an existing system without abolishing the lower layer completely. The essence of the former layer thus remains, and is filtered through to the new system, and coexists with it. This method is repeated when additional layers are added. The concept of filial piety, which we came across in our examination of the equality of the right to life, is an example of a moral principle of the *ritsuryō* Codes being passed down through filtration to the present Civil and Penal Codes. The survival of this concept of filial piety in these Codes can be understood when we remember that law in Japan has always been inseparable from morality. Here lies the reason why moral values such as sacrifice and loyalty examined earlier could easily take superiority over the individual's right to life laid down in the most modern Constitution in Japan.

To bring this present study to a close, we can note that, as with earlier attempts to modify foreign ideas to suit Japanese taste, the foreign concept of the right to life has been modified in the course of internalization both by structures inherent in Japanese society and by that society's tendency to emphasize particular social nexuses which stand against the right to life provision. Being influenced by these structures and tendency, it has become possible for infringements of the constitutional provision to occur. For Japanese law, the value of life itself is not absolute, and the legal position reflects Japanese values generally.

Notes

PREFACE

1 Ishimoda Shō, *Kodaihō to chūseihō* (Early Law and Medieval Law), vol. 8 of *Ishimoda Shō chosakushū*, (Collected Works of Ishimoda Shō) (Tōkyō, 1989), pp. 33–4.

1 INTRODUCTION

1 The Constitution of Japan was promulgated on 3 November 1946, and came into force on 3 May 1947.
2 The legal scholar J.A. Jolowicz has succinctly summarized the core characteristic of a right as follows: 'If the existence and nature of a right can only be deduced from the remedies available to the victims of a "wrong", it follows that a "right", so far as the law is concerned, is co-extensive with its protection through the action of the law, that is with the availability of a legal remedy in the courts. We may say that a man has certain rights, and we commonly do say just that, but if by our statement we mean more than that in certain circumstances he can secure redress from another through the medium of judicial decision, then we are using the word "right" in a sense that involves reference to something outside the prevailing positive law of the society in which we live.' 'The Judicial Protection of Fundamental Rights Under English Law' (The Cambridge–Tilburg Law Lectures, 2nd Series, 1979) (Deventer, the Netherlands, 1980), pp. 1–48, at p. 10. A right is thus 'coextensive with its judicial protection' (ibid., p. 11).
3 Fundamental human rights enshrined in the Constitution are conferred not only on Japanese but also on non-Japanese in Japan. See Lawrence W. Beer, 'Freedom of Expression: The Continuing Revolution', in Percy R. Luney, Jr. and Takahashi Kazuyuki (eds), *Japanese Constitutional Law* (Tokyo, 1993), pp. 221–54, at p. 252, note 68.
4 For a discussion of natural rights theories see *inter alios* John Finnis, *Natural Law and Natural Rights* (Oxford, 1980); Margaret MacDonald, 'Natural Rights', in Jeremy Waldron (ed.), *Theories of Rights* (Oxford, 1984), pp. 21–40.
5 This theory was advanced by Ueki Emori (1857–92), Baba Tatsui (1850–88) and Katō Hiroyuki (1836–1916). Katō, however, changed his belief

and publicly criticized this natural rights theory in 1881. See Matsumoto Sannosuke (tr. J. Victor Koschmann), 'The Idea of Heaven: A Tokugawa Foundation for Natural Rights Theory', in Najita Tetsuo and Irwin Scheiner (eds), *Japanese Thought in the Tokugawa Period 1600–1868*: *Methods and Metaphors* (Chicago and London, 1978), pp. 181–99, at pp. 182–4.

6 In this book we shall refer to the *Dai Nippon Teikoku Kenpō* as the 'Meiji Constitution'.

7 The concept of *seizonken* was introduced into Japan at the beginning of the Taishō period (1912–25) by the political scientist Fukuda Tokuzō.

8 The *Asahi Case* (*Asahi soshō*) reflects this growing interest in material comforts. The case concerned Asahi Shigeru, a hospital in-patient, who, in July 1956, received income monthly from his brother to provide for his everyday essentials. In July, the state paid ¥1,500 monthly to the hospital to help cover hospital costs. In August of that year, however, the state requested him to pay ¥900 from his ¥1,500 monthly income to help pay the medical costs. Asahi took the Minister of Health and Welfare to court, claiming that this request infringed both article 25 of the Constitution and the *Seikatsu hogohō* (The Protection of Everyday-Living Law) (No. 144) of 1947. The Tokyo District Court found in his favour, arguing that ¥600 was not sufficient income to live on every month (Tokyo District Court Decision, 19 October 1957: *Gyōreishū* 11.10.2921. The Minister of Health and Welfare appealed the decision, and the Tokyo High Court overturned the decision of the lower court (Decision of the Tokyo High Court, 24 May 1964: *Minshū* 21.5.1043). Whilst an appeal to the Grand Bench of the Supreme Court was pending, Asahi died, and the Supreme Court held that his relative could not continue the action as the original complainant had passed away. For an article on the welfare system in Japan see Tabata Hirokuni, 'Japanese Welfare State: Its Structure and Transformation', *Annals of the Institute of Social Science* (Institute of Social Science, University of Tokyo), no. 32 (1990), pp. 1–29. On welfare rights in Japan, see Ōsuka Akira, 'Welfare Rights', in Percy R. Luney, Jr. and Takahashi Kazuyuki (eds), *Japanese Constitutional Law*, op. cit., pp. 269–87.

2 LAW AND RIGHTS IN JAPAN

1 The text of the Potsdam Declaration may be found in Supreme Commander for the Allied Powers, *Political Reorientation of Japan, September 1945 to September 1948* (Westport, Conn., 1970), vol. 2, Appendix A: 3, p. 413.

2 This was W.A. Martin's translation into Chinese of Henry Wheaton's book, *Elements of International Law* (Boston, 1863). See Carmen Blacker, *The Japanese Enlightenment: A Study of the Writings of Fukuzawa Yukichi* (Cambridge, 1964), p. 105. Frequent references to '*kenri*' occur in Mitsukuri's writings. Thus, in an article on 'Liberty' in the *Journal of the Japanese Enlightenment* he writes: 'The translation of "liberty" is *jiyū*. It means to accord to people the free exercise of their rights (*kenri*) without restriction by others': William Reynolds Braisted (tr.), *Meiroku Zasshi: Journal of the Japanese Enlightenment* (Tokyo, 1976), p. 117.

3 An explanation of the term 'right' is given by Nishimura Shigeki in his article, 'An Explanation of "Right"': Third of a Series of Expositions on

Foreign Words', in the October 1875 issue of *Meiroku Zasshi*: William
Reynolds Braisted (tr.), op. cit., pp. 510–13.

4 Ishida Takeshi, *The Introduction of Western Political Concepts Into
Japan: Non-Western Societies' Response to the Impact of the West*, Nissan
Occasional Paper Series, No. 2, Nissan Institute of Japanese Studies, the
University of Oxford (Oxford, 1986), p. 12. The Japanese human rights
law specialist Lawrence W. Beer similarly observes that 'the choice of
Kenri to refer to rights was not a particularly felicitous one, because in all
previous uses of the character *Ken* in compounds, *Ken* implied might or
power . . .'; see Lawrence W. Beer, 'The Public Welfare Standard and
Freedom of Expression in Japan', in Dan Henderson (ed.), *The Constitution of Japan: Its First Twenty Years, 1947–67* (Seattle, 1968), pp. 205–
38, at p. 217, footnote 37. The constitutional lawyer Takayanagi Kenzō
has argued that the concept of 'right' prevailed in a limited sense historically. He notes: 'Japanese legal historians . . . point out that there was a
concept and a term corresponding to a right. At the end of the Heian
period (810–1185 A.D.) the word *shiki*, which originally meant "office"
and connotated a duty, came to mean a "right in land". This usage,
however, became obsolete in the Tokugawa period, except in the term
kabu shiki which meant "rights of a licensed trader". In such circumstances, it was quite natural that Meiji students of Western jurisprudence
had to coin a new term *ken ri* (power plus interest) in order to express the
concept of a right.' Takayanagi Kenzō, 'A Century of Innovation: The
Development of Japanese Law, 1861–1961', in Arthur Taylor von Mehren,
Law in Japan: The Legal Order in a Changing Society (Cambridge, Mass.,
1963), pp. 5–40, at p. 24. Jean-Pierre Lehmann points out that 'Mitsukuri's
ri was not the same as that in common usage today when using the term
Kenri. Mitsukuri's *ri* is that of reason, principle, as in *giri* or *tenri*.' Jean-
Pierre Lehmann, 'Native Custom and Legal Codification: Boissonade's
Introduction of Western Law to Japan', *Proceedings of the British Asso-
ciation for Japanese Studies*, vol. 4 (part 1: History and International
Relations [ed. Gordon Daniels]) (1979), pp. 33–72, at p. 39, footnote 15.
On the translation of '*kenri*', see further Tawaragi Kōtarō, 'Nihonjin no
hōishiki ni okeru "kenri" to "kengi"' (Concerning '*Kenri*' and '*Kengi*' in
the Japanese Sense of Law), *Hōgaku Kenkyū* (Legal Studies) (Faculty of
Law, Keiō University), vol. 65, no. 12 (1992), pp. 271–88.

5 *Fukuzawa zenshū* (The Collected Works of Fukuzawa) (Tōkyō, 1926),
vol. 5, p. 413 (quoted in Carmen Blacker, op. cit., p. 107). On Fukuzawa's
views on law and rights, see further Matsuoka Hiroshi, 'Fukuzawa Yukichi ni okeru "hō" oyobi "kenri" ni kansuru ichi kōsatsu' (A Study on
Fukuzawa Yukichi's Views on 'Law' and 'Rights'), *Hōgaku Kenkyū*
(Legal Studies) (Faculty of Law, Keiō University), vol. 65, no. 12
(1992), pp. 217–41.

6 On the Japanese enlightenment see, for example, Kenneth B. Pyle, 'Meiji
Conservatism', in Marius B. Jansen (ed.), *The Nineteenth Century* (vol. 5
of *The Cambridge History of Japan*) (Cambridge, 1989), pp. 674–720; see
particularly pp. 674–7.

7 This is based on Takikawa Masajirō's classification, derived from his
analysis of the foreign influences exerted on Japan and its legal system.

Takikawa Masajirō, *Nihon hōseishi* (A History of the Japanese Legal System) (Tōkyō, 1985), *ge* (vol. 2).

8 The text of the *Kojiki* is found in *Kojiki* (Records of Ancient Matters), with textual notes and articles by Aoki Kazuo, Ishimoda Shō *et al.*, vol. 1 of *Nihon shisō taikei* (Series on Japanese Thought) (Tōkyō, 1982). For an English translation of the text see Basil Hall Chamberlain, *The Kojiki: Records of Ancient Matters* (Rutland, V., 1982).

9 The text of the *Nihon shoki* is found in *Nihon shoki* (The Chronicles of Japan), vols 67 and 68 of *Nihon koten bungaku taikei* (Japanese Classics Series), with comments and notes by Sakamoto Tarō, Ienaga Saburō *et al.* (Tōkyō, 1967). For an English translation, see W.G. Aston, *Chronicles of Japan from the Early Times to A.D. 697* (London, 1896).

10 The text of the *Norito* is found in *Kojiki/Norito* (Records of Ancient Matters/Purification Prayers), vol. 1 of *Nihon koten bungaku taikei* (Japanese Classics Series), eds. Kurano Kenji and Takeda Yukichi (Tōkyō, 1963), pp. 365–463. For English translations see Felicia Gressitt Bock, *Engi Shiki: Procedures of the Engi Era, Books VI–X* (Tokyo, 1972), pp. 65–105; Donald L. Philippi, *Norito: A New Translation of the Ancient Japanese Ritual Prayers* (Tokyo, 1959).

11 We find in the *Norito* the following eight items of *amatsutsumi*:

1 *ahanachi* (breaking down the ridges);
2 *mizoume* (covering up the ditches);
3 *hihanachi* (releasing the irrigation sluices);
4 *shikimaki* (double planting);
5 *kushisashi* (setting up the stakes);
6 *ikihagi* (or *ikehagi*) (skinning alive);
7 *sakahagi* (skinning backwards);
8 *kusohe* (defecation)

See *Kojiki/Norito*, op. cit., p. 424. Yōko Williams, in her paper, 'The Concept of *Tsumi*', delivered at the Japan Anthropology Workshop on 'Ceremony and Ritual' held at Leiden University, the Netherlands, 26–30 March 1990, noted that items 1–5 were characterized as offences against the agricultural community: these included destroying the water-supply facilities, destroying the harvest, and acts affecting the ownership of land. Items 6, 7 and 8, she argued, constituted blasphemy against the sacred order.

12 We find in the *Norito* the following fourteen items of *kunitsutsumi*:

1 *ikihadadachi* (to cut living skin);
2 *shihadadachi* (to cut dead skin);
3 *shirahito* (white person);
4 *kokumi* (skin excrescences);
5 *ono ga haha o okasu tsumi* (*tsumi* of violating one's own mother);
6 *ono ga ko o okasu tsumi* (*tsumi* of violating one's own child);
7 *haha to ko o okasu tsumi* (*tsumi* of violating both one's own mother and child);
8 *ko to haha o okasu tsumi* (*tsumi* of violating both one's child and mother);
9 *kemono o okasu tsumi* (*tsumi* of transgression with animals);

10 *haumushi no wazawai* (woes from creeping insects);

11 *takatsukami no wazawai* (woes from the Deities on High);

12 *takatsutori no wazawai* (woes from the birds on high);

13 *kemono taoshi* (killing animals by putting a curse on them);

14 *majinai mono o naseru tsumi* (*tsumi* of witchcraft).

See *Kojiki/Norito*, op. cit., p. 424. Yōko Williams, in her paper, 'The Resolution of *Tsumi*', delivered at the Japan Anthropology Workshop's International Symposium on 'Rethinking Japanese Religion' held at Newnham College, the University of Cambridge, 3–5 April 1991, argued that such crimes as murder and wounding, and sins such as incest and natural calamities, were inseparable. She argued that the concept of *kunitsutsumi* was older than *amatsutsumi*.

13 In the Taika Reform, an attempt was made to lessen the power and importance of the old clans and adopt a centralized bureaucratic administrative system.

14 On the *Yōrō* Code, see further Chapter 4, note 17.

15 *Ōnin no ran* was brought about from the need to determine the heir to Shōgun Ashikaga Yoshimasa (1436–90). As a result of this war, the Muromachi *bakufu* lost ultimate power, leading the way to rule by the so-called *sengoku daimyō* (wartime feudal lords).

16 The position of *kebiishi* was established after the Kusuko no hen (*coup d'état* of Kusuko) of 810, which proved the inability of the *kuge* officers to maintain social order in Kyoto. Gradually, members of the *bushi* class were appointed to the position.

17 This is also called the *Goseibai shikimoku*. These items were the first of the structured laws of the feudal Houses. It consists of fifty-one items, and was the written ethics of feudal law, based on examples of the past and customary law of feudal society. As the power of the feudal Houses increased, these fifty-one items became insufficient to cater for the needs of society, and further items were added. These additions were called *Shikimoku tsuika* (Laws as Added).

18 The so-called Sengoku jidai was the latter half of the Muromachi period (1399-1573), a period when the Muromachi *bakufu* lost ultimate power to the regional lords, and each regional ruler began to practise power independently over his region.

19 Examples of such laws are the *Jinkaishū* (A Collection of Dust) of the Date family, and the *Hyakkajō* (One Hundred Provisions) of Chōsokabe Motochika.

20 The *Kuge shohatto* (Laws for *Kuge*), *Buke shohatto* (Laws for the *Daimyō*) and *Shoshi hatto* (Laws for Vassals and *Hatamoto* [Direct Retainers of the Shōgun]) are examples of laws modelled on the *Jōei shikimoku*. The *Kujikata osasamegaki* (Provisions Concerning Public Matters) is an example of such a collection of case-law.

21 Takikawa Masajirō, *Nihon hōseishi*, op. cit., *jō* (vol. 1); *ge* (vol. 2).

22 Ibid.

23 The early *ritsuryō* administrative system consisted of the *jingikan*, the *dajōkan*, and eight ministries under the *dajōkan*.

24 This was called *keiritsu* (Penal Code).

25 The term '*Kyū keihō*' is commonly employed to differentiate it from the *Keihō* (Penal Code of 1907), currently in force in amended form.

26 See further Iwatani Jūrō, 'Futatsu no futsubun keihō sōan to Boasonādo' (Two Drafts of the Penal Code in French and Boissonade), *Hōgaku Kenkyū* (Keiō University Faculty of Law), vol. 64, no. 1 (1991), pp. 57–80.

27 Kenneth B. Pyle, op. cit., pp. 688–9, summarizes the effects of the unequal treaties as follows: 'The treaties to which the bakufu had submitted represented an infringement of Japanese sovereignty. They permitted foreign residents and trade in certain leased territories and ports, and under the system of extraterritoriality, foreign residents were subject to the jurisdiction of their consular courts. Japanese tariffs were under international control.' For a discussion on treaty revision negotiations, see Inoue Kiyoshi, *Jōyaku kaisei* (Amending the Treaties) (Tōkyō, 1955).

28 See Johannes Siemes, *Herman Roesler and the Making of the Meiji State* (Tokyo, 1966). For a discussion on the contribution of Germany to the modernization of Japan at this period, see Bernd Martin, 'The German Role in the Modernization of Japan', *Oriens Extremus*, vol. 33, no. 1 (1990), pp. 77–88. Other foreign specialists who advised the Japanese on constitutional matters included the American Henry Willard Denison (1880–1914) and the Englishman Piggott. For a discussion by the historian Gordon Daniels on the American E.H. House, see 'E.H. House, Japan's American Advocate', *Proceedings of the British Association for Japanese Studies*, vol. 5, part 1 (1980), pp. 3–10 and 207–8. For a British perspective on Meiji Japan, see Gordon Daniels, 'The British Role in the Meiji Restoration: A Reinterpretive Note', *Modern Asian Studies*, vol. 2, part 4, October (1968), pp. 291–313; Gordon Daniels, 'The Japanese Civil War (1868): A British View', *Modern Asian Studies*, vol. 1, part 3, July (1967), pp. 241–63. For a brief discussion on the Westernization of Japanese law during the Meiji period, see Noda Yoshiyuki, *Introduction to Japanese Law* (Tokyo, 1976), pp. 41–62.

29 Meiji Constitution, article 31.

30 'The Constitution of the Empire of Japan', in A. Stead (ed.), *Japan by the Japanese* (London, 1904), pp. 32–63, at pp. 43–4.

31 The *Nippon kokkenan* was presented to Prince Arisugawa in 1878. By article 3 of Chapter 6 ('The People and their Rights and Duties'), 'All people living in the Empire shall have their lives and property protected, whether they may be Japanese subjects or foreigners . . .' Quoted in Fujii Shin'ichi, *The Constitution of Japan: A Historical Survey* (Tokyo, 1965), p. 94.

32 'Arbitrary power over life and property', he believed, 'would . . . throw the subjects into confusion and lead to misery. Unless their lives and property are protected by law, the peace and order of the country cannot be hoped for. Without this guarantee, the Imperial rule would sooner be called tyrannical than autocratic . . . In order . . . to achieve the desired results of constitutional government, protection should be extended to the honour, the liberty, and the lives and property of the subjects.' Quoted in Fujii Shin'ichi, ibid., p. 197. No specific protection of the right to life appeared in the *Teikoku kenpō sōan* (A Draft of the Imperial Constitution).

33 According to Hozumi Yatsuka, an authorized constitution is ordained by a Sovereign of his own free will; a contractual constitution, on the other hand, arises from an agreement among sovereign individuals. See Uesugi Shinkichi (ed.), *Hozumi Yatsuka hakase ronbunshū* (Collected Essays of Dr Hozumi Yatsuka), rev. edn. (ed. Hozumi Shigetaka), (Tōkyō, 1943), p. 4, p. 991.

34 Article 73(1) reads: 'When it has become necessary in future to amend the provisions of the present Constitution, a project to the effect shall be submitted to the Imperial Diet by Imperial Order.' By article 73(2), 'In the above case, neither House can open the debate, unless a majority of not less than two-thirds of the Members present is obtained.' Cf. also the Preamble, which notes: 'When in the future it may become necessary to amend any of the provisions of the present constitution, We or Our successors shall assume the initiative right, and submit a project for the same to the Imperial Diet. The Imperial Diet shall pass its vote upon it, according to the conditions imposed by the present Constitution, and in no other wise shall Our descendants or Our subjects be permitted to attempt any alternative thereof.' Miyasawa Toshiyoshi argues that 'Japan's surrender . . . brought about a constitutional change that could not be legally effected under the Meiji Constitution. In this sense, from the viewpoint of legal scholarship, Japan's surrender constitutes a revolution': *Kenpō* (Constitutional Law) (Tōkyō, 1962), rev. edn, reprinted in Tanaka Hideo (ed.), *The Japanese Legal System: Introductory Cases and Materials* (Tokyo, 1976), pp. 681–4, at p. 682. For B.J. George, if the Constitution was in form an amended version of the Meiji Constitution, its content was 'revolutionary'. The adoption of the present Constitution, he argues, 'signaled, of course, a revolution in the assumption on which Japanese constitutional law rested and the establishment both of constitutional or human rights and of a mechanism to enforce them': 'Rights of the Criminally Accused', in Percy R. Luney, Jr. and Takahashi Kazuyuki (eds), *Japanese Constitutional Law* (Tokyo, 1993), pp. 289–318, at p. 291. Okudaira Yasuhiro observed that the American-influenced Constitution 'meant a "revolution" in the legal system as well as in the social structure': *Some Consideration on the Constitution of Japan*, University of Tokyo Institute of Social Science Occasional Papers in Law and Society, no. 3 (1987), p. 1. On the *tennō* system, for example, Okudaira observes: 'The constitutional modification of the *tennō* system was done in a wholesome and almost revolutionary manner': 'Forty Years of the Constitution and Its Various Influences: Japanese, American, and European', in Percy R. Luney, Jr. and Takahashi Kazuyuki (eds), *Japanese Constitutional Law*, op. cit., pp. 1–38, at p. 3. For John Maki, the principle of popular sovereignty as enshrined in both the Preamble and in article 1 of the Constitution was 'revolutionary': 'The Constitution of Japan: Pacifism, Popular Sovereignty, and Human Rights', in Percy R. Luney, Jr. and Takahashi Kazuyuki (eds), *Japanese Constitutional Law*, op. cit., pp. 39–55, at p. 45. On the 'revolution' in the field of freedom of expression, see Lawrence W. Beer, 'Freedom of Expression: The Continuing Revolution', in Percy R. Luney, Jr. and Takahashi Kazuyuki (eds), *Japanese Constitutional Law*, op. cit., pp. 221–54. See also Lawrence

W. Beer, 'Constitutional Revolution in Japanese Law, Society and Politics', *Modern Asian Studies*, vol. 16, no. 1 (1982), pp. 33–67.

35 John M. Maki (tr. and ed.), *Japan's Commission on the Constitution: The Final Report* (Seattle, 1980), p. 353.

36 Article 81.

37 This is not to say, however, that all types of freedoms and rights enshrined in the Constitution have been protected to the same degree. On the differing treatment of socio-economic and fundamental human rights, for example see Okudaira Yasuhiro, 'Forty Years', op. cit., p. 9.

38 On freedom of expression, see Lawrence W. Beer, 'The Public Welfare Standard', op. cit., pp. 205–38; Lawrence W. Beer, *Freedom of Expression in Japan: A Study in Comparative Law, Politics, and Society* (Tokyo, 1984); Lawrence W. Beer, 'Freedom of Expression: The Continuing Revolution', op. cit., pp. 221–54.

39 On privacy, see Saeki Hitoshi, 'Puraibashii to meiyo no hogo' (The Protection of Privacy and Individual Dignity), *Hōgaku kyōkai zasshi*, vol. 101, no. 7 (1984), pp. 1–66; vol. 101, no. 8 (1984), pp. 22–63; vol. 101, no. 9 (1984), pp. 88–155; vol. 101, no. 11 (1984), pp. 1–83. Other perceived new 'rights', however, have not enjoyed such success. The environmental 'right' is a case in point. See Julian Gresser, Fujikura Kōichirō and Morishima Akio, *Environmental Law in Japan* (Cambridge, Mass., 1981).

40 The tradition of duty consciousness can be clearly observed in the laws of the Tokugawa period, where the perception of 'rights' was viewed in terms of duty to others. Through obedience to the required behaviour centred on Confucian relationships, the individual found in the fulfilling of his duties 'conciliable rights' to protect him. See Dan F. Henderson, *Conciliation and Japanese Law: Tokugawa and Modern*, vol. 1 (Seattle, 1965); Dan F. Henderson, 'The Evolution of Tokugawa Law', in John W. Hall and Marius B. Jansen (eds), *Studies in the Institutional History of Modern Japan* (Princeton, N.J., 1968), pp. 203–30. On 'conciliable rights' and 'reciprocal duty consciousness', see Lawrence W. Beer, *Freedom of Expression in Japan*, op.cit., ch. 3, 'Social Patterns and Freedom of Expression', pp. 100-28. The emphasis on duty to the detriment of individual rights has persisted. Of the situation in 1970, Richard Minear observed: 'Evidence from contemporary Japan indicates that even today "rights' consciousness" is weak.' *Japanese Tradition and Western Law: Emperor, State, and Law in the Thought of Hozumi Yatsuka* (Cambridge, Mass., 1970), p. 179.

41 The stubborn resistance of the Japanese Cabinet and the drafters of the first government draft of the Constitution to 'allow' the Japanese people unrestricted rights and freedoms reflects their desire to continue the tradition of duty consciousness. They sought to insert such limitations as 'as provided by law' and 'to the extent that they do not conflict with the public peace and order' to restrict individual rights. See 'First Government Draft of the Constitution, 4 March 1946', in Supreme Commander for the Allied Powers, *Political Reorientation of Japan*, op. cit., Appendices vol. (vol. 2), pp. 625–30. See D.C.S. Sissons, 'Human Rights Under the Japanese Constitution', *Papers on Modern Japan* (Department of International Relations, Australian National Uni-

versity, Canberra, 1965), pp. 50–69, at p. 51. On the drafting of the Japanese Constitution see *Kenpō chōsa kai* (Commission on the Constitution), *Kenpō seitei no keika ni kansuru shoiinkai hōkokusho* (Report of the Sub-Committee on the Process of the Enactment of the Constitution) (Tōkyō, 1961).

42 By article 20 of the Meiji Constitution, 'Japanese subjects are amenable to service in the Army or Navy, according to the provisions of law.' By article 21, 'Japanese subjects are amenable to the duty of paying taxes, according to the provisions of law.'

43 See B.J. George, 'Rights of the Criminally Accused', op. cit., p. 311, note 19.

44 Article 27.

45 Article 26.

46 Article 27(3).

47 Article 24.

48 Article 30. B.J. George notes that this duty is 'qualitatively different' from the four duties noted above, 'and continued from the Meiji Constitution': 'Rights of the Criminally Accused', op. cit., p. 311, note 19.

49 Article 12.

50 John M. Maki, *Japan's Commission on the Constitution*, op. cit., p. 280.

51 Ibid., pp. 102, 280–1.

52 Ibid., p. 281.

53 Ibid., pp. 273–4.

54 The term '*kihonteki jinken*' (fundamental human rights) appears in articles 11 and 97 of the Japanese Constitution. By article 97, 'The fundamental human rights guaranteed by this Constitution to the people of Japan are fruits of the age-old struggle of man to be free; they have survived the many exacting tests for durability and are conferred upon this and future generations in trust, to be held for all time inviolate.' By article 11, 'The people shall not be prevented from enjoying any of the fundamental human rights. These fundamental human rights guaranteed to the people in this Constitution shall be conferred upon the people of this and future generations as eternal and inviolate rights.'

55 In *Ōkuri* v. *Kageyama* (1956) (10 *Minshū* 785), for example, Justice Irie noted: 'Of course, the liberties guaranteed in the Constitution are not absolute nor unlimited; limitation thereof up to a certain point would not be considered unconstitutional where there exists a sufficient reason for holding it as absolutely necessary for the public welfare or for other constitutional requirements.'

56 See p. 11, this volume.

57 Article 13.

58 Article 11.

59 See Ōsuka Akira, 'Constitutional Protection and Guarantee of Rights and Freedoms: The Case of Japan', *Waseda Bulletin of Comparative Law*, vol. 7 (1988), pp. 1–14.

60 Ashibe Nobuyoshi, 'Human Rights and Judicial Power', in Lawrence W. Beer (ed.), *Constitutional Systems in Late Twentieth Century Asia* (Seattle and London, 1992), pp. 224–69, at p. 233.

61 In the early stages of the development of the public welfare doctrine by
the courts, there were attempts to define the concept in abstract terms. In
a Supreme Court decision of 1950, the public welfare was perceived in
the following terms: 'The maintenance of order and respect for the
fundamental human rights of the individual – it is precisely these things
which contribute the content of the public welfare' (Supreme Court
Grand Bench Decision, 11 October 1950. 4 *Keishū* 2012, 2014: *Japan
v. Sugino*).

In 1972, the Supreme Court established the rule of 'double standards'
on the protection of human rights: that while economic freedoms, such as
property rights, could be restricted by broad political discretion on the
part of the judiciary, 'spiritual' freedoms, such as the freedom of expression, were to be afforded a preferred position (Supreme Court Grand
Bench Decision, 22 November 1972: *Keishū* 26 9 586.)

Despite this, whilst imposing restrictions on such freedoms as the
freedom of expression, the Supreme Court has, on more than one occasion, held economic regulations unconstitutional. Thus in 1975, regulations relating to the location of a chemist's shop were held
unconstitutional as they were irrelevant to the legislative purpose
(Supreme Court Grand Bench Decision, 30 April 1975: *Minshū* 29 4
572). In 1987, provisions dealing with common ownership of forests in
the Forest Law were held to be in contravention of article 29 of the
Constitution (Supreme Court Grand Bench Decision, 22 April 1987:
Hanrei Jihō 1227 21). On these cases, see further Nakamura Mutsuo,
'Freedom of Economic Activities and the Right to Property', in Percy R.
Luney, Jr. and Takahashi Kazuyuki (eds), *Japanese Constitutional Law*,
op. cit., pp. 255–67, at pp. 259–60, 261–3.

It is important to remember that, whilst the public welfare doctrine has
been employed by the courts to limit individual rights, over the years the
courts have both applied and interpreted the doctrine in a more limited
fashion. And, as we have noted, the Supreme Court itself defined it as
including – and not in opposition to – fundamental human rights and
freedoms. Summarizing the position, John Maki observes that, 'Generally, the Supreme Court has utilized the public welfare doctrine to
maintain a reasonable balance between the individual's enjoyment of
rights and freedoms and the well-being of other individuals and of society
itself': 'The Constitution of Japan', op. cit., p. 52.

62 The political scientist J.A.A. Stockwin, for example, notes that 'the
"public welfare" in articles 12 and 13 presumably refers to the whole
of chapter 3.' *Japan: Divided Politics in a Growth Economy* (London,
1982), 2nd edn, p. 210. Some commentators have argued that certain
areas of human rights should be outside the scope of the public
welfare doctrine. Commissioner Yabe observed in the Final Report
of the Commission on the Constitution: 'Freedoms relating to the
internal life of the individual such as the freedoms of thought and
conscience cannot, I believe, be limited in the name of the public
interest': John M. Maki, *Japan's Commission on the Constitution*, op.
cit., p. 279.

63 John Finnis, *Natural Law and Natural Rights* (Oxford, 1980), p. 198.

64 The human rights lawyer Lawrence Repeta has gone so far as to argue

that, in practice, 'the individual rights as proclaimed in the Constitution are accorded virtually no protection against violation under color of government authority': 'The International Convention on Civil and Political Rights and Human Rights Law in Japan', *Law in Japan*, vol. 20 (1987), pp. 1–28, at p. 26. This position, however, clearly exaggerates the degree to which the contemporary Japanese state is 'hostile' to individual rights.

3 ASPECTS OF THE BOUNDARIES OF LIFE

1 The Civil Code of Japan (Law No. 89), 27 April 1909, article 1(3). *Shiken* (private rights) include property rights, rights of status and rights of exclusive use. See J.E. De Becker, *Annotated Civil Code of Japan* (Washington DC, 1909), 1st edn, vol. 1, p. 3. The unborn child, however, is recognized as a personality in respect to its claims for compensation for damage in relation to an unlawful act committed against the life of its parents and its right of succession. By article 721 of the Civil Code, 'A child *en ventre sa mere* shall, in respect of his demand of compensation for damages, be deemed to have already been born.'

2 Elsewhere, similarly, this question has arisen, and has been resolved in different ways. The European Court of Human Rights, for example, has held that a foetus does not enjoy the protection of constitutional provisions entrenching a 'right to life': *Borowski* v. *Attorney General of Canada* (1987) 4 DLR (4th) 112, *Semble Paton* v. *United Kingdom* (1980) 3 EHRR 408. In some of the states of the United States, however, the foetus is acknowledged as having a constitutional right to life. In the state of Illinois, for example, we read: 'The unborn child is a human person . . . entitled to the right to life from conception under the laws and Constitution of this State' (Ill. Ann. Stat. ch. 38, 81–2, Smith-Hurd Supp. 1989). See also Susan Prall, 'Privacy II: State Attempts to Regulate Abortion', *Annual Survey of American Law* (1988), pp. 385–427, at p. 422. For a comparative dimension to the issue, see, for example, Mary Ann Glendon, *Abortion and Divorce in Western European Law: American Failures, European Challenges* (Cambridge, Mass., 1987); Barbara Hinkson Craig and David M. O'Brien, *Abortion and American Politics* (Chatham, N.J., 1993).

3 In the report *Fertility and the Family*, the Glover Report on Reproductive Technologies to the European Commission of 1989, the term 'unborn child' is taken to 'include all stages of development up to birth' (p. 94). The terms 'pre-embryo', 'embryo' and 'foetus' are defined thus:

> '*Pre-embryo*: the product of conception, from fertilization to nidation, i.e. up to implantation in the uterine cavity. This stage lasts about 10 days.
> *Embryo*: the product of conception during the stage from implantation in the uterine cavity up to six weeks after fertilization.
> *Foetus*: the product of conception from the end of the embryonic stage to birth' (p. 94).

4 This is the position under English law. For murder to have been committed, the child must be alive: *Poulton* (1832) 5 C & P 329, *per* Littledale J; *Brain* (1834) 6 C & P 349 (Park J); *Sellis* (1837) 7 C & P 850 (Coltman

J.). There is no requirement for the umbilical cord to be severed, or that the after-birth be expelled: *Reeves* (1839) 9 C & P 25 (Vaughan J); *Trilloe* (1842) 2 Mood CC 260 (Erskine J). In their book, *Criminal Law* (London, 1988, 6th edn), J.C. Smith and Brian Hogan make the point that 'there is . . . some uncertainty about the precise moment at which the child comes under the protection of the law of murder, though the question does not seem to have troubled the courts in recent years' (p. 310). The Criminal Law Reform Committee has recommended that the test to be adopted by the courts to determine birth in law should be that the child should have been born and have an existence independent of the mother. See Smith and Hogan, ibid., p. 310.

5 Ōba Shigema, *Keihō kakuron* (Theories on Criminal Law) (Tōkyō, 1923), vol. 1 (*jōkan*), 11th edn, p. 27.

6 *Daishinin hanketsu* (Judgment of the Great Council of State), 13 December 1919. *Daishinin keiji hanketsu roku* (Records of Criminal Judgments of the Great Council of State), Record 25, p. 1367.

7 This approach also finds support amongst many academics. Supporters include Ōno Seiichirō, *Shintei keihō kōgi kakuron* (New Revised Lectures on the Theories of Criminal Law) (Tōkyō, 1950), 3rd ed., p. 157; Takikawa Kōtatsu, *Keihō kakuron* (Theories on Criminal Law) (Tōkyō, 1951), p. 22; Kimura Kameji, *Keihō kakuron* (Theories on Criminal Law) (Tōkyō, 1959), rev. edn, p. 11; Dandō Shigemitsu, *Keihō kōyō kakuron* (The Core of the Theories on Criminal Law) (Tōkyō, 1985), rev. edn, p. 363; Uematsu Tadashi, *Keihō gairon II kakuron* (An Outline of Theories of Criminal Law II) (Tōkyō, 1975), rev. edn, p. 247; Fukuda Taira, *Keihō kakuron* (Theories on Criminal Law) (Tōkyō , 1988) completely rev. edn, p. 174; Kagawa Tatsuo, *Keihō kōgi kakuron* (Lectures on the Theories on Criminal Law) (Tōkyō, 1982), p. 292; Nishihara Haruo, *Hanzai kakuron* (Theories on Crime) (Tōkyō, 1983), 2nd edn, p. 9; Saitō Seiji, *Keihō kōgi kakuron I* (Lectures on the Theories on Criminal Law I) (Tōkyō, 1979), new rev. edn., p. 32; Ōtani Hiroshi, *Keihō kōgi kakuron* (Lectures on the Theories on Criminal Law) (Tōkyō, 1983), p. 2.

8 By article 218(1), a person who is responsible for old, young, disabled or ill persons, and leaves them alone, thereby denying them the protection needed, shall be punished by a term of imprisonment for between three months and five years. Article 218(2) provides that, where they are the person's, or his wife's, lineal descendants, punishment shall be for a period between six months' and seven years' imprisonment. For other discrepancies in punishment between lineal and non-lineal ascendants see Chapter 4.

9 Supreme Court Decision, 19 January 1989. 42 *Keishū* 1. See also Uchida Fumiaki *et al.*, *Chikujō hanrei keihō* (Cases and Notes on Criminal Law) (Tōkyō, 1990), pp. 182–3.

10 The maximum and minimum penalties laid down in Chapter 27 of the Penal Code for 'crimes of bodily injury' are as shown in the table opposite.

Article	Crime	Punishment	
		Maximum	*Minimum*
204	Bodily injury	10 years	Minor fine
205(1)	Death resulting from bodily injury of non-lineal ascendants	15 years (art. 12(1))	2(+) years
205(2)	Death resulting from bodily injury of lineal ascendants	Life	3(+) years
206	Abetting bodily injury	1 year	Minor fine
208	Violence	2 years	Minor fine

The Code's *dataizai* provisions have, from time to time, been the subject of review. In 1931, for example, the Committee for the Revision of the Abortion Law was established to consider the matter. (See Ishii Michiko, 'The Abortion Problem and Family Law in Japan: A Reconsideration of Legalized Abortion Under the Eugenic Protection Law', *Annals of the Institute of Social Science* (Institute of Social Science, University of Tokyo), no. 26 (1984), pp. 64–77, at p. 70; p. 77, footnote 21.) In 1961, minor revisions to the provisions were incorporated into the Draft Penal Code. (The 'Crimes of Abortion' in the 1961 Draft Penal Code are found in Chapter 28, articles 288–92. Article 290 criminalizes *inter alia* 'Abortion by Habitual Offender or for Gain'. For an English translation see B.J. George (ed.), *A Preparatory Draft for the Revised Penal Code of Japan 1961* [Littleton, Colo., 1964], pp. 87–8.) Neither attempt, however, could change in the slightest the abortion provisons of the Penal Code.

11 Between 1947 and 1949, over 8.5 million births were recorded. See Ministry of Health and Welfare, *Shōwa 54 nen jinkō tōkei* (Statistics of Demographic Trends) (Tōkyō, 1979), vol. 1, p. 48.

12 By 1950 nearly 6.25 million people had returned to Japan. See Ministry of Health and Welfare, *Kōseishō 20 nen shi* (Twenty Years of the Ministry of Health and Welfare) (Tōkyō, 1965). Cited in Ishii Michiko, op. cit., p. 76, footnote 19.

13 *Nihon bosei hogo i kyōkai* (The Japan Gynaecological Association for the Protection of Mothers), *Shitei ishi hikken* (Designated Physician's Handbook) (Tōkyō, 1966), p. 10.

14 *Naikaku sōridaijin* (The Prime Minister), *Sanji seigen ni kansuru seron chōsa: shōwa 45 nen sangatsu* (Opinion Survey on Birth Control: March 1970) (Tōkyō, 1970), p. 19.

15 The available statistics can be tabulated as follows:

Year	Abortions (000's)	Year	Abortions (000's)
1950	489	1980	598
1960	1,063	1985	550
1970	732	1988	498

Source: Ikushima Eizaburō, 'Jinkō kōsei no shōrai yosoku', (Future Prediction on the Composition of the Population), in Fukuoka-ken ishikai (Fukuoka Prefecture Association of Medical Doctors), *Kazoku keikaku: yūsei hogohō shidōsha kōshū* (Family Planning: Lectures for Practitioners of the Eugenic Protection Law). Paper delivered at a conference held by the Fukuoka-ken ishikai in Fukuoka City on 20 April 1991 (Fukuoka, 1991), pp. 3–7, at p. 3.

16 Glover Report, op. cit., pp. 98–101.
17 The Report explains that, 'Up to this stage, more than one individual can be formed, while no such indeterminacy remains later.' This 'boundary' is also 'linked to the beginning of the nervous system, and so to the possibility of consciousness' (ibid., p. 100).
18 'This proposed criterion', observes the Glover Report, 'is the point where enough of the nervous system has developed to make it likely that consciousness is present' (ibid., p. 100).
19 *Seichō no ie* is a right-wing religious sect formed in the pre-war period. Its political and social agenda can be summarized as follows:

1 Anti-communism.
2 Return to the Meiji Constitution.
3 Emperor as head of state (rather than as symbol of state).
4 The displaying of the Japanese flag.
5 The Yasukuni *jinja* (Yasukuni shrine) protects the state.
6 Anti-abortion.

Whilst the first five elements demonstrate *Seichō no ie*'s right-wing stance politically, its anti-abortion leaning stems from its philosophy of worshipping life itself. Its anti-abortion stance is a necessary consequence of this philosophy.

Seichō no ie's belief as regards the value of the life of the unborn child can be gleaned from the writings of Taniguchi Seichō, the adopted son-in-law of the founder of *Seichō no ie*, Taniguchi Masaharu (b. 1893). Taniguchi Seichō writes of the *taiji*: 'We must respect human life . . . [the unborn child] is a fine human life . . . It is the same as "human life". The only difference is that it still resides in the mother's womb and is connected to her body through an umbilical cord' (Taniguchi Seichō, *Nani ga taisetsu ka?* [What's Important?] (Tōkyō, 1975), p. 38. Quoted in Samuel Coleman, *Family Planning in Japanese Society: Traditional Birth Control in a Modern Urban Culture* [Princeton, N.J., 1983], p. 63). It is the woman's duty to obey the 'command of heaven' and to carry out her 'great mission' of giving birth to her child. (Taniguchi Seichō, ibid., pp. 3–4). Of abortion, he observes: 'the damage to the mother's body from abortion surgery is truly frightful . . . This is the counteraction (*hansayō*) of the anger of the foetus' soul having been set adrift from darkness into darkness . . .' (ibid., pp. 59–60).

The soul of the aborted foetuses are consoled through the Buddhist practice of *mizuko kuyō* (consolation for the unborn child). See further, Anne Page Brooks, '*Mizuko Kuyō* and Japanese Buddhism', *Japanese Journal of Religious Studies*, vol. 8, nos. 3–4, September–December, (1981), pp. 119–47; Emiko Ohnuki-Tierney, *Illness and Culture in Contemporary Japan: An Anthropological View* (Cambridge, 1984), pp. 78–81; Hoshino Eiki and Takeda Dōshō, 'Indebtedness and Comfort: The Undercurrents of *Mizuko Kuyō* in Contemporary Japan;, *Japanese Journal of Religious Studies*, vol. 14, no. 4, December (1987), pp. 305–20; Bardwell Smith, 'Buddhism and Abortion in Contemporary Japan; *Mizuko Kuyō* and the Confrontation with Death', *Japanese Journal of Religious Studies*, vol. 15, no. 1, March (1988), pp. 3–24. See also William R. LaFleur, 'Contestation and Consensus: The Morality of Abortion in Japan', *Philosophy East and West*, October (1990), pp. 529–42.

Seichō no ie's policy of actively pursuing political campaigns to support its ideology on the question of abortion contradicts the traditional Japanese religions, such as Buddhism and Shinto, in this respect. There is present in Japanese Buddhism a tendency not to interfere with the conduct of individuals, or to accuse them for their conduct; rather, Japanese Buddhism embraces human frailty. Traditional Shintoism distances itself even further from the moral affairs of individuals. These philosophies tend to bring shallow criticism from Western authors on account of what they see as the relative lack of critical opposition from these religious sectors to issues such as abortion. See Lawrence Lader, *Abortion* (Boston, 1966), p. 133; Luke Lee, 'International Status of Abortion Legalization', in Howard J. Osofsky and Joy D. Osofsky (eds), *The Abortion Experience: Psychological and Medical Impact* (Hagerstown, Md., 1973), pp. 338–64, at p. 349; Edward Pohlman, *Psychology of Birth Planning* (Cambridge, Mass., 1969), pp. 29, 403; Irene Taeuber, *The Population of Japan* (Princeton, N.J., 1958), p. 29. Similar criticism has been made by some Japanese authors. See, for example, Muramatsu Minoru, 'Medical Aspects of the Practice of Fertility Regulation', in Muramatsu Minoru (ed.), *Japan's Experience in Family Planning – Past and Present* (Tokyo, 1967), pp. 57–82, at pp. 78–9; Ōta Tenrei, *Datai kinshi to yūsei hogohō* (Abortion Prohibition and the Eugenic Protection Law) (Tōkyō, 1967), p. 2; Ōta Tenrei, *Nihon sanji chōsetsu hyakunen shi* (A Hundred Year History of Birth Control in Japan) (Tōkyō, 1976), p. 329.

20 Glover Report, op. cit., p. 108.

21 Ibid.

22 See *Mainichi Shinbun* (*Mainichi* Newspaper), 4 September 1989.

23 The period up to which the unborn child cannot sustain life outside its mother's womb is *tsūjō ninshin man 23 shū izen* (before the full 23 weeks, including the 23rd week).

24 The period up to which the unborn child cannot sustain life outside its mother's womb is *tsūjō ninshin man 22 shū miman* (before the full 22 weeks).

25 *Nichibo ihō* (The Monthly Digest of the *Nihon bosei hogo i kyōkai*), vol. 42, no. 481, 1 April (1990), p. 111.

26 Ibid.
27 British Association Study Group, *Social Concern and Biological Advances* (London, 1974). Quoted in William A.R. Thomson, *A Dictionary of Medical Ethics and Practice* (Bristol, 1977), p. 80.
28 The *Memorandum* issued by the Honorary Secretary of the Conference of Medical Royal Colleges and their Faculties in the United Kingdom on 15 January 1979 observed: 'Cessation of respiration and cessation of the heart beat are examples of organic failure occurring during the process of dying, and since the moment that the heart beat ceases is usually detectable with simplicity by no more than clinical means, it has for many centuries been accepted as the moment of death itself, without any serious attempt being made to assess the validity of this assumption.' See British Medical Association, *The Handbook of Medical Ethics* (London, 1980), pp. 67–8.
29 Ibid., p. 68.
30 Ibid.
31 Ibid., p. 69.
32 For a discussion of *nōshi* in Japan see 'Tokushū: nōshi o meguru sho-mondai' (Special Issue: Various Problems Concerning Brain Death) *Hōritsu no hiroba*, vol. 38, no. 8 (1985), pp. 4–45; Morioka Masahiro, '*Nōshi to wa nan de atta ka*' (What Was Brain Death?), in *Nihon rinri gakkai kenkyū happyō yōshi* (Japan Ethics Association Outline of Presentation), Japan Ethics Association 39th Annual Conference, held at Waseda University, 14–15 October 1988), p. 7, cited in Carl B. Becker, 'Buddhist Views of Suicide and Euthanasia', *Philosophy East and West*, October (1990), pp. 543–56. An interesting survey by the *Asahi Shinbun* (*Asahi* Newspaper) conducted in March 1988 revealed that 43 per cent of those members of the public polled agreed with the brain death theory, whilst 42 per cent disagreed. In an earlier *Yomiuri Shinbun* (*Yomiuri* Newspaper) opinion poll in November 1987, 46.2 per cent favoured the brain death theory, whilst 28.3 per cent did not. See Umeda Toshirō, 'Transplants Forbidden', *Japan Quarterly*, vol. 36, no. 2, April–June (1989), pp. 146–54, at pp. 149–50. For a recent article discussing *inter alia* the debate on brain death and organ transplantation in the context of informed consent and patients' rights in Japan, see Robert B. Leflar, 'Informed Consent and Patients' Rights in Japan', *Houston Law Review*, vol. 33, no. 1 (1996), pp. 1–112.
33 Representative of those who take this view is the philosopher Umehara Takeshi. For Umehara's view on death, see Umehara Takeshi (ed.), *Nōshi wa shi de nai* (Brain Death is Not Death) (Kyōto, 1992); on his view on life, see Umehara Takeshi, *Bukkyō no shisō I* (Buddhist Thought, I) (vol. 5 of *Umehara Takeshi chosakushū* (Collected Works of Umehara Takeshi) (Tōkyō, 1982), pp. 48–9. I am grateful to Dr Nakamura Yukiyasu of the First Surgical Department of Kurume University's Medical Faculty for this information.
34 See further, Report of the Committee on Brain Death, in Tachibana Takashi, *Nōshi rinchō hihan* (Criticism on the Report of the Committee on Brain Death) (Tōkyō, 1992), p. 246. This has been the traditional view, which is still held generally.

35 Edmund Davies, 'A Legal Look at Transplants', *Proceedings of the Royal Society of Medicine*, vol. 62 (1969), p. 633.
36 Yasuhira Masakichi, *Kaisei keihō kakuron* (Revised Theories on Criminal Law) (Tōkyō, 1960), p. 15.
37 Takikawa Haruo and Takeuchi Tadashi, *Keihō kakuron kōgi* (Lectures on the Theories of Criminal Law) (Tōkyō, 1965), p. 3.
38 Kagawa Tatsuo, op. cit., p. 293.
39 Ōba Shigema, op. cit., p. 36.
40 Fukuda Taira, op. cit., p. 174.
41 Fujiki Hideo, *Keihō kōgi kakuron* (Lectures on the Theories of Criminal Law) (Tōkyō, 1976), pp. 189, 190.
42 Ōtani Hiroshi, op. cit., p. 12.
43 Nakatani Kinko, *Keihō kōgi kakuron* (Lectures on the Theories of Criminal Law), *jō* (vol. 1) (Tōkyō, 1983), p. 12.
44 Uematsu Tadashi, op. cit., p. 247.
45 Dandō Shigemitsu, op. cit., p. 367.
46 Hirano Ryūichi, *Keihō gaisetsu* (An Outline of Criminal Law) (Tōkyō, 1977), p. 156.
47 Saitō Seiji, op. cit., p. 34.
48 By article 202 of the 1907 Penal Code, 'Every person who has instigated or assisted another person to commit suicide or has killed a person at such person's request or with his consent shall be punished with penal servitude or imprisonment for not less than six months nor more than seven years.'
49 See *Kojiki* (Records of Ancient Matters), original text, with translation into contemporary Japanese and notes by Tsugita Masaki, vol. 3 (*ge*) (Tōkyō, 1984), pp. 83–5.
50 These include *Shinjū ten no Amajima* (Love Suicides at Amajima) of 1721; *Sonezaki shinjū* (Love Suicides at Somezaki) of 1703; *Imamiya shinjū* (Love Suicides of Imamiya) of 1711; *Ikudama shinjū* (Love Suicides at Ikudama) of 1715; *Shinjū yoigoshin* (Love Suicides on the Eve of the Koshin Festival) of 1722; and *Shinjū yaibawa kōri no tsuitachi* (Love Suicides in Midsummer With an Icy Blade) of 1709. For the Japanese texts of the major *shinjū* plays see Shigetomo Ki *et al.* (eds), *Chikamatsu jōrurishū* (A Collection of Chikamatsu's Ballad-Dramas), *jō* (vol. 1) and *ge* (vol. 2), in *Nihon koten bungaku taikei* (Japanese Classics Series) (Tōkyō, 1958), vols. 49 and 50. For an English translation of Chikamatsu's *Sonezaki shinjū*, see Donald Keene (tr.), *Major Plays of Chikamatsu* (New York, 1961), pp. 39–90. For a translation of *Shinjū ten no Amajima*, see Donald Keene, ibid., pp. 387–425.
51 On Dazai Osamu, see Alan Wolfe, *Suicidal Narrative in Modern Japan: The Case of Dazai Osamu* (Princeton, N.J., 1990); David Brudnoy, 'The Immutable Despair of Dazai Osamu', *Monumenta Nipponica*, vol. 23 (1968), pp. 457–74.
52 If there was no such intention, the person is guilty of murder. See the Decision of the Supreme Court, 21 November 1958. *Keishū* 12-15-3519.
53 The crime of murder differs from such crimes in that, whilst the former requires there to have been an intention to kill, the latter do not necessarily require this. Thus in the case of causing death from bodily injury, the Supreme Court has distinguished this crime (provided in articles 205(1)

and 205(2) of the 1907 Penal Code) from the crime of murder (provided by articles 199 and 200 of the Code) as follows: 'the only subjective difference concerning murder and the crime of causing death as a result of bodily injury is whether or not there existed an intention to kill . . .' Decision of the First Petty Bench of the Supreme Court, 13 April 1979. 33 *Keishū* 179.

54 In a sense, *anrakushi* (as well as *jisatsu*) is the individual's ultimate 'right', reflecting as it does a 'right' to die. In law, terminating the life of a dying patient, under strict conditions, is not a criminal offence. In a 1962 High Court case the Court held that euthanasia should be allowed only under strict conditions. These were: (1) the patient should be suffering from an incurable disease, with death imminent; (2) when suffering from unbearable pain; (3) euthanasia should be performed only for the purpose of relieving the patient's agony; (4) the patient has consented to the act, consent having been given when fully conscious and able to express his/her will; (5) in general, it should be performed by a medical doctor; (6) the method used should be ethically appropriate: High Court Criminal Records, vol. 15, no. 9, 22 December 1962, p. 674.

In the recent Yokohama District Court decision of 28 March 1995, the Court held that euthanasia was permissible where the following four conditions were present: (1) the patient suffered from unbearable physical pain; (2) nearing the time of death; (3) there was no means of easing the patient's pain; (4) the patient has expressed a will to die. See, for example, the *Nishi Nihon Shinbun*, 28 March 1995 (evening edition), p. 1.

Anrakushi is a frequently encountered theme in Japanese literature. Perhaps the best-known work dealing with this subject is Mori Ōgai's (1862–1922) *'Takasebune'* (Convict Boat). See further, Yatome Fumimaro, 'Iwayuru anrakushi ni tsuite no ichi kōsatsu: Mori Ōgai *"Takasebune"* o tōshite (Euthanasia in Mori Ōgai's *'Takasebune'*), *Dōhō Daigaku Kiyō* (Bulletin of Dōhō University) (Institute of Liberal and General Education), no. 4 (1990), pp. 131–46.

55 For a discussion of *songenshi* see, for example, Saitō Seiji *Keihō ni okeru seimei no hogo: nōshi, songenshi, zōki ishoku, taiji no shōgai* (The Protection of Life in Criminal Law: Brain Death, Death with Dignity, Internal Organ Transplants and Damage to Foetuses) (Tōkyō, 1987), p. 293; Miano Akira, *Anrakushi kara songenshi e* (From Mercy Killing to Death with Dignity) (Tōkyō, 1984), p. 397. The February 15th issue of the *Jurisuto*, no. 1061 (1995) devotes much space to the issue of *songenshi*, and is a useful contribution to the ongoing discussion on the subject (see pp. 7–73).

56 1 QB 276; [1978] 2 All ER 987. Sir George Baker held that the common law did not concede legal personality to the unborn child. The husband had no right at law or in equity which the court could protect.

57 *C* v. *S* [1987] 1 All ER 1230. Both Heilbron J. and the Court of Appeal held that the father's consent to abortion was unnecessary. Heilbron J. followed Sir George Baker's view in *Paton* v. *B.P.A.S. Trustees* and concluded that: 'a child, after it has been born, and only then in certain circumstances based upon his or her having a legal right, may be a party to an action brought with regard to such matters [as arise before birth]. In other words, the claim crystallises on the birth, at which date, but not

before, the child attains the status of a legal person, and thereupon can [complain about those matters]' ([1987] 1 All ER, at p. 1234). Leave to appeal the case to the House of Lords was refused by the Appeal Committee of the House of Lords. See further, Noel Williams, 'Taiji no seimei wa dare no mono ka? – Igirisu dewa dō kangaerarete iru ka?' (The Foetus's Life is Whose? How is this Matter Viewed in Britain?). A paper presented at a public lecture delivered at Daitō Bunka University, Tokyo, 28 September 1996.

58 See Samuel Coleman, op. cit., pp. 21–3.
59 Takikawa Kōtatsu, op. cit., p. 57.
60 Susan Treggiari, *Roman Marriage: Iusti Coniuges from the Time of Cicero to the Time of Ulpian* (Oxford, 1991), p. 11. Additionally, women owed the state children, and children qualified the father for certain privileges. Thus, for example, during the Flavian period, the constitutional law of the Latin town of Malaga laid down its rules for its council as follows: 'In this senate [if] two or more have the same number of votes, let [the presiding magistrate] give preference and announce as selected first . . . a man who has children over one who has none . . .' S. Riccobono *et al.*, *Fontes Iuris Romani Antejustiniani* (Florence, 1968–9), 2nd edn, vol. 1. 23. 56, AD 82–3, quoted in Treggiari op. cit., p. 67. In the Institutes of Gaius (?*c.* 161) we read that *orbi* (those who have no children), 'according to the Papian Law lose half of inheritances and legacies on account of the fact that they have no children . . .' Gaius 2.286a, quoted in Treggiari, ibid., p. 72.
61 See Shimazu Ichirō, 'Cases and Legislation Concerning Artificial Insemination: A Comparative Study of Japanese Law', *Hitotsubashi Journal of Law and Politics*, vol. 7 (1974), pp. 8–28.
62 Susan Orpett Long, *Family Change and the Life Course in Japan* (Ithaca, N.Y., 1987), p. 88.
63 Ōhashi Yukako, 'My Body Belongs to Me: Women Fight Against a Retrogressive Revision of the Eugenic Law', *AMPO Japan – Asia Quarterly Review*, vol. 18, nos. 2/3 (1986), pp. 94–9, at p. 99.
64 The most important recent contribution to the debate on capital punishment in Japan is Dandō Shigemitsu's book, *Shikei haishiron* (A Theory on the Abolition of the Death Penalty), 4th edn. (Tōkyō, 1995).
65 In Japan, social sanctions have been – and continue to be – an important means of social control. See further John O. Haley, 'Sheathing the Sword of Justice in Japan: An Essay on Law Without Sanctions', *Journal of Japanese Studies*, vol. 8, no. 2 (1982), pp. 265–81. See also John Haley, 'Introduction: Legal vs Social Controls', *Law in Japan*, vol. 17 (1984), pp. 1–6.
66 Where the convicted prisoner becomes insane subsequent to trial, a stay of execution of the death penalty may be granted even after the Minister of Justice has issued the order to execute the prisoner; and no execution may be carried out 'unless the order of the Minister of Justice is given after the condition of mental derangement has recovered'. Code of Criminal Procedure, 1948 (as amended by Law no. 268 of 31 July 1952), article 479.
67 Where the convicted prisoner is pregnant, a stay of execution may be granted, and no execution may be carried out 'unless the order of the

Minister of Justice is given after . . . the delivery has been made'. Code of Criminal Procedure, 1948 (as amended by Law no. 268 of 31 July 1952), article 479.

68 By article 51 of the Juvenile Law 1948, persons under the age of 18 when they committed a capital offence cannot be sentenced to death. In such cases, the death penalty is reduced to life imprisonment. Under Japanese law, juveniles are persons under the age of 20 (Juvenile Law 1948, article 2). In respect of capital punishment, 18 years of age is the same as that provided by article 6(5) of the International Covenant on Civil and Political Rights, where those below the age of 18 are exempt from the death penalty. It is interesting to note that this exemption was first introduced by Japan when the article was in its draft stage (A/C.3/L. 650). Although Japan suggested that the phrase punishments 'imposed on minors', be inserted into the text, this was later changed to 'children and young persons'. In article 6(5) the phrase 'persons below 18 years of age' now appears. See B.G. Ramcharan, 'The Drafting History of Article 6 of the International Covenant on Civil and Political Rights', in B.G. Ramcharan (ed.), *The Right to Life in International Law* (Dordrecht, 1985), pp. 42–56, at pp. 47, 49. In the Annual Report of the Inter-American Commission on Human Rights, 1986–1987, we read that, 'The rule prohibiting the execution of juvenile offenders has acquired the authority of *jus cogens*' (p. 168). See Theodore S. Orlin, 'The Prohibition of the Death Penalty: An Emerging International Norm?' in Allan Rosas and Jan Helgesen (eds), *Human Rights in a Changing East–West Perspective* (London, 1990), pp. 136–73, at p. 137.

69 Since 1983, the Japanese courts have followed the ruling of the Supreme Court in the *Nagayama Norio Case*. In that case, the criteria to be applied in determining whether or not to impose the death sentence was held to be as follows: 'Under the present legal system which retains the death penalty, when various circumstances are considered such as the nature of the crime, its motivation and its mode, especially the persistency and cruelty of the method of killing, the significance of the result, especially the number of victims, the feeling of the family of the victims, the impact on society, the offender's age, criminal record and circumstances after conviction, if its liability is considered heavy and the death penalty is regarded as unavoidable from the viewpoint of proportionality as well as deterrence the imposition of the death penalty is allowed.' Quoted in Amnesty International, *Japan: The Death Penalty and the Need for More Safeguards Against Ill-Treatment of Detainees* (Tokyo, 1991), pp. 49–50. For a study on how the general standard articulated in *Japan* v. *Nagayama* has been applied by the courts since 1983, see Masumoto Hirofumi, 'Shikei hanketsu no gutaiteki ryōkei kijun no kentō: Nagayama daiichiji saikōsai hanketsu igo no hanketsu o sozai ni shite' (An Examination of the Standards Employed for Death Penalty Sentencing From Concrete Examples: A Review of Cases Since *Japan* v. *Nagayama* (1983)', *Nara Daigaku Kiyō* (Memoirs of Nara University), no. 23 (1995), pp. 29–50.

70 1907 Penal Code, article 11(2).

71 See Ōno Masayoshi 'Contradictions in the Functions of Criminal Law', *Osaka University Law Review*, no. 14 (1966), pp. 25–34, at p. 25.

72 See Tanaka Hideo (ed.), *The Japanese Legal System: Introductory Cases and Materials* (Tokyo, 1976), p. 829. Urabe Noriho, for example, notes: 'As for Article 31 of the Constitution, there are some arguments as to whether it has the same meaning as the due process clauses of the fifth and fourteenth amendments of the United States Constitution because those due process clauses are concerned both with procedure and substance. But it is understood almost unanimously that Article 31 requires at least "procedural due process" in restricting the people's rights and liberties': Urabe Noriho, 'Rule of Law and Due Process: A Comparative View of the United States and Japan', in Percy R. Luney, Jr. and Takahashi Kazuyuki (eds), *Japanese Constitutional Law* (Tokyo, 1993), pp. 173–86, at p. 177. Whilst it is a generally held view that articles 32–9 of the present Constitution provide the individual with due process protection in relation to criminal proceedings, the issue of whether, and to what extent, procedural due process exists in areas other than criminal law is controversial. See further Okudaira Yasuhiro, 'Forty Years of the Constitution and its Various Influences: Japanese, American, and European', in Percy R. Luney, Jr. and Takahashi Kazuyuki (eds), ibid., pp. 1–38, at pp. 13–16. On due process in relation to property rights see Ukai Nobushige and Nathaniel L. Nathanson, 'Protection of Property Rights and Due Process of Law in the Japanese Constitution', in Dan Fenno Henderson (ed.), *The Constitution of Japan: Its First Twenty Years, 1947–67* (Seattle and London, 1968), pp. 239–55.

73 Ronald Dworkin, *Taking Rights Seriously* (Cambridge, Mass., 1978), pp. 132–6.

74 Takayanagi Kenzō, 'A Century of Innovation – The Development of Japanese Law, 1868–1961', in Arthur Taylor von Mehren, *Law in Japan: The Legal Order in a Changing Society* (Cambridge, Mass., 1963), pp. 5–40. Reprinted in Tanaka Hideo, op. cit., pp. 163–93, at p. 164.

75 Hirano Ryūichi, 'The Accused and Society: Some Aspects of Japanese Criminal Law', in Arthur Taylor von Mehren (ed.) *Law in Japan: The Legal Order in a Changing Society* (Cambridge, Mass., 1963), pp. 274–96, at p. 292. The Code adheres to the principle of justice without discrimination on grounds of social class, and no punishment without a previous law.

76 Ishii Ryōsuke (ed.), *Japanese Legislation in the Meiji Era* (tr. William J. Chambliss), vol. 10: *Legislation* (Tokyo, 1958), p. 18.

77 Chapter 2, 'Crimes Concerning Insurrection.'

78 Chapter 3, 'Crimes Concerning Foreign Aggression.'

79 Chapter 9, 'Crimes of Arson and Fire Caused by Negligence.'

80 Chapter 11, 'Crimes of Traffic Obstruction.'

81 Chapter 15, 'Crimes Relating to Pollution of Drinking Water.'

82 Chapter 26, 'Crimes of Homicide.'

83 Chapter 36, 'Crimes of Larceny and Robbery.'

84 Supreme Court Decision, 26 November 1969. *Ex parte R.K.B. Mainichi hōsō co.* 23 *Keishū* 1490. See Tanaka Hideo (ed.), op. cit., pp. 740–3, at p. 742.

85 Protection of the individual's rights at the pre-trial stage is found in articles 33, 34, 35 and 36 of the Constitution. These include *inter alia*

a prohibition on 'torture' and 'cruel' punishments by 'any public officer' (article 36); the requirement of a search warrant to enter and search premises (article 35); and a prohibition on detention 'without adequate cause' (article 34).

86 See further Matsui Shigenori, *Saiban o ukeru kenri* (Right of Access to the Courts) (Tōkyō, 1993).

87 For an English translation of the early Supreme Court judgment of 22 December 1948 (2 *Keishū* 1853) by D.C.S. Sissons see John M. Maki (ed.) *Court and Constitution in Japan: Selected Supreme Court Decisions, 1948–60* (Seattle, 1964), pp. 207–9. For a brief discussion on delays in court proceedings, see Tanaka Hideo, op. cit., pp. 475–81.

88 *Pak* v. *Japan*. Supreme Court Decision of 20 December 1972. 26 *Keishū* 631. Quoted in Tanaka Hideo, op. cit., pp. 478–81, at p. 478. The Court considered that the following factors should be taken into account when deciding on whether an infringement of the constitutional guarantee to a speedy trial has taken place: this 'is to be determined not merely by the length of time which has elapsed, but also by taking into account the causes and the reasons for the delay, by considering whether such delay was in fact unavoidable, by considering how much damage was inflicted upon the interests designed to be protected under the said constitutional guarantee, as well as by making an all-over observation of various other factors. For instance, we will not hold that there have been such extraordinary circumstances in a case which is of such a complicated nature as would reasonably require a considerable length of time for hearing and decision. Nor will we so hold in a case where the primary cause for such delay was on the defendant's side, such as the defendant's failure to appear in court or his efforts to prolong the trial. Such conduct on the part of the defendant is tantamount to a waiver of his right to a speedy trial . . .' (ibid., p. 479).

89 See Matsui Shigenori, 'A Comment Upon the Role of the Judiciary in Japan', *Osaka University Law Review*, no. 35 (1988), pp. 17–28; Percy R. Luney, Jr., 'The Judiciary: Its Organization and Status in the Parliamentary System', in Percy R. Luney, Jr. and Takahashi Kazuyuki (eds), *Japanese Constitutional Law*, op. cit., pp. 123–49.

90 Code of Criminal Procedure, article 289.

91 Tanaka Hideo comments that 'Article 38, Paragraph 1 of the Constitution, if literally interpreted, seems to cover only testimony against oneself. But the widely accepted view equates it with a clause providing for the privilege against self-incrimination' (op. cit., p. 824). Cases brought before the Supreme Court involving article 38(1) and privilege against self-incrimination include: (a) Supreme Court Decision of 26 July 1954 (8 *Keishū* 1151); (b) Supreme Court Decision of 20 February 1957 (11 *Keishū* 802); and (c) Supreme Court Decision of 2 May 1962 (16 *Keishū* 495 – *Saitō* v. *Japan*). For English translations of the case of *Saitō* v. *Japan*, see Itō Hiroshi and Lawrence Ward Beer, *The Constitutional Case Law of Japan: Selected Supreme Court Decisions, 1961–70* (Seattle, 1978), pp. 164–6; Tanaka Hideo, op. cit., pp. 823–4. See further B.J. George, 'The "Right of Silence" in Japanese Law', in Dan Fenno Henderson (ed.), *The Constitution of Japan*, op. cit., pp. 257ff.

92 For cases on this area of law see *inter alia* (a) Supreme Court Decision of 1 August 1951 (5 *Keishū* 1684); (b) Supreme Court Decision of 10 July 1953 (7 *Keishū* 1474); (c) Supreme Court Decision of 1 July 1966 (20 *Keishū* 537 – *Abe* v. *Japan*). For translations of the *Abe* v. *Japan* case, see Tanaka Hideo, op. cit., pp. 820–2; Itō and Beer, op. cit., pp. 167–8. For a more recent case, see Supreme Court Decision of 29 February 1984 (38 *Keishū* 479).

93 See *inter alia* the cases of: (a) Supreme Court Decision of 29 July 1948 (2 *Keishū* 1021); (b) Supreme Court Decision of 28 May 1958 (12 *Keishū* 1718).

94 In a 1950 case (Supreme Court Decision of 27 September 4 *Keishū* 1805) it was held that it was constitutional to give to the procurator the right to appeal even against a judgment of acquittal. For an English translation of what if often referred to as the *Kojima Double Jeopardy Case* (*Kojima* v. *Japan*, Supreme Court Decision of 13 July 1966, 20 *Keishū* 6), see Itō and Beer, op. cit., pp. 154–7. B.J. George, commenting on the English translation of the term '*ichiji fusairi*' as 'double jeopardy', cautions against its use: 'Although the term *ichiji fusairi* is usually translated as "double jeopardy", the concept is closer to the Roman law concept of *non bis in idem* than to Anglo-American double jeopardy, so that the latter term ought not be used for *ichiji fusairi* lest it create confusion on the part of uninitiated persons': B.J. George, 'Rights of the Criminally Accused', in Percy R. Luney, Jr. and Takahashi Kazuyuki (eds), *Japanese Constitutional Law*, op. cit., pp. 289–318, at p. 316, note 99.

95 Takikawa Masajirō, *Nihon gyōkei shi* (A History of Japanese Penology) (Tōkyō, 1964), p. 20.

96 Rules of Criminal Procedure (Supreme Court Rules no. 32 of 1948, as amended), articles 235–50.

97 The number of cases tried by jury is given by Okahara in his article, 'Baishinhō no teishi ni kansuru hōritsu ni tsuite' (On the Act to Suspend the Operation of the Jury Act), *Hosōkai Zasshi*, vol. 4 (1943), pp. 10ff. (cited in Tanaka Hideo, op. cit., p. 482, footnote a). These are as follows (year, with number of cases tried by jury in parentheses): 1928 (31), 1929 (143), 1930 (66), 1931 (60), 1932 (55), 1933 (36), 1934 (26), 1935 (18), 1936 (19), 1937 (15), 1938 (4), 1939 (4), 1940 (4), 1941 (1), 1942 (2).

Although the jury system is not now in operation, constitutionally speaking it has not been abolished. Okudaira Yasuhiro, for example, observed that, 'the constitutional silence does not imply that trial by jury is prohibited': 'Forty Years', op. cit., p. 12.

98 Rules of Criminal Procedure (Supreme Court Rules no. 32 of 1948, as amended), articles 251–70.

99 Code of Criminal Procedure (Law no. 131 of 1948, as amended), articles 454–60. Only the Attorney General can file this appeal.

100 Ibid., articles 435–53.

101 By article 16 of the Meiji Constitution, 'The Emperor orders amnesty, pardon, commutation of punishments and rehabilitation.'

102 'By general amnesty, which is granted by a Cabinet order specifying certain offenses, convictions lose their effect and the right of prosecution

is extinguished.' Alfred Oppler, 'The Judicial and Legal System', chapter 6 of SCAP's report on the *Political Reorientation of Japan, September 1945 to September 1948* (Westport, Conn., 1970), vol. 1, p. 234.

103 'General commutation of punishment, granted by a Cabinet order which specifies the offenses or penalties to be commuted, mitigates the penalties, while special commutation of punishment is granted by the Cabinet with the same effect to individual persons who have been condemned' (ibid.).

104 'General rehabilitation is granted by Cabinet orders specifying the conditions to be applied to those convicted criminals who have been deprived of, or suspended from, their civil rights or qualifications because of their conviction. Rehabilitation restores the deprived or suspended rights or qualifications' (ibid.).

105 'By special amnesty, which is granted individually to specified persons, convictions lose effect' (ibid.).

106 'Reprieve exempts a criminal from the execution of penalty and is granted individually' (ibid.).

107 Amnesty is, however, rarely granted in practice.

108 Supreme Court Decision of 19 July 1985 (1158 *Hanrei Jihō* 28). For a discussion in English on this case, see the comments by Nomura Minoru and Nakazora Toshimasa in *Waseda Bulletin of Comparative Law*, vol. 7 (1988), p. 91.

109 Hirasawa died in prison in 1987, aged 95.

110 Supreme Court Decision of 12 May 1948 (2 *Keishū* 191). For an English translation of this case, see John M. Maki, *Court and Constitution in Japan*, op. cit., pp. 156–64; quoted on p. 158.

111 Ibid., p. 157.

112 Ibid., p. 159.

113 Ibid. For a discussion of these methods of executing the death penalty in the Tokugawa period, see Ishii Ryōsuke, *Edo no keibatsu* (Punishment in the Edo Era) (Tōkyō, 1964).

114 Supreme Court Decision of 6 April 1955 (9 *Keishū* 663).

115 *Ichikawa et al* v. *Japan*. Supreme Court Decision of 19 July 1961 (15 *Keishū* 7). For an English translation, see Itō and Beer, op. cit., pp. 161–4. The technicalities involved in executing the death penalty are described in the Order in question thus: 'in carrying out the capital punishment by hanging . . . tie both hands behind the back . . . blindfold the face . . . bring the person up onto the platform and make him stand on the centreboard . . . put the rope around his neck . . . open the trap door . . . let the convicted hang in the air . . .'

116 For a discussion on this point, see Lawrence Repeta, 'The International Convention on Civil and Political Rights and Human Rights Law in Japan: Introduction to the First Five Issues of "Citizens' Human Rights Reports" by the Japan Civil Liberties Union', *Law in Japan*, vol. 20 (1987), pp. 1–28, at pp. 4–7.

117 Article 6(6).

118 Under Japanese law, similarly, pregnant women *per se*, we remember, are exempt from the death penalty. See note 67, this chapter.

119 For a list of these states see Roger Hood, *The Death Penalty: A World-Wide Perspective* (Oxford, 1989), p. 169.
120 2 *Keishū* 191. See John M. Maki, *Court and Constitution in Japan*, op. cit., p. 158.
121 Ibid., p. 163.
122 Ibid., p. 158.
123 Ibid.
124 Ibid., p. 161.
125 Ibid.
126 Japan's reliance on public opinion in Japan to justify its retentionist stance is seen, for example, in its statement to the Human Rights Committee of the United Nations. There we read: 'the representative of Japan informed the Committee that the Legislative Council, one of the advisory bodies to the Minister of Justice, had recently studied the question of capital punishment and had concluded that its abolition would be unwarranted in view of the continued commission of brutal crimes and the fact that a large majority of Japanese people favoured the retention of the death penalty' (A/37/40 para. 82). See Theodore S. Orlin, op. cit., p. 149.

An opinion poll conducted by the Mainichi Press in 1956, for example, revealed that the verdict of the learned judges in the 1955 case was in keeping with views held by the population at large. Chiba Masaji, in her analysis of the statistics, notes that 59.3 per cent of the 2,904 people polled favoured retention of the death penalty, with only 23.8 per cent favouring its abolition ('Results and Problems of K.O.L. Research in Japan', A Preliminary Report to the Symposium of the International Research Committee on Sociology of Law in Noordwijk, the Netherlands, September 1972; quoted in Alfred Oppler, *Legal Reform in Occupied Japan: A Participant Looks Back* [Princeton, N.J., 1976], p. 127, footnote 23). Another poll in the same year – this time organized by the government – revealed an even stronger desire amongst those polled to retain capital punishment (ibid., p. 127, footnote 23). The figures revealed that 65 per cent opposed abolition, whilst only 18 per cent favoured abolition. In a government poll conducted in 1967, the figures were even higher, with 70 per cent of those polled favouring the retention of the death penalty: Ōno Masayoshi, 'Capital Punishment and Penal Reform', *Osaka University Law Review*, no. 22 (1975), pp. 1–18, at p. 17.

This trend has continued up to the present. An opinion poll conducted in 1989 reveals that those who desired to retain capital punishment outnumbered those who wished to see its abolition. In the poll conducted by the Prime Minister's Office, 66.5 per cent of the general public expressed their desire to retain the death penalty. Of these, the majority were motivated to respond as they did from the belief that the number of violent crimes committed was on the increase (although official statistics for 1988, for example, revealed that the number of murders and armed robberies had actually decreased: Amnesty International, op. cit., p. 51). In 1993, a *Yomiuri Shinbun* poll of 2,100 respondents revealed that 63.9 per cent believed capital punishment should be continued (*The Daily Yomiuri*, 1 June 1993).

127 Tsuda Mamichi, 'On the Death Penalty', in William Reynolds Braisted (tr. with an introduction), *Meiroku Zasshi: Journal of the Japanese Enlightenment*) (Tokyo, 1976), pp. 498–500. Boissonade, likewise, opposed the death penalty in Japan. See further, Yano Yūko, 'Boasonādo no shikei haishiron ni kansuru ichi kōsatsu' (An Essay on Boissonado's Theory on the Abolition of the Death Penalty), *Hōgaku Seijigaku Ronkyū* (Journal of Law and Political Studies), Graduate School of Law, Keiō University, no. 17 (Summer 1993), pp. 71–105.

128 The practice of the displaying of the head was abolished in 1879. Decapitation was abolished by the 1880 Old Penal Code.

129 Tabata, for example, argues that the spirit of the Constitution demands its abolition: 'To abolish capital punishment by the people's accord and not to maintain it', he notes, 'is the spirit of the Constitution.' That spirit, he argues, is embodied in articles 9 and 11 of the Constitution (quoted and cited in Ōno Masayoshi, 'Capital Punishment and Penal Reform', op. cit., p. 15). Masaki, similarly, cites the contradiction between the pacifist provision of article 9 and the retention of the death penalty (quoted and cited in Ōno Masayoshi, ibid., p. 16). On pacifism and the right to live in peace generally, see Fukase Tadakazu, *Sensō hōki to heiwateki seizonken* (The Renunciation of War and the Right to Live in Peace) (Tōkyō, 1987). For a historical perspective on peace and article 9, see Klaus Schlichtmann, 'The Ethics of Peace: Shidehara Kijūrō and Article 9 of the Constitution', *Japan Forum*, vol. 7, no. 1 (1995), pp. 43–67.

130 See further Robert L. Ramseyer, 'The *Sōka Gakkai*', in Richard K. Beardsley (ed.), *Studies in Japanese Culture: 1*, The University of Michigan Centre for Japanese Studies Occasional Paper no. 9 (Ann Arbor, Mich., 1965), pp. 141–92.

131 Richard L. Gage (ed.), *Arnold Toynbee and Daisaku Ikeda – Choose Life: A Dialogue* (Oxford, 1976), p. 148.

132 Capital punishment was abolished for a period of 247 years from the first year of *Kōnin*, 810.

133 Ishio Yoshihisa, *Nihon kodaihō no kenkyū* (Research on Early Japanese Law) (Tōkyō, 1968), p. 172.

134 Hirano Ryūichi, 'The Accused and Society', op. cit., p. 290.

135 Paul Sieghart, *The Lawful Rights of Mankind: An Introduction to the International Legal Code of Human Rights* (Oxford, 1985), p. 110.

136 See further, Gino J. Naldi, 'The Prohibition on the Death Penalty in International Law', *Netherlands International Law Review*, vol. 38 (1991), pp. 373–84; Theodore S. Orlin, op. cit.

137 David Lyons, *Ethics and the Rule of Law* (Cambridge, 1984), p. 145.

138 Alfred C. Oppler, *Legal Reform in Occupied Japan*, op. cit., p. 126.

139 Joel Feinberg, *Doing and Deserving* (Princeton, N.J., 1970).

140 Immanuel Kant (tr. John Ladd), *Metaphysical Elements of Justice* (New York, 1965).

141 In comments on the Second Protocol to the International Covenant on Civil and Political Rights Aiming at the Abolition of the Death Penalty of 28 July 1981, Japan defended its retentionist stance by claiming that, in addition to capital punishment being regarded as an 'effective deterrent' to cruel crimes by the general population, 'the majority of the

Japanese citizens support retention of the death penalty as a just punishment for criminals who have committed particular heinous crimes' (UN Doc. A/36/441, p. 11, reprinted CN 4/Sub 2/1987/20, p. 25). This is reflected in an opinion poll conducted by the *Yomiuri Shinbun* in 1993. It found that 40.5 per cent of those who supported the retention of capital punishment did so because they believed that 'it is natural for those who commit serious crimes to pay the supreme penalty' (see note 126, this chapter).

142 The Tokugawa period, however, was an exception. Applying Confucianism as its governing theory, the Tokugawa regime incorporated retribution and *adauchi* (personal 'revenge') as an element in its system of ruling. In legislation governing the conduct of the *bushi* class, we read that *adauchi* had to be sought by those individuals, or their families, that had suffered at the hands of aggressors. Thus, for example, the children of parents killed by an assailant were obligated to take personal revenge against the assailant. The famous episode of the 46 *rōnin* (masterless *samurai*) is but one example of followers taking revenge for the injustice suffered by their master. The taking of such revenge did not, however, bring immunity from further action by the authorities. Those who murdered as revenge, for example, were themselves to be punished for their crime.

It is a common criticism of retributive theories that they fail to show why the state should have an exclusive right to punish. Robert Nozick (*Anarchy, State and Utopia* [New York, 1974]), in an attempt to resolve the difficulty, has argued that punishment can be justified if those individuals in society who are wronged by others 'transfer' the right to punish those wrongdoers to the state. The case of personal revenge in Tokugawa Japan is interesting in that the opposite is the case. Here the state 'transfers' the right to punish wrongdoers to those individuals directly affected by the wrongdoing. The state, nevertheless, maintains its right to punish those to whom it has 'transferred' such a right.

143 See David Lyons, op. cit., pp. 157–8.

144 Alfred C. Oppler, *Legal Reform in Occupied Japan*, op. cit., p. 126.

145 Quoted in Ōno Masayoshi, 'Capital Punishment and Penal Reform', op. cit., p. 6.

146 John M. Maki (tr. and ed.), *Japan's Commission on the Constitution: The Final Report* (Seattle, 1980), p. 282.

147 Ibid.

148 Two studies in particular may be mentioned which demonstrate that, as a deterrent, capital punishment is no more effective than long-term imprisonment. The first study is Sellin's comparison of abolitionist and retentionist states in the United States. This is to be found in the appendices of the Gowers Commission *Report of the British Royal Commission on Capital Punishment, 1949–53*, Cmnd. 8932 (London, 1953). The second relates to the murder rate in New Zealand between 1924 and 1962 (a period which saw capital punishment abolished twice. In force between 1924 and 1935, and in abeyance between 1935 and 1941, it was abolished in 1941. Capital punishment was restored in 1951, and operated until it was abolished yet again in 1961). For a graph illustrating murder rates and the death penalty in New Zealand between

1924 and 1962, see Nigel Walker, *Crime and Punishment in Britain* (Edinburgh, 1968), 2nd rev. edn, p. 240. Judy Wakabayashi makes a mention of twenty-two studies worldwide which concluded that capital punishment was no greater a deterrent than long sentences (Judy Wakabayashi, 'The Death Penalty in Japan', *Japan Forum*, vol. 6, no. 2 (1994), pp. 189–205, at p. 189).

149 Ōno Masayoshi, 'Capital Punishment and Penal Reform', op. cit., p. 6.

150 Wakabayashi provides the following statistics relating to recent death sentences and executions in Japan:

	1979	1980	1981	1982	1983	1984	1985	1986	1987	1988	1989	1990	1991	1992	Dec. 1993
District Court level	5	8	1	11	5	6	9	5	6	10	2	2	3	1	4
High Court level	1	2	1	8	4	5	5	7	8	4	5	2	4	4	1
Supreme Court level	4	4	3	0	0	3	1	0	6	7	5	7	4	4	4
New confirmed sentences	4	7	3	1	1	3	2	0	8	11	5	6	5	5	6
Executions	1	1	1	1	1	1	3	2	2	2	1	0	0	0	7
Total confirmed sentences	20	26	28	28	27	27	26	24	29	38	40	46	51	56	55

Judy Wakabayashi, op. cit., p. 191. Every year since 1993 executions have remained in single figures.

151 In the 1993 *Yomiuri Shinbun* survey (op. cit., note 141), only 2.4 per cent of those polled who supported the retention of capital punishment considered that, '[u]nder the current judicial system, there is no danger of sentencing an innocent person to death'. Of those who opposed its retention, 32 per cent stressed their opposition on the ground that it was 'irreparable if an innocent person is executed'.

152 Takikawa Masajirō, *Nihon gyōkei shi* op. cit., pp. 21–2.

153 Jeremy Bentham, *An Introduction to the Principles of Morals and Legislation*, eds. J.H. Burns and H.L.A. Hart, (London, 1970).

4 THE EQUALITY OF THE RIGHT TO LIFE

1 By article 1, 'All human beings are born free and equal in dignity and rights . . .' By article 2, 'Everyone is entitled to all the rights and freedoms set forth in this Declaration, without distinction of any kind, such as race, colour, sex, language, religion, political or other opinion, national or social origin, property, birth or other status . . .' By article 7, 'All are equal before the law and are entitled without any discrimination to equal protection of the law. All are entitled to equal protection against any discrimination in violation of this Declaration and against any incitement to such discrimination.'

2 Hedley Bull, *The Anarchical Society: A Study of Order in World Politics* (London, 1977), p. 7.

3 See Mitani Taichirō, 'The Establishment of Party Cabinets, 1898–1932', in Peter Duus (ed.), *The Twentieth Century*, vol. 6 of *The Cambridge History of Japan* (Cambridge, 1988), pp. 55–96, at p. 62. The independence of the judiciary – one of the three separable powers – was soon tested in the Ootsu incident of 11 May 1891. On this day, the

Russian Crown Prince, Nikolai Aleksandrovitch (1868–1918), who later became Tsar Nikolai II, was attacked by a Japanese policeman, Tsuda Sanzō, and injured in Ootsu City. The Japanese government put pressure on the Head of the Great Court of Judicature (*Daishinin inchō*), Kojima Iken, to hand down the death penalty. However, Judge Kojima resisted government pressure, and did not hand down the death penalty, arguing that the crime of treason against the Crown Prince did not apply to a foreign prince. The accused was tried for the 'ordinary' crime of attempted murder. The tripartite separation of powers was emphasized by the legal scholar Uesugi Shinkichi (1878–1929), who stressed the separation of the judiciary from the legislature: Uesugi Shinkichi, *Teikoku kenpō chikujō kōgi* (A Lecture on Items of the Imperial Constitution) (Tōkyō, 1935), pp. 164–5. In contrast to Uesugi Shinkichi, the constitutional law scholar Minobe Tatsukichi (1873–1948) argued that the legislature had superiority over the other branches. 'Our Constitution,' he argued, 'unlike the American Constitution, is not based on the principle that the legislative, the judicial, and the executive branches occupy positions equal to one another. The actions of the legislative branch express the highest will of the state, and the judicial and the administrative branch are not equal to it but stand below it'. Minobe Tatsukichi, *Kenpō satsuyō* (Interpreting the Constitution) (Tōkyō, 1926), p. 506. See Mitani Taichirō, op. cit., pp. 86–7. For a discussion in English on Minobe Tatsukichi see Frank O. Miller, *Minobe Tatsukichi: Interpreter of Constitutionalism in Japan* (Berkeley and Los Angeles, 1965).

4 The state's role is not, however, confined to the protection of human life, but also extends to giving assistance to the victims or the families of victims of crime. It is given the task of reducing suffering to the family or victims of attacks which result in death or serious injury to the victim. In Japan, machinery was set up by the Act to Provide Payment of Benefits to Victims of Crime, which became law in 1981. By article 1, the Act provides 'for the payment of benefits by the state to the bereaved family of those who have met with an untimely death or to those who have suffered heavy injuries due to a criminal act injuring a man's life or body.'

5 As amended and supplemented by various laws.

6 See articles 118(2), 124(2), 126(3), 127, 145, 146, 181, 196, 199, 200, 202, 205(1), 205(2), 210, 211, 213, 214, 216, 219, 221, 240, 241 and 260.

7 See *inter alia* articles 204, 181, 222, 223, 240 and 216.

8 Article 35.

9 Article 36.

10 Article 37.

11 Article 38.

12 Article 39.

13 Article 40.

14 Article 41.

15 Article 42.

16 Yoshida submitted three reasons for the retention of these articles: 'the position of the emperor under the New Constitution; second the position of the Imperial Family in relation to ordinary individuals and third, the special provisions which . . . exist in a monarchy such as England for the protection of the King'. Following a rebuttal of the first two points,

MacArthur continues: 'As for your third point, there is no statutory provision in British law comparable to Article 73 and 75 of the Japanese Penal Code. In fact, under the statute of 5 and 6 Victoria, Chapter 61, assault upon the British Monarch is punishable as a misdemeanor. Although the ancient Statute of Treasons, ordained prior to representative government during the reign of Edward III, took a more serious view of violence against the King's person and, because a mediaeval sovereign then embodied in his person all the powers of state, it included such acts of violence within the crime of treason. This six hundred year old statute, last revised a century ago, is a remnant of and derived from the age of Germanic feudalism and there is no record of its modern application, nor is there the slightest analogy to the situation now existing in Japan . . .' (Supreme Commander for the Allied Powers, *Political Reorientation of Japan, September 1945 to September 1948*, vol. 2 [Appendices volume] (Westport, Conn., 1970), Appendix C: 23, pp. 679–80).

The perception that the Imperial family requires special protection of the right to life in law remains. In the case of *Japan* v. *Daidoji et al.* of 13 November 1979, the Tokyo District Court imposed a harsher penalty for the attempted murder of the Emperor than that allowed for the same crime committed against ordinary persons. As Beer observes, however, 'Critics pointed out the absence of a basis for such a distinction in either the Constitution or in criminal law': Lawrence W. Beer, 'The Present Constitutional System of Japan', in Lawrence W. Beer (ed.), *Constitutional Systems in Late Twentieth Century Asia* (Seattle and London, 1992), pp. 175–223, at p. 220, note 123.

17 The *ritsuryō* we are using as our text is the *Yōrō* Code, which is modelled on the following Codes (dates of coming into force in parentheses): *Ōmi ryō* (671[?]), *Asuka kiyomigahara ryō* (689), *Taihō ritsuryō* (702) and *Yōrō ritsuryō* (757). Whilst these are the generally accepted dates, there is dispute, however, as to the exact dating of the compilation of the *Ōmi ryō* and the *Asuka kiyomigahara ryō*. Aoki Kazuo even denies the compilation of the *Ōmi ryō*. For further discussion see Inoue Mitsusada, *Inoue Mitsusada chōsakushū* (The Collected Works of Inoue Mitsusada), vol. 2 (Tōkyō, 1986), pp. 97–106.

18 See commentary on the *ritsuryō* in Inoue Mitsusada *et al.* (eds), *Ritsuryō* (Laws and Ordinances), *Nihon shisō taikei* (Series on Japanese Thought), vol. 3 (Tōkyō, 1976), p. 490.

19 Ibid. See notes on page 18 of the *Ritsuryō*.

20 Ibid., pp. 15–16.

21 Ibid., pp. 488–9.

22 These *rokugi* (six considerations) were:

1   Relatives of the Emperor.
2   Ones who served the Emperor for a long time and were treated with respect by him.
3   Those of great virtue.
4   Those of great ability as commanders and politicians.
5   Those who had shown most success in fighting for one's country, or who had gone to a foreign country as messengers without fear for their lives;

6 Officials higher than the third rank of officers.
See *Ritsuryō*, ibid., pp. 19–20.

23 Ibid., p. 35.

24 Only after the late seventh century do we find distinction made between *zan* (cutting) and *kō* (hanging): ibid., p. 487. One interpretation of why cutting was considered a more severe penalty than hanging is to be found in the *Hōsō shiyōshō* (Details of Legal Matters) text from the Heian period. In vol. 1 (*kan jō*) of the work we read that, whilst in the case of *kō* the punishment was not executed immediately (thereby allowing the possibility of remission), in the case of *zan* no such possibility could be entertained for the penalty was immediately executed. See Kuwahara Jitsuzō, *Chūgoku no kōdō* (The Way of Piety in China) (Tōkyō, 1977), p. 52.

25 *Taisha* is believed to be a reference to the *Isejingū* shrine. See the commentary to the *ritsuryō* in Inoue Mitsusada *et al.*, op. cit., p. 17.

26 Ibid., p. 16.

27 Ibid. See the commentary on the text.

28 Ibid. See the commentary on the text.

29 Ibid., p. 18.

30 Ibid., p. 17.

31 For details of this law, see Takikawa Masajirō, *Nihon hōseishi* (A History of the Japanese Legal System) (Tōkyō, 1985), *ge* (vol. 2), p. 44.

32 *Hikimawashi no ue haritsuke*. See Kuwahara Jitsuzō, op. cit., p. 92.

33 For a discussion of the views of four prominent Japanese Confucian thinkers of the Tokugawa period – Hayashi Razan (1583–1657), Kumazawa Banzan (1619–91), Yamaga Sokō (1622–85) and Asami Keisai (1652–1711) – see I.J. McMullen, 'Rulers or Fathers? A Casuistical Problem in Early Modern Japanese Thought', *Past and Present*, no. 116, August (1987), pp. 56–97.

34 Hugh D. Baker, for example, observes that, in traditional China, 'the individual must put family before state.' See his *Chinese Family and Kinship* (London, 1979), p. 122. Incidents illustrating the Chinese view on the matter are noted in Kuwahara Jitsuzō, op. cit., pp. 106–8. In one example, a son, who reported his father's plot to kill the Emperor, was subsequently condemned to death for his act of filial impiety in reporting his own father to the authorities.

35 Robert Bellah, for example, observes that, in Japan, 'the first duty is to one's lord rather than to one's family'. See his *Tokugawa Religion: The Cultural Roots of Modern Japan* (New York, 1957), p. 18. For further references on this point see I.J. McMullen, op. cit., p. 57, footnote 4. I.J. McMullen has demonstrated that 'the Japanese response to Chinese ideology was not uniform' (p. 97). He has shown how, 'at the ideological level, a small but respectable number of articulate Japanese Confucians dissented from the tendency of the dominant samurai tradition, and tried to preserve what they considered a healthier balance between familial and political values'. However, '[t]hey did not prevail' (p. 97).

36 See further Paul Heng-Chao Ch'en, *The Formation of the Early Meiji Legal Order: The Japanese Code of 1871 and its Chinese Foundation* (Oxford, 1981), pp. 3–11.

37 For an English translation of the Code, see Paul Heng-Chao Ch'en, ibid., pp. 83–184.

38 The provision in the Code on the crime of 'parricide' reads as follows: 'Any person found guilty of planning to kill his or her grandfather or grandmother, whether paternal or maternal, his or her own father or mother, paternal uncle or aunt, elder brother or sister; and any woman found guilty of planning to kill her husband, or husband's parent or grandparent, shall be sentenced to death by decapitation, provided that such a plan has actually been attempted; and to death by decapitation followed by the display of the decapitated head if the offence has proved mortal . . .' (ibid., p. 132).

39 Supreme Court Decision, 11 October 1950. 4 *Keishū* 2037. For an English translation see John M. Maki (ed.), *Court and Constitution in Japan: Selected Supreme Court Decisions, 1948–60* (Seattle, 1964), pp. 129–55. See also Kurt Steiner, 'A Japanese Cause Célèbre: The Fukuoka Parricide Case', *American Journal of Comparative Law*, vol. 5 (1956), pp. 106–11.

40 John M. Maki (ed.), *Court and Constitution in Japan*, op. cit., p. 132.

41 In early Roman law, for example, the head of the legal unit of the family – the *paterfamilias* – had the power of life and death (*ius vitae necisque*) over his children (whatever their ages). See Barry Nicholas, *An Introduction to Roman Law* (Oxford, 1962), pp. 65–7.

42 Ōtsuka Hitoshi, *Keihō gaisetsu* (An Outline of Criminal Law) (Tōkyō, 1987), p. 16.

43 Under the Italian Penal Code, the crimes of murder and injury resulting in the death of lineal ascendants (as well as descendants) are punished more severely than those of cases involving non-lineal ascendants (and non-lineal descendants). In the case of murder, whereas article 575 provides punishment by imprisonment for not less than 21 years, articles 576 and 577 provide a punishment of life imprisonment if the act was committed *inter alia* 'against an ascendant or descendant'. By article 577, if the act was committed against 'a spouse, brother, or sister, an adoptive father, mother or child, or against a direct relation by marriage', imprisonment for between 20 and 30 years is to be imposed. Punishment for assault and personal injury resulting in death is provided in article 584. Non-lineal descendants (and ascendants) who cause the death of an individual are to be imprisoned for a period between 10 and 18 years. Where a descendant causes the death of an ascendant (or an ascendant causes the death of a descendant), on the other hand, the assailant is to be more severely punished, punishment being increased 'from one-third to one-half' if the aggravating circumstances designated in article 576 occur. By article 585, an increase of 'up to one-third' is called for if any of the aggravating circumstances designated in article 577 occur. For an English translation of the Italian Penal Code see Edward Wise (ed. and tr.), *Italian Penal Code* (London, 1978).

44 This system was adopted from the family system of the *bushi* class of the Tokugawa period. For an account of the *ie* in Japanese history, see Murakami Yasusuke, '*Ie* Society as a Pattern of Civilization', *Journal of Japanese Studies*, vol. 10, no. 2 (1984), pp. 281–363.

45 Whilst in principle the system sought to secure the continuity of the *ie*

through patrilineal descent, in line with the Confucian ideal, it also served a wider social function. In the period before the end of the Second World War, the *ie* system contributed to the political and ideological unity of society. In his discussion of non-agnatic adoption in seventeenth- and eighteenth-century Japan, I.J. McMullen contrasts the 'high Confucian norm' (p. 134) prohibiting non-agnatic adoption in China with the practice in Japan. He notes: 'The Japanese priorities, in short, were the reverse of Confucian theory: maintenance of its social role across generations was in practice a more important criterion than agnatic descent in the organization of the Japanese *ie*' (see I.J. McMullen, 'Non-Agnatic Adoption: A Confucian Controversy in Seventeenth- and Eighteenth-Century Japan', *Harvard Journal of Asiatic Studies*, vol. 35 (1975), pp. 133–89).The practice of non-agnatic adoption was allowed in law during the Meiji period to continue the *ie*.

46 *Aizawa* v. *Japan*. Supreme Court Decision, 4 April 1973. 27 *Keishū* 265. Quoted in Tanaka Hideo (ed.), *The Japanese Legal System: Introductory Cases and Materials* (Tokyo, 1976), p. 727.

47 '[T]he only subjective difference between homicide and the crime of causing death as a result of bodily injuries', noted the Supreme Court, 'is whether or not there existed an intent to kill . . .': First Petty Bench Decision of the Supreme Court, 13 April 1979 (Case no. (a) 2113 of 1977). 33 *Keishū* 179.

48 This contrasts with the position under the Civil Code, where the term *hizoku* is to be found.

49 Here, we see the idea of the adopted member of the family being placed equally with the 'original' members. The relationship between the adopted child and adopted parents is seen as constituting the same bond as the blood-related parent–child relationship. In the case of *sonzoku satsujin*, however, the adopted children under the Penal Code suffered a more severe penalty than those involved in 'ordinary' murder.

50 The Penal Code of 1907, article 12(1). By article 12(1): 'Imprisonment at forced labour shall be either for life or for a fixed term, and a fixed term of imprisonment at forced labour shall be from one month to 15 years.'

51 Alfred Oppler, *Legal Reform in Occupied Japan: A Participant Looks Back* (Princeton, N.J., 1976), p. 121.

52 John M. Maki (ed.), *Court and Constitution in Japan*, op. cit., p. 143.

53 See note 39, this chapter.

54 John M. Maki (ed.), op. cit., pp. 130–1.

55 Ibid., p. 132.

56 Ibid., p. 146.

57 Ibid., p. 131.

58 Ibid., p. 132.

59 Ibid., p. 150.

60 Ibid., p. 152.

61 Supreme Court Decision, 27 May 1964. 18 *Minshū* 676. Quoted in Tanaka Hideo (ed.), op. cit., p. 722.

62 See *inter alios* Hirano Ryūichi, *Keihō gaisetsu* (An Outline of Criminal Law) (Tōkyō, 1977), p. 157; Uchida Fumiaki, *Keihō kakuron* (Theories on Criminal Law) (Tōkyō, 1984), 2nd edn, p. 12, footnote 6; Yoshikawa Tsuneo, *Keihō kakuron* (Theories on Criminal Law) (Tōkyō, 1982), p.

28; Saitō Seiji, *Keihō kōgi kakuron* (Lectures on the Theories on Criminal Law) (Tōkyō, 1979), rev. edn, p. 238; and Ōtani Hiroshi, *Keihō kōgi kakuron* (Lectures on the Theories on Criminal Law) (Tōkyō, 1983), p. 18, p. 48, footnote 1.

63 John M. Maki (ed.), op. cit., p. 140.

64 By article 25(1), 'When any one of the following persons has been sentenced to imprisonment with forced labour or imprisonment for not more than three years . . . the execution of the sentence may be suspended for a period from one year to five years as from the day when the decision has become final: (1) A person not previously sentenced to imprisonment or a graver punishment; (2) A person who, although previously sentenced to imprisonment or a graver punishment, has not again been sentenced to imprisonment or a graver punishment within five years from the day when the execution of the former punishment was completed or remitted.'

65 Thus, in the case which came before the Nagoya High Court in 1962, for example, the son who, out of mercy, had obeyed his father's pleas to end his life, had the minimum penalty imposed on him, reflecting the unfortunate circumstances of the case. See Chapter 3, note 5.

66 See note 46, this chapter. On this case see Uchida Fumiaki *et al.*, *Chikujō hanrei keihō* (Cases and Notes on Criminal Law) (Tōkyō, 1990), pp. 170–1. For a discussion on the case in English see Tanaka Hideo (ed.), op. cit., pp. 725–9.

67 Tanaka Hideo (ed.), op. cit., p. 726

68 Ibid., p. 727.

69 Ibid.

70 Ibid.

71 Ibid., p. 726.

72 Ibid., p. 727.

73 Justice Tanaka argued that, 'to respect the dignity of each individual and to protect equality of individuals as human beings is the first principle of democracy . . . Article 14, Paragraph 1 is meant to invalidate every sort of differential treatment that conflicts with this fundamental principle of the Constitution. The enumeration of grounds for differential treatment therein should be understood as merely exemplary' (ibid., pp. 725–6).

74 Justice Ōsumi argued that 'Article 200 . . . stands on the moral principle of a hierarchical society holding that a lineal ascendant should be respected . . . simply because he or she is a lineal ascendant . . . A moral principle to govern parent–child relationships is not fit for enforcement by law. Moreover, to enforce the above-mentioned moral principle by law . . . is tantamount to creating an unreasonable discrimination based upon one's status' (ibid., p. 727).

75 Ibid., p. 728.

76 Justice Hozumi himself was of the opinion that a moral principle such as filial piety should not find expression in law, 'not because he thinks so little of filial piety but because he thinks so much of it that he feels that law should not be allowed to touch it' (John M. Maki (ed.), op. cit., p. 144).

77 *Chūō Korōn*, vol. 60, no. 9, September (1950), pp. 78ff. Cited in Kurt Steiner, op. cit., p. 107, footnote 7.

78 Article 24 reads: '(1) Marriage shall be based only on the mutual consent of both sexes and it shall be maintained through mutual cooperation with the equal rights of husband and wife as a basis. (2) With regard to choice of spouse, property rights, inheritance, choice of domicile, divorce and other matters pertaining to marriage and the family, laws shall be enacted from the standpoint of individual dignity and the essential equality of the sexes.'

79 John M. Maki (ed. and tr.), *Japan's Commission on the Constitution: The Final Report* (Seattle, 1980), p. 285.

80 Otto von Gierke, in his critical study of Laband's work, considered the proposition, 'law is law and nothing else', as appropriate to describe a major part of his legal theory: 'Labands Staatsrecht und die Deutsche Rechtswissenschaft' (The State Rights of Laband and German Studies on Law), in *Schmollers Jahrbuch für Gesetzgebung, Verwaltung und Volkswirtschaft im Deutschen Reich*, vol. 7, no. 4 (1883), pp. 1097–1195. Richard Minear summarizes the chief characteristics of Laband's legal positivism as follows: 'a definition of law as sovereign command; an absolute dependence on reason for the creation of a science of law; the separation of law from ethics; the positing of a personality for the state, a fragile concept which all too easily resolved itself into the theoretical personal rule of an absolute monarch; and a denial of fundamental liberties except as specifically guaranteed by law'. See his *Japanese Tradition and Western Law: Emperor, State, and Law in the Thought of Hozumi Yatsuka* (Cambridge, Mass., 1970), p. 54.

81 In his book, *The Province of Jurisprudence Determined* (ed. H.L.A. Hart [London, 1954]), John Austin wrote that, 'The appropriate subject of Jurisprudence . . . is positive law: Meaning by positive law . . . law established or "positum", in an independent political community, by the express or tacit authority of its sovereign or supreme government' (p. 365). For Austin, any law 'properly so called' is 'a rule laid down for the guidance of an intelligent being by an intelligent being having power over him' (p. 10). Only law sanctioned by the sovereign is law 'properly so called'. Law becomes command, the command of the sovereign. For him, jurisprudence 'has no immediate concern' with 'the goodness or badness of laws' (p. 366). 'The existence of law', writes Austin, 'is one thing; its merit or demerit is another.' For a critical discussion of his views on the connection between law and morality, see H.L.A. Hart, 'Positivism and the Separation of Law and Morals', *Harvard Law Review*, vol. 71 (1958), pp. 593–629.

82 Uesugi Shinkichi (ed.), *Hozumi Yatsuka hakase ronbunshū* (Collected Essays of Dr Hozumi Yatsuka) (Tōkyō, 1913), rev. edn (ed. Hozumi Shigetaka [Tōkyō, 1943]), p. 329. Quoted in Minear, op. cit., pp. 87–8.

83 Law as sovereign command is one of the main principles of the positivist conception of law.

84 Richard Minear, op. cit., p. 90.

85 Ibid., p. 88.

86 David Lyons, *Ethics and the Rule of Law* (Cambridge, 1984), p. 61.

87 Ibid.

88 Ibid.

89 Ibid., p. 62.

90 See Italian Penal Code, articles 576, 577, 585.
91 See Argentinian Penal Code, article 80(1).
92 Ōtsuka Hitoshi, op. cit., p. 16. Similar sentiments were voiced by Justice Hozumi. 'There are, of course,' he observed, 'many cases in which nothing could be more hateful than killing a person who bears the appellation, "parent", but cases may also not be rare in which we may shed tears of sympathy for a person who commits patricide in an extreme situation' (John M. Maki (ed.), *Court and Constitution in Japan*, op. cit., p. 140). See also Kumagai Fumie, 'Filial Violence: A Peculiar Parent–Child Relationship in the Japanese Family Today', *Journal of Comparative Family Studies*, vol. 21, no. 3 (Special Issue, Summer 1981), pp. 337–50.

5 THE SOCIAL VALUE OF DEATH

1 The traditional unitary model relies on the unity of decision-making within an organization. Sargant Florence conceived the model in terms of an hour-glass, showing a focus of decision on the managing director, and a vertical line of authority from shareholders to employees: *Ownership Control and Success of Large Companies* (London, 1961), p. 19. Alan Fox found it helpful to compare the unitary model to that of a 'team, unified by a common purpose'. Viewed as an unitary system, it has 'one source of authority and one focus of loyalty': *Industrial Sociology and Industrial Relations*, Research Paper no. 3 for the Royal Commission on Trade Unions and Employers' Associations (London, 1966), pp. 2–3.
2 Article 52(1) of the Commercial Code defines a 'company' as 'an association incorporated for the purpose of engaging in commercial transaction as a business'. By article 52(2), 'an association which has for its object the acquisition of gain and is incorporated in accordance with the provisions [of the Code] shall be deemed to be a company even if it does not engage in commercial transactions as a business'. In Japanese law, there are three types of companies (article 53): *gōmei kaisha* (commercial partnership); *gōshi kaisha* (limited partnership); and *kabushiki kaisha* (limited company). In this chapter we are concerned with the *kabushiki kaisha*. For regulations governing this type of company see Chapter 4 of the Commercial Code, '*kabushiki kaisha*', articles 165–456.
3 Article 54 notes that, 'A company is a juristic person.'
4 Thus, by article 254(3), for example, directors 'shall be obligated to obey any law or ordinance and the articles of incorporation as well as resolutions adopted at a general meeting and to perform their duties faithfully on behalf of the company'.
5 Commercial Code, article 254(1).
6 Ibid., article 260(1).
7 By article 26, 'the company shall, by the resolution of the board of directors, appoint the particular director who shall represent the company'.
8 See Morimoto, *Kaishahō* (Company Law), in Katō, Takahashi and Tanigawa (eds), *Kaisha to hō* (Company and Law) (Tōkyō, 1982), at p. 97.

Cited in Robert W. Dziubla, 'Enforcing Corporate Responsibility: Japanese Corporate Directors' Liability to Third Parties for Failure to Supervise', *Law in Japan*, vol. 18 (1985), pp. 55–75, at p. 57, footnote 10.

9 Rodney Clark, *The Japanese Company* (New Haven, Conn., 1979), p. 108.

10 On this theory, see the work of Befu Harumi: 'A Theory of Social Exchange as Applied to Japan', in Sugimoto Yoshio and Ross E. Mouer (eds), *Constructs for Understanding Japan* (London, 1989), pp. 39–66; 'Power in Exchange: The Strategy of Control and Patterns of Compliance in Japan', *Asian Profile*, vol. 2 nos. 5/6, October–December (1974), pp. 601–22; 'Power in the Great White Tower', in R.D. Fogelson and R.M. Adams, *The Anthropology of Power* (New York, 1977), pp. 77–87; 'The Group Model of Japanese Society and an Alternative', *Rice University Studies*, vol. 66, no. 1 (Winter, 1980), pp. 169–87.

11 Loyalty to the company has been perceived by numerous Western authors to be central to the relationship between the company and its members. Ronald Dore, for example ('Commitment – to What, by Whom and Why?', in *Social and Cultural Background of Labor–Management Relations in Asian Countries*, Proceedings of the 1971 Asian Regional Conference on Industrial Relations, held in Tokyo in March 1971, pp. 106–26) draws attention to Japan's 'traditional ethic which lays an overwhelming stress on group loyalty and the subordination of individual interests to the interests of the group to which the individual belongs' (p. 120). Some authors, however, doubt that loyalty to the company extends across the board to include all members of all types and sizes of companies. See Befu Harumi, 'A Critique of the Group Model of Japanese Society', in Ross Mouer and Sugimoto Yoshio' (eds) *Social Analysis* (Special Issue: Japanese Society: Reappraisals and New Directions), nos. 5/6, December (1980), pp. 29–43, at p. 33. Studies by Robert M. Marsh and Hiroshi Mannari (*Modernization and the Japanese Factory* [Princeton, N.J., 1976]) and Robert E. Cole (*Japanese Blue Collar: The Changing Tradition* [Berkeley, Calif., 1971]) indicate that loyalty is not always as strong as many authors assume, particularly amongst those outside the 'elite course' destined for promotion to higher positions within the company.

12 George De Vos in *Socialization for Achievement: Essays on the Cultural Psychology of the Japanese* (Berkeley, Calif., 1973) chapters 7 and 14, for example, has argued that the process of socialization amongst the Japanese has led them to sacrifice themselves and their self-interest for the sake of the wider, less selfish, purpose of group harmony. It might be added, however, that the achieving of group harmony itself entails acts of selfishness by the group to the detriment of other social groups. Thus in the case of the company, if its members sacrifice themselves for the sake of harmony, such sacrifice does not necessarily extend beyond this to include sacrifice for the wider local community, for example. The company is, in many respects, a closed community which buries its head in the sand. Nowhere is this more in evidence than in its relations with the local community. Employees and their families often resist entering into harmonious relationship with residents living in the vicinity of company dormitories, for example. When there is a clash of interest between the

two groups, local residents often suffer. Residents of company dormitories often form an impenetrable group with a capacity to act counter to the welfare of the local community generally, as well as individuals specifically.

13 Attempts have been made to dispel the 'myth' of the 'life employment' of Japanese employees. See, for example, Rodney C. Clark, 'Union–Management Conflict in a Japanese Company', in W.G. Beasley (ed.), *Modern Japan*: *Aspects of History, Literature and Society* (London, 1975), pp. 209–26, at p. 210. An important recent study is John C. Beck and Martha N. Beck's *The Change of a Lifetime*: *Employment Patterns Among Japan's Managerial Elite* (Honolulu, Hawaii, 1994). Given the recent unfavourable economic climate, there has been a trend for many companies to move away from the practice of lifetime employment and to lay off workers to protect their overall financial well-being. This has brought with it a corresponding increase in the rate of unemployment. There is growing realization amongst people that the 'lifetime' employment system is fraying at the edges. In a 1994 opinion poll conducted by the *Yomiuri Shinbun*, 61.9 per cent of those polled believed that the system was 'on its way out'; 5.8 per cent already believed that the system had ceased to exist (*The Daily Yomiuri*, 16 February 1994). Taking those working in companies *as a totality*, this opinion is – and has been – a reflection of reality. As Kamiya Masako points out, 'Research as well as statistics show that the life-long employment scheme applies only to a fraction of the working population.' Statistics for the 1970s and 1980s, for example, show that, taken as a totality, men stay on at the same institution some ten years on average, and women six years: Kamiya Masako, 'A Decade of the Equal Employment Opportunity Act in Japan: Has It Changed Society?', *Law in Japan*, vol. 25 (1995), pp. 40–83, at p. 43, note 7.

14 Ronald Dore, in *British Factory–Japanese Factory*: *The Origins of Diversity in Industrial Relations* (London, 1973), refers to such arrangement as 'welfare corporatism', (pp. 370, 375, 377, 400).

15 Hosokawa Migiwa *et al.*, *Karōshi*: *nō, shinzōkei shitsubyō no gyōmujō nintei to yobō* (*Karōshi*: Official Recognition of Brain and Heart Disease and their Prevention) (Tōkyō, 1982).

16 Okamura Chikanobu, *Karōshi to rōsai hoshō* (Compensation for Death and Illness from Overwork, and Accidents at Work) (Tōkyō, 1990), p. 14. Uehata Tetsunojō defines *karōshi* as 'a condition in which a worker's normal daily rhythms are disrupted by continuing unsound work patterns, resulting in a build-up of fatigue. The exhaustion induced by chronic overwork aggravates pre-existent health problems, such as high blood pressure and hardening of the arteries, and causes a life-threatening crisis' (quoted in Kawahito Hiroshi, 'Death and the Corporate Warrior', *Japan Quarterly*, April–June [1991], pp. 149–58, at p. 150).

17 These figures are quoted in the article 'Lawyer Laments Death by Overwork: Hiroshi Kawahito Urges Hardworking Employees to Start Taking It Easy', *The Japan Times*, 7 October 1989 (International Weekly Edition).

18 For details of the requirements for compensation under the Labour Standards Act (Law no. 49) 1947, see Okamura Chikanobu, op. cit.,

pp. 158–60. Because of the increasing number of reported incidents of *karōshi*, however, the government relaxed the strict conditions laid down for compensation claims under this Act when entertaining claims for compensation arising from *karōshi*. Thus, in the case of local government officers, for example, whereas the old standard for approving claims required the claimant to have been involved in very hard work (proved clinically) the very day he became ill, or just before he became ill, under these new regulations one week became acceptable: The *Chikōsai kikin jimukyokuchō tsūchi* (Local Government Officers' Compensation Fund for Accidents Order) 1987. Supplementary Paper no. 2 of this Order contains details of these conditions. These changes resulted from the Minister of Labour's publication of the New Standards of Approval Order of 26 October 1987 (no. 620). See Okamura Chikanobu, op. cit., pp. 151–4. On 19 December 1994 the government announced its intention of reviewing these conditions, which are still perceived as too severe for the claimant.

19 Okamura Chikanobu, for example, believes that every year some tens of thousands suffer from *karōshi* (op. cit., p. 16). Kawahito Hiroshi estimates a figure of 10,000 *karōshi* victims a year: 'Death and the Corporate Warrior', op. cit., p. 150.

20 *The Japan Times*, 7 October 1989 (International Weekly Edition).

21 Figures issued by the *Karōshi bengodan zenkoku renraku kaigi* group of lawyers, based on 1,806 hotline cases inquiring about workers' compensation (as of 16 June 1990), show that, in occupational terms, 3.8 per cent were directors; 16.9 per cent were managers; 15.4 per cent were sales and office workers; 5.6 per cent were technicians; 7.8 per cent were construction workers; 9.1 per cent were manufacturing workers; 6.7 per cent were government employees; and 34.8 per cent were engaged in other activities. Kawahito Hiroshi, 'Death and the Corporate Warrior', op. cit., p. 151. The group reports that, as at 1 May 1991, 2,092 counselling cases were conducted. It notes that the age of those dying from *karōshi* is gradually getting lower (and that there is also an increase in the number of those committing suicide from stress and overwork). In percentage terms, 25.8 per cent of those seeking consultation were in their fifties; 25.8 per cent were in their forties; and 10.4 per cent were in their thirties. See *Yomiuri Shinbun*, 1 May 1991. Cases of *karōshi* involving workers are more documented than those involving directors or managers. This is largely because the wives and families of directors and those high up the corporate ladder who fall victims of *karōshi* feel more obliged, because of the victim's high position in the company, to refrain from any form of public criticism of the company (although exceptions, of course, may be cited – see the case of Ishii Jun, manager of Mitsui's Soviet division, in Kawahito's article, 'Death and the Corporate Warrior', op. cit., p. 149). Incidents of *karōshi* amongst workers, on the other hand, are frequently taken up by trade unions, who have a vested interest in publicizing the cases and take appropriate legal action on behalf of their members and their families, For a list and discussion of cases of *karōshi* involving workers, and which were the subject of legal actions, see Okamura Chikanobu, op. cit. pp. 100-35. In a Tokyo District Court decision in March 1996, the Court acknowledged the victim's suicide as *karōshi*, and

ordered the employer to compensate the parents of the victim. On this case, see further *The Daily Yomiuri*, 29 March 1996.

22 Uehata Tetsunojō, 'Shokugyōsei sutoresu ni yoru karōshi' (Death from Overwork Due to Occupational Stress), in Hosokawa Migiwa (ed.), *Shinrōdō kagaku hen* (New Work Science: A Selection), May (1988), p. 683. His attempt at illustrating the causes of *karōshi* diagrammatically is reproduced in Okamura Chikanobu, op. cit., p. 37.

23 Ministry of Labour, *Maigetsu kinrō tōkei* (Monthly Labour Statistics) (Tōkyō, 1990).

24 See Sano Yōko, 'Seven Mysteries of Long Working Hours', *Japan Quarterly*, vol. 35, July–September (1988), pp. 248–52, at p. 248.

25 Whether there will be a decrease in the number of hours worked in all sectors of industry in the long term is arguable. The heavy industries and transport are particular examples of industries which might be slow to change their ways in this respect. Shimada Haruo points out in his article, 'The Desperate Need for New Values in Japanese Corporate Behaviour', *Journal of Japanese Studies*, vol. 17, no. 1, (1991), pp. 107–25, at p. 115, that in these industries, 'work hours . . . are far longer [than average], averaging 2,200–2,300 a year'. Twenty per cent of workers over the age of 30 work more than 3,000 hours a year (p. 116).

26 *Hitachi seisakusho Musashi kōjō jiken* (Case of Musashi Factory of Hitachi Seisakusho), Tokyo District Court, 22 May 1987. *Hanji* 906–93.

27 Tokyo High Court, 27 March 1986. 472 *Rōhan* 28. In so deciding, the High Court followed the precedent set by the Second Petty Bench of the Supreme Court in the *Shizunai Post Office Case* of 1984 (Decision by the Second Petty Bench of the Supreme Court, 27 March 1984: 430 *Rōhan* 69), where the legality of disciplinary punishments in the form of warnings and cautions imposed on postal workers because of their refusal to work overtime was disputed. An agreement existed between the union and the Ministry of Posts and Telecommunications, included in the work rules, that 'overtime work can be ordered when inevitable'. The Court held that the circumstances of the case – where an overtime order was issued to deliver the post which the appellants had refused to deliver – warranted the overtime request 'inevitable'. No consent was deemed to be required each time an overtime request is made. For a discussion of the case in English by Nakamura Kazuhisa and Matsuo Kuniyuki, see *Waseda Bulletin of Comparative Law*, vol. 6 (1987), pp. 130–3.

28 Included in the work rules must be details of working conditions, consisting of *inter alia* hours of work, rest hours, holidays, shifts, wages, matters relating to retirement and dismissal, as well as benefits. For a discussion in English on work rules and collective agreements see Hanami Tadashi, *Labour Law and Industrial Relations in Japan* (Deventer, 1985), 2nd rev. edn, pp. 65–6, 123–30.

29 Decision of the Supreme Court, 28 November 1991: *Minshū* 45.8.1270.

30 See Sengoku Tamotsu (tr. Ezaki Kōichi and Ezaki Yūko), *Willing Workers: The Work Ethics in Japan, England and the United States* (Westport, Conn., 1985), p. 10.

31 *The Japan Times* 7 October 1989 (International Weekly Edition).

32 The present author has been made particularly aware of this during his teaching experience in Japan.

33 See Sano Yōko, op. cit., p. 249.

34 Sengoku Tamotsu, op. cit., p. 10. Sano Yōko (op. cit., p. 250) introduces figures showing that, in 1986, workers took about 50 per cent of what they were entitled to, down 11 per cent from the 61 per cent figure for 1980. A study by the International Federation of Chemical, Energy and General Workers' Unions, Japanese Affiliated Federation (ICEF–JAF) in 1984 (Sano Yōko, op. cit., p. 250), similarly revealed that 2,450 of the total 5,419 respondents – which included workers at all levels of the corporate hierarchy – took less than 50 per cent of their holiday entitlement. The same would also seem to apply to *saijitsu* (national holidays). (Japan acquired a new set of national holidays in July 1948, following Japan's defeat in the war. For a discussion on the changes to national holidays in the immediate post-war period see William P. Woodard, *The Allied Occupation of Japan 1945–1952 and Japanese Religion* [Leiden, 1972], pp. 142–7). Although Japan, as compared to Britain, for example, has a relatively large number of national holidays, workers in the private sector are not automatically 'entitled' to take the day off. The ICEF–JAF survey reveals useful information as to why such a state of affairs exists. Employees were concerned that taking holidays would damage the company's financial position. In addition, many of those interviewed were conscious of the trouble which such action on their part would cause their colleagues, for this would necessarily involve the colleagues doing extra work. Another reason cited was 'tacit pressure' to refuse holidays, workers feeling 'uncomfortable' taking a holiday when no one else did.

35 See Sengoku Tamotsu, op. cit., p. 142, who observes that younger workers these days tend 'to take . . . a paid holiday for granted, and their lifestyles are influencing the older corporate employees . . .'; James Bartholomew, 'Cultural Values in Japan', in Bradley M. Richardson and Ueda Taizō (eds), *Business and Society in Japan: Fundamentals for Businessmen* (New York, 1981), pp. 244–50, at p. 249. Albert Novick, in 'Work, Work: Long Vacations Get Short Shrift', *Intersect: Where Japan Meets Asia and the World*, August (1989), observes 'a new class of young workers, who are jealous of their free time, living for exotic leisure activities' (p. 38). 'For the time being', however, he notes, 'this new species of Japanese stands as an embattled minority' (p. 38). Other authors, including Sepp Linhart ('The Use and Meaning of Leisure in Present-Day Japan', in W.G. Beasley (ed.), *Modern Japan: Aspects of History, Literature and Society* [London, 1975], pp. 198–208, at p. 199) suggest that the Japanese generally have begun to challenge the *status quo*. Linhart (p. 206) sees 'a picture of a society where the attitudes towards work and leisure are slowly changing from a very one-sided over-emphasis on work to a more balanced outlook on work and leisure, seeing both as necessary'.

36 See, for example, Kinoshita Ritsuko, *Ōkoku no tsumatachi* (Wives of a Kingdom) (Tōkyō, 1983); Saitō Shigeo, *Tsumatachi no shishūki* (Housewives' Autumn) (Tōkyō, 1982). For a review of these two books in English, see Takahashi Sachiko, 'Weary Wives: A Glance Into Japanese Homes through "Wives of a Kingdom" and "Housewives' Autumn" ', *AMPO: Japan–Asia Quarterly Review*, vol. 18, nos. 2/3 (1991), pp. 65–9. Unlike the position of the British employee, the Japanese employee 'sent

away' often leaves his wife and family at home. Often, the family is unable – or unwilling – to accompany the husband, for the children's education is seen as a primary concern of contemporary Japanese society, and a move is perceived to jeopardize the child's progress at school. Those children who do manage to accompany the father often find great difficulty adjusting to the academic pace of their Japanese counterparts when they do eventually return to Japan. For a discussion on the *kikokushijo* ('returnee children'), which constitute, in Roger Goodman's words, a 'fashionable, international Japanese elite', see Roger Goodman, *Japan's ' International Youth': The Emergence of a New Class of Schoolchildren* (Oxford, 1990); Roger Goodman, 'Deconstructing an Anthropological Text: A "Moving" Account of Returnee Schoolchildren in Contemporary Japan', in Eyal Ben-Ari *et al.* (eds), *Unwrapping Japan: Society and Culture in Anthropological Perspective* (Manchester, 1990), pp. 163–87.

37 On these places of relaxation, which form a major part of the employee's 'zone of liberty', see Sepp Linhart, '*Sakariba*: Zone of "Evaporation" Between Work and Home?', in Joy Hendry and Jonathan Webber (eds), *Interpreting Japanese Society: Anthropological Approaches* (Oxford, 1986) JASO Occasional Paper no. 5, pp. 198–210. See also Saitō Seiichirō, *Goraku to supōtsu*' (Amusements and Sports), in Umesao Tadao, *Nihonjin no seikatsu* (The Daily Life of the Japanese) (Tōkyō, 1976), pp. 127–56.

38 Decision of the Second Petty Bench of the Supreme Court, 14 April 1986: 477 *Rōhan* 6.

39 For a discussion of this case in English, see Nakamura Kazuhisa and Saitō Madoka's comments in *Waseda Bulletin of Comparative Law*, vol. 7 (1988), pp. 115–16. For a recent case where the Court turned down an appeal by a company employee protesting a work transfer (on the grounds that his transfer from Tokyo to Nagoya did not prevent him from playing a role in raising his children), see the Tokyo High Court decision of 29 May 1996: *The Daily Yomiuri*, 31 May 1996.

40 Decision of the Second Petty Bench of the Supreme Court, 5 April 1985: 39 *Minshū* 675.

41 Comment in *Waseda Bulletin of Comparative Law*, vol. 7 (1988), pp. 113, 116.

42 *Mainichi Shinbun*, 16 December 1989.

43 Ibid.

44 Michael R. Reich, 'Public and Private Responses to a Chemical Disaster in Japan: The Case of Kanemi Yushō, *Law in Japan*, vol. 15 (1982), pp. 102–29, at p. 115.

45 For a discussion of apology in the field of unfair competition, for example, see Eguchi Jun'ichi, 'The Publication of Apology ("*shazai kōkoku*") As a Remedy for Unfair Competition in Japan', *Osaka University Law Review*, no. 18 (1971), pp. 19–28.

46 Frank Gibney, *Japan: The Fragile Superpower* (New York, 1975), p. 92.

47 Robert Jay Lifton *et al.* *Six Lives/Six Deaths: Portraits From Modern Japan* (New Haven, Conn., 1979), p. 282.

48 Ibid., p. 282.

49 John O. Haley, 'Sheathing the Sword of Justice in Japan: An Essay on

Law Without Sanctions', *Journal of Japanese Studies*, vol. 8, no. 2 (1982), pp. 265–81, at p. 276.

50 Michael R. Reich, op. cit., p. 116.

51 In the *ritsu*, we read that, in relation to the *shitōkan* (four officers in the same department – namely, *Kami* [Chief Secretary], *Suke* [Second Officer], *Jō* [Third Officer], *Sakan* [Fourth Officer]), where one officer commits an official crime the other officers are to be punished as well. Takikawa Masajirō, in *Nihon hōseishi* (A History of the Japanese Legal System, *jō* [vol. 1]) (Tōkyō, 1985), suggests that this was so to let the officers watch each other's actions and detect crime (p. 205). After the *ritsuryō*, the term *renza* was used to denote vicarious liability, so that persons not comitting crimes shared responsibility with those who did. This was popular during the medieval period, as well as in the Tokugawa period.

52 *Enza* relates to the vicarious responsibility of family members for crimes committed by other family members. In the *ritsu* Code, punishment for serious crimes extended to the second degree of relationship. Crimes to which *enza* was applied were *mu hen*, *taigyaku* and *mu hon* – three items of *hachigyaku*. In cases of *mu hen* and *taigyaku*, the criminal's father and his children were punished. His official position was taken away from him, and he became a *kanko* (slave). In the case of *mu hon*, such family members as, for example, the grandparents, grandchildren, and brothers, were exiled. According to the *kyaku* (Penalties), *enza* was also applied in cases involving forged money. See Takikawa Masajirō, ibid., *jō* (vol. 1), pp. 204–5.

53 See, for example, Katō Masaaki, 'Self-Destruction in Japan: A Cross-Cultural Epidemiological Analysis of Suicide', in Takie Sugiyama Lebra and William P. Lebra (eds), *Japanese Culture and Behavior: Selected Readings* (Honolulu, 1974), pp. 359–82; George De Vos, 'Deviancy and Social Change: A Psychocultural Evaluation of Trends in Japanese Delinquency and Suicide', in Robert J. Smith and Richard K. Beardsley (eds), *Japanese Culture: Its Development and Characteristics* (New York, 1962), pp. 153–71, at p. 162. For a recent book on suicide in Japan, see Maurice Pinguet (tr. Rosemary Morris), *Voluntary Death in Japan* (Cambridge, 1993).

54 Following the sociologist Emile Durkheim's terminology, where this act is also characteristically performed as a duty, as in the case of apology suicide in the present context, this type of suicide would be referred to as 'obligatory altruistic suicide'. Emile Durkheim, *Suicide: A Study in Sociology* (tr. John A. Spaulding and George Simpson) (London, 1952), p. 221.

55 Nakamaki Hirochika, 'Rituals of the *Kōyasan*'. A Paper presented at the Japan Anthropology Workshop's International Symposium on 'Ritual and Ceremony', held at the University of Leiden, the Netherlands, 26–30 March 1990.

56 Mount Kōya has been associated with the Buddhist belief since the beginning of the ninth century.

57 For a discussion of corporate social responsibility in the Anglo-American context, see *inter alios* Michael Beesley and Tom Evans, *Corporate Social Responsibility: A Reassessment* (London, 1978); G. Goyder, *The*

Responsible Company (Oxford, 1963); E. Epstein, 'The Social Role of Business Enterprise in Britain: An American Perspective', *Journal of Management Studies*, vol. 14 (1977), pp. 281–316; Noel Williams, 'Corporate Social Responsibility and the Community', *Kenkyū hōkoku* (Bulletin) (Minami Kyūshū University), no. 25(B) (Cultural and Social Science) (1995), pp. 121–201. For a discussion of the concept, with particular reference to *karōshi*, in the Japanese context, see Kawahito Hiroshi, *Karōshi to kigyō no sekinin* (Karōshi and Corporate Social Responsibility) (Tōkyō, 1990).

58 These are the directors.

59 Milton Friedman, 'The Social Responsibility of Business Is to Increase Its Profits', in G.A. Steiner and J.F. Steiner (eds), *Issues in Business and Society*, 2nd edn, (New York, 1977), pp. 168–74.

60 F.A. Hayek, 'The Corporation in a Democratic Society: In Whose Interests Ought It and Will It be Run?', in Igor Ansoff (ed.), *Business Strategy* (Harmondsworth, 1969), pp. 225–39.

61 Maurice Cranston and Sandford Lakoff have defined pluralism as 'the assembly of autonomous groups, living in private harmony with each other, but offering individuals a wide variety of alternative opportunities for self-expression and self-fulfilment': *A Glossary of Political Ideas* (London, 1969), p. 4. For Alan Fox, the pluralistic perspective is one of a 'coalition of interests', a 'miniature democratic state composed of sectional groups with divergent interests over which the government tries to maintain some kind of dynamic equilibrium' (op. cit., p. 2).

62 To consider them would be but an extension of recognition afforded employees in English law, for example. Section 46 of the Companies Act 1980 made it clear that directors are legally obligated to consider the interests of the employees. Like any other fiduciary duty, the duty of directors in this respect is owed to the company and enforceable by the company alone. M.C. Oliver, however, has doubted the effectiveness of this provision. Oliver notes that the provision 'has been much criticised as being ineffective and indeed is illustrative, along with certain other sections of the 1980 Act, of the truth of the ancient proverb that barking dogs seldom bite' (*Company Law* [London, 1981], p. 273). The provision, however, has been seen as indicative of the direction of future developments. Savage, for example, points out that, 'The 1980 Act, albeit in a modest manner, lays the foundation for future reforms aimed at making companies and those who are responsible for running them, more accountable for their actions' (Savage, *Companies Act 1980* [London, 1980], p. 1). See now Companies Act 1985, s. 309(1).

63 For a discussion on how corporate social responsibility can best be effected in practice in Japan, see Takeuchi Akio (tr. Malcolm D.H. Smith), 'Should There Be a General Provision on the Social Responsibility of Enterprises in the Commercial Code?', *Law in Japan*, vol. 11 (1978), pp. 37–56. See also Editor's Introduction, 'Commercial Law Reform in Japan: The Current Debate', *Law in Japan*, vol. 11 (1978), pp. 103–4.

64 Matsuda, 'Kaisha no shakaiteki sekinin ni tsuite – shōhō kaisei no mondai toshite' (The Social Responsibility of Companies – A Question

of the Revision of the Commercial Code), *Shōji Hōmu*, no. 713 (1975), p. 24. Cited and quoted in Takeuchi Akio, op. cit., p. 39, footnote 2.

65 In the English *Case of Sutton's Hospital* of 1612, for example, it was held that the company 'is invisible, immortal, and rests only in intendment and consideration of the law'; companies 'cannot commit treason, nor be outlawed, nor excommunicate, for they have no souls' (1612) Co. Rep. 23a. The same theme was taken up by Templeman J. in the more recent case of *Re Armvent Ltd*, in which the learned judge observed that 'the company has no soul and no feelings': [1975] 3 All ER 441.

66 Milton Friedman, op.cit., p. 168.

6 MORAL VALUE AND JAPANESE LAW

1 Joel Feinberg, *Social Philosophy* (Englewood Cliffs, N.J., 1973), pp. 79, 86–8, 94–7.

2 John Finnis, *Natural Law and Natural Rights* (Oxford, 1980), p. 213; Paul Sieghart, *The International Law of Human Rights* (Oxford, 1983), p. 130; Paul Sieghart, *Aids and Human Rights: A UK Perspective* (London, 1989), p. 12. In respect of the state's obligation to prohibit torture, or cruel, inhuman or degrading treatment or punishment, Sieghart notes that, 'The State's obligation is absolute, and there are no qualifying clauses of any kind. As a result, **any** failure by a State to comply with its obligations in respect of **any** one of these modes of conduct amounts to a violation of this prohibition: no question of justification can ever arise' (*Aids and Human Rights*, p. 65). Legal philosophers have also held other rights to be absolute. H.L.A. Hart, for example, has argued that 'there is at least one natural right, the equal right of all men to be free' in 'Are There Any Natural Rights?' (in Jeremy Waldron [ed.], *Theories of Rights* [Oxford, 1984], pp. 77–90), at p. 77. Alan Gewirth, in his article, 'Are There Any Absolute Rights?' (in Jeremy Waldron [ed.], *Theories of Rights*, pp. 91–109), argues both that 'the right of the mother not to be tortured to death by her son is absolute' (p. 107) and that 'all innocent persons have an absolute right not to be made the intended victims of a homicidal project' (p. 108). Elsewhere, Alan Gewirth argues that the right to the non-infliction of cancer is an absolute right: 'Human Rights and the Prevention of Cancer', *American Philosophical Quarterly*, vol. 17 (1980), pp. 117–25.

3 The prohibition is also to be found in the International Covenant of Civil and Political Rights of 1976, article 7; the American Convention on Human Rights of 1978, article 5(2); the African Charter of Human Rights and People's Rights of 1986, article 5; and the European Convention on Human Rights of 1953, article 3.

4 See p. 2 in this book.

5 John Finnis, op. cit., p. 213.

6 See note 55 to Chapter 2.

7 Article 36.

8 See pp. 41–2 in this volume.

9 F. Menghistu, 'The Satisfaction of Survival Requirements', in B.G. Ramcharan (ed.), *The Right to Life in International Law* (Dordrecht, the Netherlands, 1985), pp. 63–83, at p. 63. Similar sentiments have

been expressed by *inter alios* Halûk A. Kabaalioglu, who believes that, 'There can be no doubt that "right to life" is the most important of all human rights' ('The Obligation to "Respect" and to "Ensure" the Right to Life', in B.G. Ramcharan [ed.], ibid., pp. 160–81, at p. 160). For Leo Kuper, 'The right to life must certainly be the most basic and elementary of the human rights' ('Genocide and Mass Killings: Illusion and Reality', in B.G. Ramcharan [ed.], ibid. pp 114–19, at p. 114. For D. Lasok, 'There can be nothing more fundamental than the right of life' ('The Rights of the Unborn', in J.W. Bridge *et al.* [eds.], *Fundamental Rights: A Volume of Essays to Commemorate the 50th Anniversary of the Founding of the Law School in Exeter, 1923–1973* [London, 1973], pp. 18–30, at p. 28).

10 Quoted in B.G. Ramcharan, 'The Concept and Dimensions of the Right to Life', in B.G. Ramcharan (ed.), op. cit., pp. 1–32, at p. 5.

11 B.G. Ramcharan, 'The Drafting History of Article 6 of the International Covenant on Civil and Political Rights', in B.G. Ramcharan (ed.), ibid., pp. 42–56, at p. 43.

12 Resolution 1983/43, adopted on 9 March 1983. Quoted in B.G. Ramcharan, 'The Concept and Dimensions of the Right to Life', op. cit., p. 4.

13 Quoted in J. Colon-Collazo, 'The Legislative History of the Right to Life in the Inter-American Legal System', in B.G. Ramcharan (ed.), *The Right to Life, in International Law*, pp. 33–41, at p. 35.

14 *Diez Años de Actividades*, p. 339. Quoted in J. Colon-Collazo, ibid., p. 41.

15 The International Covenant on Civil and Political Rights accords the right to life a status higher than that of most other rights, although lower than that of those absolute rights discussed above. Article 4(1) of the Covenant provides that, 'in time of public emergency which threatens the life of the nation and the existence of which is officially proclaimed . . .', the right concerned may be suspended (albeit only 'to the extent strictly required by the exigencies of the situation . . .'). The right to life, the freedom from cruel, inhuman or degrading treatment or punishment, and freedom from slavery, however, are all exempt from this provision.

16 These are found in article 2, which reads: '(1) Everyone's right to life shall be protected by law. No one shall be deprived of his life intentionally save in the execution of a sentence of a court following his conviction of a crime for which this penalty is provided by law. (2) Deprivation of life shall not be regarded as inflicted in contravention of this Article when it results from the use of force which is no more than absolutely necessary: (a) in defence of any person from unlawful violence; (b) in order to effect a lawful arrest or to prevent the escape of a person lawfully detained; (c) in action lawfully taken for the purpose of quelling a riot or insurrection.'

17 Article 4.

18 John Finnis, op. cit., p. 214.

19 CCPR/C/10/Add.1, at its 319th, 320th and 324th Session held on the 20th and 22nd October 1981: CCPR/C/Sr. 319, 320 and 324. See *Freedom of Information and Expression in Japan: A Commentary on the Report Submitted to the Human Rights Committee by the Government of Japan*

(Article 19 Publications, Commentaries on Freedom of Information and Expression, no. 14, London, 1989), pp. 7–8.

20 CCPR/Sr. 319, 320 and 324, para. 77 (ibid., pp. 7–8).

21 CCPR/C/42/Add.2, para. 2(c) (ibid., p. 8).

22 John Macquarrie, *Principles of Christian Theology* (London, 1977), rev. edn, p. 67.

23 In his work, *Fūdo: ningengakuteki na kōsatsu* (translated by G. Bownas under the title, *Climate and Culture: A Philosophical Study* [Tokyo, 1971]), Watsuji Tetsurō argues (at pp. 136–7) that the climate of Japan has helped create a distinctive culture, based on spatial relationality. He cites as an example the *ie* system, with its organizational structure and the emotions which accompany it. Members are not merely a collection of individuals, but are, in the words of Najita Tetsuo and H.D. Harootunian, 'a cooperative group of selfless human beings engaged in fundamental roles of nourishing life': 'Japanese Revolt Against the West: Political and Cultural Criticism in the Twentieth Century', in Peter Duus (ed.), *The Twentieth Century* (vol. 6 of *The Cambridge History of Japan*) (Cambridge, 1988), pp. 711–74, at p. 748.

The theme of the individual participating in relationships was reiterated recently by the legal scholar John Maki. He observed: 'The Japanese individual exists as a part of society in a mutually supportive relationship, not as an isolated individual independent of or resistant to the pressures and responsibility of society': 'The Constitution of Japan: Pacifism, Popular Sovereignty, and Fundamental Human Rights', in Percy R. Luney, Jr. and Takahashi Kazuyuki (eds), *Japanese Constitutional Law* (Tokyo, 1993), pp. 39-55, at p. 51. He sees this element as constituting one consideration which may have led to the inclusion of the public welfare in the present Japanese Constitution.

24 For a discussion in English of Nishida's views in this respect see Yuasa Yasuo, *The Body: Toward an Eastern Mind-Body Theory* (tr. Nagatomo Shigenori and Thomas P. Kasulis) (New York, 1987), pp. 49–74.

25 Alasdair MacIntyre, 'Individual and Social Morality in Japan and the United States: Rival Conceptions of the Self', *Philosophy East and West*, October (1990), pp. 489–96, at p. 495.

26 Ibid., p. 496.

27 J. Victor Koschmann, 'Introduction: Soft Rule and Expressive Protest', in J. Victor Koschmann (ed.), *Authority and the Individual in Japan: Citizen Protest in Historical Perspective* (Tokyo, 1978), pp. 1–30, at p. 14.

28 Armando Martins Janeira, *The Epic and the Tragic Sense of Life in Japanese Literature: A Comparative Essay on Japanese and Western Culture* (Rutland, Vt. and Tokyo, 1967), p. 47.

29 Christian Bay, 'A Human Rights Approach to Transnational Politics', *Universal Human Rights*, vol. 1, no. 1 (January–March 1979), p. 24.

30 The idea of hell was a popular conception in Buddhism during the Kamakura period (1185–1392), for example. However, the idea of hell and punishment did not find fertile soil in Japan. Yoel Hoffmann observes of the early Buddhist writings: '[they] contain blood-chilling descriptions of the many and cruel torments awaiting the wicked after death – but the Japanese, in the innocent and optimistic manner so characteristic of them, soon found the means of salvation: it would be

sufficient to call Buddha's name before dying in order to be saved from hell. Moreover, dying itself was seen as a process of purification and atonement; at death, everyone became a Buddha': *Japanese Death Poems Written by Zen Monks and Haiku Poets on the Verge of Death* (Rutland, Vt. and Tokyo, 1986), pp. 36–7. On the attitude of the early Japanese to life and death, see Ōmine Akira (tr. Unno Taitetsu), 'The Genealogy of Sorrow: Japanese View of Life and Death', *The Eastern Buddhist*, vol. 25, no. 2 (1992), pp. 14–29.

31 Takami Jun (1907–65) captures this feeling in his poem, 'At the Boundary of Life and Death'. He asks:

> At the boundary of life and death
> what exists I wonder?
>
> . . . .
>
> On the life-death boundary . . . might there not be
> something hung like a wonderful rainbow,
> even though my surroundings
> and also my self
> were a devastated jungle?

(Edith Marcombe and Sawa Yūki [tr.], *Anthology of Modern Japanese Poetry* [Rutland Vt., 1972], p. 107.)

32 John Finnis lists seven basic values which he considers comprise the 'basic forms of human good'. These are: life, knowledge, play, aesthetic experience, sociability (friendship), practical reasonableness, and 'religion'. See John Finnis, op. cit., pp. 85–90.

33 Onodera Isao, 'Ai wa ooku no tsumi o oou' (Love Covers Up Many Sins), *Seiki* (The Century), vol. 36, no. 412, September (1984), pp. 59–69.

34 For a social anthropological view on *ba* see, for example, Nakane Chie's understanding. For her, 'my term *frame* is the English translation of the Japanese *ba*, the concept from which I originally evolved my theory, but for which it is hard to find the exact English counterpart. *Ba* means "location", but the normal usage of the term connotates a special base on which something is placed according to a given purpose': Nakane Chie, *Japanese Society* (London, 1970), p. 1.

35 Yamaori Tetsuo, *Kami to hotoke* (Gods and Buddha) (Tōkyō, 1983), pp. 29–30.

36 Onodera Isao, op. cit. The perseverance of the Japanese concept of *basho*, as Onodera points out elsewhere (see 'Bashoteki ronri to kirisutokyōteki sekai kan: toporogii shingaku e no ishikiron' [Nishida's Logic of *Topos* and the Christian World-View: A Tentative Approach to Topological Theology], *Katorikku kenkyū* [Catholic Studies], vol. 8, no. 25 [June 1974], pp. 48–83), can be seen in Nishida's philosophy of *mu no basho* ('place of nothingness'). In Nishida's theory of *mu no basho*, others and self, or subject and object, mingle together in this 'place of nothingness', where one's consciousness and judgement are formed. Yamaori Tetsuo (op. cit., pp. 31–2) suggests that Nishida's theory is influenced by traditional perceptions of *basho*.

37 The issue of the relation between the increasing power of women in Japan and an increasing interest in the welfare of husbands was raised by Dr Ann Waswo, Fellow of St Antony's College, Oxford, in the discussion

following the present author's reading of a paper on 'The Right to Life Under the Japanese Constitution', delivered at a Nissan Institute Seminar of the University of Oxford on 17 May 1991. In one sphere of activity – work – women have not fared well. On the reality facing women at work ten years after the Equal Employment Opportunity Act came into effect, see Kamiya Masako, 'A Decade of the Equal Employment Opportunity Act in Japan: Has It Changed Society?' *Law in Japan*, vol. 25 (1995), pp. 40–83.

38 On this debate see J. von Stein, *Thibaut und Savigny: zum 100 jährigen Gedächtnis des Kampfes um ein einheitliches bürgerliches Recht für Deutschland, 1814–1914* (Thibaut and Savigny: On the Centenary of the Struggle for a Uniform Civil Law for Germany, 1814–1914) (Berlin, 1914).

39 We see the influence of foreign law in the *Dai Nippon Teikoku Kenpō* (The Meiji Constitution); the *Minpō* (the original draft which was drawn up by Boissonade de Fontarbie, who followed the natural law tradition, and whose intention was to incorporate and maintain Japanese customs); the adopted *Kaisei minpō* (Amended Civil Code, based on the German historical law school, which emphasized the needs of the time); the *Shōhō* (drawn up by Roesler); and the *Keihō* (which was promulgated on 17 July 1880, and came into force on 1 January 1882, which was derived from French models).

40 On the debate between the French and British schools of law see Arashi Yoshito, 'Nihon hōseishi no kōryū to Takikawa hakase' (The Rise of the Japanese Legal System and Dr Takikawa), in Takikawa Masajirō, *Nihon hōseishi* (A History of the Japanese Legal System) (Tōkyō, 1985), *ge* (vol. 2), pp. 281–96.

41 One author who argued along these lines was Masujima. See his article, 'Modern Japanese Legal Institutions', *Transactions of the Asiatic Society of Japan*, vol. 18 (1890), pp. 229–58. See also Robert Johnston Kramer, 'The Politics of Legal Modernization: The Roman and the Japanese Experiences', Ph.D. thesis, New York University (1975), pp. 151–2.

42 However, as a result, the *Kaisei minpō* amendment lessened, rather than increased, the emphasis on Japanese customs. See Arashi Yoshito, op. cit., pp. 287–9.

Bibliography

Abe Haruo (1963) 'The Accused and Society: Therapeutic and Preventative Aspects of Criminal Justice in Japan', in Arthur Taylor von Mehren (ed.), *Law in Japan: The Legal Order in a Changing Society*, Cambridge, Mass.: Harvard University Press, pp. 324–63.

Amnesty International(1991) *Japan: The Death Penalty and the Need for More Safeguards Against Ill-Treatment of Detainees*, Tokyo.

Anzai Kazuhiro (1988) 'Nō to sono ishiki' (The Brain and its Consciousness), in *Nihon rinri gakkai kenkyū happyō yōshi* (Japan Ethics Association Outline of Presentation), 39th Annual Conference, Waseda University, 14–15 October 1988, p. 6.

Aoki Kazuo *et al.* (eds) (1982) *Kojiki* (Records of Ancient Matters), vol. 1 of *Nihon shisō taikei* (Series on Japanese Thought), Tōkyō.

Arashi Yoshito (1985) 'Nihon hōseishi no kōryū to Takikawa hakase' (The Rise of the Japanese Legal System and Dr Takikawa), in Takikawa Masajirō, *Nihon hōseishi* (A History of the Japanese Legal System), *ge* (vol. 2), Tōkyō, pp. 281–96.

Ashibe Nobuyoshi (1992) 'Human Rights and Judicial Power', in Lawrence W. Beer (ed.), *Constitutional Systems in Late Twentieth Century Asia*, Seattle and London: University of Washington Press, pp. 224–69.

Aston, W.G. (1896) *Chronicles of Japan from the Earliest Times to A.D. 697*, London: George Allen & Unwin.

Austin, John (1954) *The Province of Jurisprudence Determined* (ed. H.L.A. Hart), London: Weidenfeld & Nicolson.

Baker, Hugh D. (1979) *Chinese Family and Kinship*, London: The Macmillan Press.

Bartholomew, James (1981) 'Cultural Values in Japan', in Bradley M. Richardson and Ueda Taizō (eds), *Business and Society in Japan: Fundamentals for Businessmen*, New York: Praeger Publishers, pp. 244–50.

Bay, Christian (1979) 'A Human Rights Approach to Transnational Politics', *Universal Human Rights*, vol. 1, no. 1 (January–March).

Beck, John C. and Martha N. Beck (1994) *The Change of a Lifetime: Employment Patterns Among Japan's Managerial Elite*, Honolulu, Hawaii: University of Hawaii Press.

Becker, Carl B. (1990) 'Buddhist Views of Suicide and Euthanasia', *Philosophy East and West*, October, pp. 543–56.

Beer, Lawrence Ward (1968) 'The Public Welfare Standard and Freedom of Expression in Japan', in Dan Henderson (ed.), *The Constitution of Japan: Its First Twenty Years, 1947–67*, Seattle: University of Washington Press, pp. 205–38.

—— (1982) 'Constitutional Revolution in Japanese Law, Society and Politics', *Modern Asian Studies*, vol. 16, no. 1, pp. 33–67.

—— (1984) *Freedom of Expression in Japan: A Study in Comparative Law, Politics, and Society*, Tokyo, New York and San Francisco: Kodansha International.

—— (1992) 'The Present Constitutional System of Japan', in Lawrence W. Beer (ed.), *Constitutional Systems in Late Twentieth Century Asia*, Seattle and London: University of Washington Press, pp. 175–223.

—— (1993) 'Freedom of Expression: The Continuing Revolution', in Percy R. Luney, Jr. and Takahashi Kazuyuki (eds), *Japanese Constitutional Law*, Tokyo: University of Tokyo Press, pp. 221–54.

Beesley, Michael and Tom Evans (1978) *Corporate Social Responsibility: A Reassessment*, London: Croom Helm.

Befu Harumi (1974) 'Power in Exchange: The Strategy of Control and Patterns of Compliance in Japan, *Asian Profile*, vol. 2, nos. 5/6 (October–December), pp. 601–22.

—— (1977) 'Power in the Great White Tower', in R.D. Fogelson and R.M. Adams, *The Anthropology of Power*, New York: Academic Press, pp. 77–87.

—— (1980) 'A Critique of the Group Model of Japanese Society', in Ross Mouer and Sugimoto Yoshio (eds), *Social Analysis*, (Special Issue: Japanese Society: Reappraisals and New Directions), nos. 5/6 (December), pp. 29–43.

—— (1980) 'The Group Model of Japanese Society and an Alternative', *Rice University Studies*, vol. 66, no. 1 (Winter), pp. 169–87.

—— (1989) 'A Theory of Social Exchange as Applied to Japan', in Sugimoto Yoshio and Ross E. Mouer (eds), *Constructs for Understanding Japan*, London: Kegan Paul International, pp. 39–66.

Bellah, Robert (1957) *Tokugawa Religion: The Cultural Roots of Modern Japan*, New York: The Free Press.

Bentham, Jeremy (1970 [1789]) *An Introduction to the Principles of Morals and Legislation*, eds. J.H. Burns and H.L.A. Hart, London: Athlone Press.

Blacker, Carmen (1964) *The Japanese Enlightenment: A Study of the Writings of Fukuzawa Yukichi*, Cambridge: Cambridge University Press.

Bock, Felicia Gressitt (1970–2), *Engi Shiki: Procedures of the Engi Era* Bks 1–V; Bks VI–X, Tokyo: Sophia University Press.

British Association Study Group (1974) *Social Concern and Biological Advances*, London.

British Medical Association (1980) *The Handbook of Medical Ethics*, London: BMA.

Brooks, Anne Page (1981) '*Mizuko Kuyō* and Japanese Buddhism', *Japanese Journal of Religious Studies*, vol. 8, nos. 3/4 (September–December), pp. 119–47.

Brudnoy, David (1968) 'The Immutable Despair of Dazai Osamu', *Monumenta Nipponica*, vol. 23, pp. 457–74.

Bull, Hedley (1977) *The Anarchical Society: A Study of Order in World Politics*, London: Macmillan.

Chamberlain, Basil Hall (1982) *The Kojiki: Records of Ancient Matters*, Rutland, Vt. and Tokyo: Charles E. Tuttle.

Ch'en, Paul Heng-Chao (1981) *The Formation of the Early Meiji Legal Order: The Japanese Code of 1871 and its Chinese Foundation*, Oxford: Oxford University Press.

Clark, Rodney, C. (1975) 'Union-Management Conflict in a Japanese Company', in W.G. Beasley (ed.), *Modern Japan: Aspects of History, Literature and Society*, London: George Allen & Unwin, pp. 209–26.

—— (1979) *The Japanese Company*, New Haven, Conn.: Yale University Press.

Cole, Robert E. (1971) *Japanese Blue Collar: The Changing Tradition* Berkeley, Calif.: University of California Press.

Coleman, Samuel (1983) *Family Planning in Japanese Society: Traditional Birth Control in a Modern Urban Culture*, Princeton, N.J.: Princeton University Press.

Colon-Collazo, J. (1985) 'The Legislative History of the Right to Life in the Inter-American Legal System', in B.G. Ramcharan (ed.), *The Right to Life in International Law*, Dordrecht: Martinus Nijhoff Publishers, pp. 33–41.

Conference of Medical Royal Colleges and their Faculties in the UK (1979) 'Diagnosis of Death', *Lancet*, no. 1, pp. 261–2.

Craig, Barbara Hinkson and David M. O'Brien (1993) *Abortion and American Politics*, Chatham, N.J.: Chatham House.

Cranston, Maurice and Sandford Lakoff (1969) *A Glossary of Political Ideas*, London: Basic Books.

Daniels, Gordon (1967) 'The Japanese Civil War (1868): A British View', *Modern Asian Studies*, vol. 1, part 3, (July), pp. 241–63.

—— (1968) 'The British Role in the Meiji Restoration: A Reinterpretive Note', *Modern Asian Studies*, vol. 2, part 4, (October), pp. 291–313.

—— (1980) 'E.H. House, Japan's American Advocate', *Proceedings of the British Association for Japanese Studies*, vol. 5, part 1, pp. 3–10, 207–8.

Dandō Shigemitsu (1985) *Keihō kōyō kakuron* (The Core of the Theories on Criminal Law), rev. edn., Tōkyō.

—— (1995) *Shikei haishiron* (A Theory of the Abolition of the Death Penalty), 4th edn, Tōkyō.

Davies, Edmund (1969) 'A Legal Look at Transplants', *Proceedings of the Royal Society of Medicine*, vol 62.

De Becker, J.E. (1979 [1909]) *Annotated Civil Code of Japan*, Washington, DC: University Publications of America.

De Vos, George (1962) 'Deviancy and Social Change: A Psychocultural Evaluation of Trends in Japanese Delinquency and Suicide', in Robert J. Smith and Richard K. Beardsley (eds), *Japanese Culture: Its Development and Characteristics*, New York: Wenner-Gren Foundation, pp. 153–71.

—— (1973) *Socialization for Achievement: Essays on the Cultural Psychology of the Japanese*, Berkeley, Calif.: University of California Press.

Dore, Ronald P. (1971) 'Commitment – to What, by Whom and Why?', in *Social and Cultural Background of Labor–Management Relations in Asian*

Countries, Proceedings of the 1971 Asian Regional Conference on Industrial Relations, Tokyo, March 1971, pp. 106–26.

—— (1973) *British Factory–Japanese Factory: The Origins of Diversity in Industrial Relations*, London: George Allen & Unwin.

Durkheim, Emile (1952) *Suicide: A Study in Sociology* (tr. by John A. Spaulding and George Simpson), London: Routledge & Kegan Paul.

Dworkin, Ronald (1978) *Taking Rights Seriously*, Cambridge, Mass.: Harvard University Press.

Dziubla, Robert W. (1985) 'Enforcing Corporate Responsibility: Japanese Corporate Directors' Liability to Third Parties for Failure to Supervise', *Law in Japan*, vol. 18, pp. 55–75.

Editor's Introduction (1978) 'Commercial Law Reform in Japan: The Current Debate', *Law in Japan*, vol. 11, pp. 103–4.

Eguchi Jun'ichi (1971) 'The Publication of Apology (*"shazai kōkoku"*) As a Remedy for Unfair Competition in Japan', *Osaka University Law Review*, no. 18, pp. 19–28.

Epstein, E. (1977) 'The Social Role of Business Enterprise in Britain: An American Perspective', *Journal of Management Studies*, vol. 14, pp. 281–316.

Feinberg, Joel (1970) *Doing and Deserving*, Princeton, N.J.: Princeton University Press.

—— (1973) *Social Philosophy*, Englewood Cliffs, N.J.: Prentice-Hall.

Finnis, John (1980) *Natural Law and Natural Rights*, Oxford: Clarendon Press.

Florence, Sargant (1961) *Ownership Control and Success of Large Companies*, London: Sweet and Maxwell.

Fox, Alan (1966) *Industrial Sociology and Industrial Relations*, Research Paper no. 3 for the Royal Commission on Trade Unions and Employers' Associations, London: HMSO.

Freedom of Information and Expression in Japan: A Commentary on the Report Submitted to the Human Rights Committee by the Government of Japan (1989) Commentaries on Freedom of Information and Expression, no. 14, London: Article 19 Publications.

Friedman, Milton (1977) 'The Social Responsibility of Business Is to Increase its Profits', in G.A. Steiner and J.F. Steiner (eds), *Issues in Business and Society*, 2nd edn., New York: Random House, pp. 168–74.

Fujii Shin'ichi (1965) *The Constitution of Japan: A Historical Survey*, Tokyo.

Fujiki Hideo (1976) *Keihō kōgi kakuron* (Lectures on the Theories on Criminal Law), Tōkyō.

Fukase Tadakazu (1987) *Sensō hōki to heiwateki seizonken* (The Renunciation of War and the Right to Live in Peace), Tōkyō.

Fukuda Taira (1988) *Keihō kakuron* (Theories on Criminal Law), rev. edn., Tōkyō.

Gage, Richard L. (ed.) (1976) *Arnold Toynbee and Daisaku Ikeda – Choose Life: A Dialogue*, Oxford: Oxford University Press.

George, B.J. (1964) *A Preparatory Draft for the Revised Penal Code of Japan, 1961*, Littleton, Colo.: Fred B. Rothman & Co.

—— (1969) 'The "Right of Silence" in Japanese Law', in Dan Fenno

Henderson (ed.), *The Constitution of Japan: Its First Twenty Years, 1947–67*, Seattle: University of Washington Press, pp. 257ff.

—— (1993) 'Rights of the Criminally Accused', in Percy R. Luney, Jr. and Takahashi Kazuyuki (eds), *Japanese Constitutional Law*, Tokyo: University of Tokyo Press, pp. 289–318.

Gewirth, Alan (1980) 'Human Rights and the Prevention of Cancer', *American Philosophical Quarterly*, vol. 17, pp. 117–25.

—— (1984) 'Are There Any Absolute Rights?', in Jeremy Waldron (ed.), *Theories of Rights*, Oxford: Oxford University Press, pp. 91–109.

Gibney, Frank (1975) *Japan: The Fragile Superpower*, New York: Norton.

Glendon, Mary Ann (1987) *Abortion and Divorce in Western European Law: American Failures, European Challenges* Cambridge, Mass.: Harvard University Press.

Glover Report on Reproductive Technologies to the European Commission (1989) *Fertility and the Family*, London: Fourth Estate.

Goodman, Roger (1990) *Japan's 'International Youth': The Emergence of a New Class of Schoolchildren*, Oxford: Oxford University Press.

—— (1990) 'Deconstructing an Anthropological Text: A "Moving" Account of Returnee Schoolchildren in Contemporary Japan', in Eyal Ben-Ari, Brian Moeran and James Valentine (eds), *Unwrapping Japan: Society and Culture in Anthropological Perspective*, Manchester: Manchester University Press, pp. 163–87.

Gowers Commission (1953) *Report of the British Royal Commission on Capital Punishment, 1949–53*, Cmnd. 8932, London: HMSO.

Goyder, G. (1963) *The Responsible Company*, Oxford: Oxford University Press.

Gresser, Julian, Fujikura Kōichirō and Morishima Akio (1981) *Environmental Law in Japan*, Cambridge, Mass.: MIT Press.

Haley, John O. (1982) 'Sheathing the Sword of Justice in Japan: An Essay on Law Without Sanctions', *Journal of Japanese Studies*, vol. 8, no. 2, pp. 265–81.

—— (1984) 'Introduction: Legal vs Social Controls', *Law in Japan*, vol. 17, pp. 1–6.

Hanami Tadashi (1985) *Labour Law and Industrial Relations in Japan*, 2nd rev. edn., Deventer: Kluwer Law and Taxation Publishers.

Hart, H.L.A. (1958) 'Positivism and the Separation of Law and Morals', *Harvard Law Review*, vol. 71, pp. 593–629.

—— (1984) 'Are There Any Natural Rights?', in Jeremy Waldron (ed.), *Theories of Rights*, Oxford: Oxford University Press, pp. 77–90.

Hayek, F.A.(1969) 'The Corporation in a Democratic Society: In Whose Interests Ought It and Will It Be Run?', in Igor Ansoff (ed.), *Business Strategy*, Harmondsworth: Penguin Books, pp. 225–39.

Henderson, Dan Fenno (1965) *Conciliation and Japanese Law: Tokugawa and Modern*, vol. 1, Seattle: University of Washington Press.

—— (1968) 'The Evolution of Tokugawa Law', in John W. Hall and Marius B. Jansen (eds), *Studies in the Institutional History of Modern Japan*, Princeton, N.J.: Princeton University Press, pp. 203–30.

Higuchi Norio (1995) 'Jinkō seishoku to oyako kankei' (Artificial Insemination and the Parent–Child Relationship), *Jurisuto* (Jurist), no. 1059, 1 January, pp. 129–36.

Hirano Ryūichi (1963) 'The Accused and Society: Some Aspects of Japanese Criminal Law', in Arthur Taylor von Mehren (ed.), *Law in Japan: The Legal Order in a Changing Society*, Cambridge, Mass.: Harvard University Press, pp. 274–96.

—— (1977) *Keihō gaisetsu* (An Outline of Criminal Law), Tōkyō.

Hoffmann, Yoel (1986) *Japanese Death Poems Written by Zen Monks and Haiku Poets on the Verge of Death*, Rutland, Vt. and Tokyo: Charles E. Tuttle.

Hood, Roger (1989) *The Death Penalty: A World-Wide Perspective*, Oxford: Oxford University Press.

Hoshino Eiki and Takeda Dōshō (1987) 'Indebtedness and Comfort: The Undercurrents of *Mizuko Kuyō* in Contemporary Japan', *Japanese Journal of Religious Studies*, vol. 14, no. 4 (December), pp. 305–20.

Hosokawa Migiwa, Uehata Tetsunojō and Tajiri Shunichirō (1982) *Karōshi: nō, shinzōkei shitsubyō no gyōmujō nintei to yobō* (*Karōshi*: Official Recognition of Brain and Heart Disease and their Prevention), Tōkyō.

Ikushima Eizaburō (1991) 'Jinkō kōsei no shōrai yosoku' (Future Prediction on the Composition of the Population), in Fukuoka-ken ishikai (Fukuoka Prefecture Association of Medical Doctors), *Kazoku keikaku: yūsei hogohō shidōsha kōshū* (Family Planning: Lectures for Practitioners of the Eugenic Protection Law). Paper delivered at a Conference held by the Fukuoka-ken ishikai in Fukuoka City on 20 April 1991, pp. 3–7.

Inoue Kiyoshi (1955) *Jōyaku kaisei* (Amending the Treaties), Tōkyō.

Inoue Mitsusada (1986) *Inoue Mitsusada chosakushū* (The Collected Works of Inoue Mitsusada), vol. 2, Tōkyō.

Inoue Mitsusada *et al.* (eds) (1976) *Ritsuryō* (Laws and Ordinances), *Nihon shisō taikei* (Series on Japanese Thought), vol. 3, Tōkyō.

Ishida Takeshi (1975) 'Fundamental Human Rights and the Development of Legal Thought in Japan', *Law in Japan*, vol. 8, pp. 39–66.

—— (1986) *The Introduction of Western Political Concepts Into Japan: Non-Western Societies' Response to the Impact of the West*, Nissan Occasional Paper Series, no. 2, Nissan Institute of Japanese Studies, the University of Oxford.

Ishii Michiko (1984) 'The Abortion Problem and Family Law in Japan: A Reconsideration of Legalized Abortion Under the Eugenic Protection Law', *Annals of the Institute of Social Science* (Institute of Social Science, University of Tokyo), no. 26, pp. 64–77.

Ishii Ryōsuke (ed.) (1958) *Japanese Legislation in the Meiji Era* (tr. William J. Chambliss), vol. 10: *Legislation*, Tokyo: Pan-Pacific Press.

—— (1964) *Edo no keibatsu* (Punishment in the Edo Era), Tōkyō.

Ishimoda Shō (1989) *Kodaihō to chūseihō* (Early Law and Medieval Law), vol. 8 of *Ishimoda Shō chosakushū* (Collected Works of Ishimoda Shō), Tōkyō.

Ishio Yoshihisa (1968) *Nihon kodaihō no kenkyū* (Research on Early Japanese Law), Tōkyō.

Itō Hirobumi (1904) 'The Constitution of the Empire of Japan', in A. Stead (ed.), *Japan by the Japanese*, London: Heinemann, pp. 32–63.

Itō Hiroshi and Lawrence Ward Beer (1978) *The Constitutional Case Law of Japan: Selected Supreme Court Decisions, 1961–70*, Seattle: University of Washington Press.

Iwatani Jūrō (1991) 'Futatsu no futsubun keihō sōan to Boasonādo' (Two Drafts of the Penal Code in French and Boissonade), *Hōgaku Kenkyū* (Keiō University Faculty of Law), vol. 64, no. 1, pp. 57–80.

Janeira, Armando Martins (1967) *The Epic and the Tragic Sense of Life in Japanese Literature: A Comparative Essay on Japanese and Western Culture*, Rutland, Vt. and Tokyo: Charles E. Tuttle.

Jolowicz, J.A. (1980) 'The Judicial Protection of Fundamental Rights Under English Law', Cambridge–Tilburg Law Lectures, 2nd Series, Deventer: Kluwer, pp. 1–48.

Kabaalioglu, Halûk A. (1985) 'The Obligation to "Respect" and to "Ensure" the Right to Life', in B.G. Ramcharan (ed.), *The Right to Life in International Law*, Dordrecht: Martinus Nijhoff Publishers, pp. 160–81.

Kagawa Tatsuo (1982) *Keihō kōgi kakuron* (Lectures on the Theories on Criminal Law), Tōkyō.

Kamiya Masako (1995) 'A Decade of the Equal Employment Opportunity Act in Japan: Has It Changed Society?', *Law in Japan*, vol. 25, pp. 40–83.

Kant, Immanuel (1965 [1797]) *Metaphysical Elements of Justice* (tr. John Ladd), New York: Bobbs-Merrill.

Katō Masaaki (1974) 'Self-Destruction in Japan: A Cross-Cultural Epidemiological Analysis of Suicide', in Takie Sugiyama Lebra and William P. Lebra (eds), *Japanese Culture and Behavior: Selected Readings*, Honolulu: University of Hawaii, pp. 359–82.

Kawahito Hiroshi (1990) *Karōshi to kigyō no sekinin* (*Karōshi* and Corporate Responsibility), Tōkyō.

—— (1991) 'Death and the Corporate Warrior', *Japan Quarterly*, April–June, pp. 149–58.

Keene, Donald (tr.) (1961) *Major Plays of Chikamatsu*, New York: Columbia University Press.

Kenpō chōsa kai (1961) (Commission on the Constitution), *Kenpō seitei no keika ni kansuru shoiinkai hōkokusho* (Report of the Sub-Committee on the Process of the Enactment of the Constitution), Tōkyō.

Kimura Kameji (1959) *Keihō kakuron* (Theories on Criminal Law), rev. edn, Tōkyō.

Kinoshita Ritsuko (1983) *Ōkoku no tsumatachi* (Wives of a Kingdom), Tōkyō.

Koschmann, J. Victor (1978) 'Introduction: Soft Rule and Expressive Protest', in J. Victor Koschmann (ed.), *Authority and the Individual in Japan: Citizen Protest in Historical Perspective*, Tokyo: University of Tokyo Press, pp. 1–30.

Kramer, Robert Johnston (1975) The Politics of Legal Modernization: The Roman and the Japanese Experiences, Ph.D. thesis, New York University.

Kumagai Fumie (1981) 'Filial Violence: A Peculiar Parent–Child Relationship in the Japanese Family Today', *Journal of Comparative Family Studies*, vol. 21, no. 3 (Special Issue, Summer), pp. 337–50.

Kuper, Leo (1985) 'Genocide and Mass Killings: Illusion and Reality', in B.G. Ramcharan (ed.), *The Right to Life in International Law*, Dordrecht: Martinus Nijhoff Publishers, pp. 114–19.

Kurano Kenji and Takeda Yukichi (eds) (1963) *Kojiki/Norito* (Records of Ancient Matters/Purification Prayers), vol. 1 of *Nihon koten bungaku taikei* (Japanese Classics Series), Tōkyō.

Kuwahara Jitsuzō (1977) *Chūgoku no kōdō* (The Way of Piety in China), Tōkyō.

Lader, Lawrence (1966) *Abortion*, Boston: Beacon Press.

LaFleur, William R. (1990) 'Contestation and Consensus: The Morality of Abortion in Japan', *Philosophy East and West*, October, pp. 529–42.

Lasok, D. (1973) 'The Rights of the Unborn', in J.W. Bridge *et al.* (eds), *Fundamental Rights: A Volume of Essays to Commemorate the 50th Anniversary of the Founding of the Law School in Exeter 1923–1973*, London: Sweet and Maxwell, pp. 18–30.

Lee, Luke (1973) 'International Status of Abortion Legalization', in Howard J. Osofsky and Joy D. Osofsky (eds), *The Abortion Experience: Psychological and Medical Impact*, Hagerstown, Md.: Harper & Row, pp. 338–64.

Leflar, Robert B. (1996) 'Informed Consent and Patients' Rights in Japan', *Houston Law Review*, vol. 33, no. 1, pp. 1–112.

Lehmann, Jean-Pierre (1979) 'Native Custom and Legal Codification: Boissonade's Introduction of Western Law to Japan', *Proceedings of the British Association for Japanese Studies*, vol. 4, part 1: *History and International Relations* (ed. Gordon Daniels), pp. 33–72.

Lifton, Robert Jay, Katō Shūichi and Michael R. Reich (1979) *Six Lives/Six Deaths: Portraits from Modern Japan*, New Haven, Conn.: Yale University Press.

Linhart, Sepp (1975) 'The Use and Meaning of Leisure in Present-Day Japan', in W.G. Beasley (ed.), *Modern Japan: Aspects of History, Literature and Society*, London: George Allen & Unwin, pp. 198–208.

—— (1986) '*Sakariba*: Zone of "Evaporation" Between Work and Home?', in Joy Hendry and Jonathan Webber (eds), *Interpreting Japanese Society: Anthropological Approaches*, JASO Occasional Paper, no. 5, Oxford: JASO, pp. 198–210.

Long, Susan Orpett (1987) *Family Change and the Life Course in Japan*, Cornell University East Asian Papers, no. 44, Ithaca, N.Y.: Cornell University Press.

Luney, Percy R. Jr. (1993) 'The Judiciary: Its Organization and Status in the Parliamentary System', in Percy R. Luney, Jr. and Takahashi Kazuyuki (eds), *Japanese Constitutional Law*, Tokyo: University of Tokyo Press, pp. 123–49.

Lyons, David (1984) *Ethics and the Rule of Law*, Cambridge: Cambridge University Press.

MacDonald, Margaret (1984) 'Natural Rights', in Jeremy Waldron (ed.), *Theories of Rights*, Oxford: Oxford University Press, pp. 21–40.

MacIntyre, Alasdair (1990) 'Individual and Social Morality in Japan and the United States: Rival Conceptions of the Self', *Philosophy East and West*, October, pp. 489–96.

McMullen, I.J. (1975) 'Non-Agnatic Adoption: A Confucian Controversy in Seventeenth- and Eighteenth-Century Japan', *Harvard Journal of Asiatic Studies*, vol. 35, pp. 133–89.

—— (1987) 'Rulers or Fathers? A Casuistical Problem in Early Modern Japanese Thought', *Past and Present*, no. 116 (August), pp. 56–97.

Macquarrie, John (1977) *Principles of Christian Theology*, rev. edn, London: SCM Press.

Maki, John M. (ed.) (1964) *Court and Constitution in Japan: Selected Supreme Court Decisions, 1948–60*, Seattle: University of Washington Press.

—— (tr. and ed.) (1980) *Japan's Commission on the Constitution: The Final Report*, Seattle: University of Washington Press.

—— (1993) 'The Constitution of Japan: Pacifism, Popular Sovereignty, and Fundamental Human Rights', in Percy R. Luney, Jr. and Takahashi Kazuyuki (eds), *Japanese Constitutional Law*, Tokyo: University of Tokyo Press, pp. 39–55.

Marcombe, Edith and Sawa Yūki (tr.) (1972) *Anthology of Modern Japanese Poetry*, Rutland, Vt.: Charles E. Tuttle.

Marsh, Robert M. and Hiroshi Mannari (1976) *Modernization and the Japanese Factory*, Princeton, N.J.: Princeton University Press.

Martin, Bernd (1990) 'The German Role in the Modernization of Japan', *Oriens Extremus*, vol. 33, no. 1, pp. 77–88.

Masujima, R. (1890) 'Modern Japanese Legal Institutions', *Transactions of the Asiatic Society of Japan*, vol. 18, pp. 229–58.

Masumoto Hirofumi (1995) 'Shikei hanketsu no gutaiteki ryōkei kijun no kentō: Nagayama daiichiji saikōsai hanketsu igo no hanketsu o sozai ni shite' (An Examination of the Standards Employed for Death Penalty Sentencing from Concrete Examples: A Review of Cases Since *Japan* v. *Nagayama* [1983]), *Nara Daigaku Kiyō* (Memoirs of Nara University), no. 23, pp. 29–50.

Matsui Shigenori (1988) 'A Comment Upon the Role of the Judiciary in Japan', *Osaka University Law Review*, no. 35, pp. 17–28.

—— (1993) *Saiban o ukeru kenri* (Right of Access to the Courts), Tōkyō.

Matsumoto Sannosuke (tr. J. Victor Koschmann) (1978) 'The Idea of Heaven: A Tokugawa Foundation for Natural Rights Theory', in Najita Tetsuo and Irwin Scheiner (eds), *Japanese Thought in the Tokugawa Period, 1600–1868: Methods and Metaphors*, Chicago and London: University of Chicago Press.

Matsuoka Hiroshi (1992) 'Fukuzawa Yukichi ni okeru "hō" oyobi "kenri" ni kansuru ichi kōsatsu' (A Study on Fukuzawa Yukichi's Views on 'Law' and 'Rights'), *Hōgaku Kenkyū* (Legal Studies) (Faculty of Law, Keiō University), vol. 65, no. 12, pp. 217–41.

Menghistu, F. (1985) 'The Satisfaction of Survival Requirements', in B.G. Ramcharan (ed.), *The Right to Life in International Law*, Dordrecht: Martinus Nijhoff Publishers, pp. 63–83.

Miano Akira (1984) *Anrakushi kara songenshi e* (From Mercy Killing to Death with Dignity), Tōkyō.

Miller, Frank O. (1965) *Minobe Tatsukichi: Interpreter of Constitutionalism in Japan*, Berkeley and Los Angeles: University of California Press.

Minear, Richard H. (1970) *Japanese Tradition and Western Law: Emperor, State, and Law in the Thought of Hozumi Yatsuka*, Cambridge, Mass.: Harvard University Press.

Ministry of Health and Welfare (1965) *Koseishō 20 nen shi* (Twenty Years of the Ministry of Health and Welfare), Tōkyō.

—— (1979) *Showa 54 nen jinkō tōkei* (Statistics of Demographic Trends), vol. 1, Tōkyō.

Ministry of Labour (1990) *Maigetsu kinrō tōkei* (Monthly Labour Statistics), Tōkyō.
Minobe Tatsukichi (1926) *Kenpō satsuyō* (Interpreting the Constitution), Tōkyō.
Mitani Taichirō (1988) 'The Establishment of Party Cabinets, 1898–1932', in Peter Duus (ed.), *The Twentieth Century* (vol. 6 of *The Cambridge History of Japan*), Cambridge: Cambridge University Press, pp. 55–96.
Mitsukuri Rinshō (1976) 'Liberty', in William Reynolds Braisted (tr. with introduction), *Meiroku Zasshi: Journal of the Japanese Enlightenment*, Tokyo: Tokyo University Press, pp. 117–19.
Morioka Masahiro (1988) 'Nōshi to wa nan de atta ka' (What Was Brain Death?), in *Nihon rinri gakkai kenkyū happyō yōshi* (Japan Ethics Association Outline of Presentation), Japan Ethics Association 39th Annual Conference, Waseda University, 14–15 October, p. 7.
Murakami Yasusuke (1984) '*Ie* Society as a Pattern of Civilization', *Journal of Japanese Studies*, vol. 10, no. 2, pp. 281–363.
Muramatsu Minoru (1967) 'Medical Aspects of the Practice of Fertility Regulation', in Muramatsu Minoru (ed.), *Japan's Experience in Family Planning – Past and Present*, Tokyo: Family Planning Federation of Japan, pp. 57–82.
Najita Tetsuo and H.D. Harootunian (1988) 'Japanese Revolt Against the West: Political and Cultural Criticism in the Twentieth Century', in Peter Duus (ed.), *The Twentieth Century* (vol. 6 of *The Cambridge History of Japan*) Cambridge: Cambridge University Press, pp. 711–74.
Nakamaki Hirochika (1990) 'Rituals of the *Kōyasan*'. A Paper presented at the Japan Anthropology Workshop's International Symposium on 'Ritual and Ceremony', held at the University of Leiden, the Netherlands, 26–30 March.
Nakamura Kazuhisa and Matsuo Kuniyuki (1987) Comment in *Waseda Bulletin of Comparative Law*, vol. 6, pp. 130–3.
Nakamura Kazuhisa and Saitō Madoka (1988) Comment in *Waseda Bulletin of Comparative Law*, vol. 7, pp. 113–16.
Nakamura Mutsuo (1993) 'Freedom of Economic Activities and the Right to Property', in Percy R. Luney, Jr. and Takahashi Kazuyuki (eds), *Japanese Constitutional Law*, Tokyo: University of Tokyo Press, pp. 255–67.
Nakane Chie (1970) *Japanese Society*, London: Weidenfeld and Nicolson.
Nakatani Kinko (1983) *Keihō kōgi kakuron* (Lectures on the Theories of Criminal Law), *jō* (vol. 1), Tōkyō.
Naldi, Gino J. (1991) 'The Prohibition on the Death Penalty in International Law', *Netherlands International Law Review*, vol. 38, pp. 373–84.
Nicholas, Barry (1962) *An Introduction to Roman Law*, Oxford: Clarendon Press.
Nihon bosei hogo i kyōkai (1966) (The Japan Gynaecological Association for the Protection of Mothers), *Shitei ishi hikken* (Designated Physician's Handbook), Tōkyō, p. 10.
—— (1990) *Nichibo ihō* (Monthly Digest), vol. 42, no. 481 (1 April), p. 111.
Nishihara Haruo (1983) *Hanzai kakuron* (Theories on Crime), 2nd edn., Tōkyō.
Nishimura Shigeki (1976) 'An Explanation of "Right": Third in a Series of Expositions on Foreign Words', in William Reynolds Braisted (tr. with

introduction), *Meiroku Zasshi: Journal of the Japanese Enlightenment*, Tokyo: Tokyo University Press, pp. 510–13.

Noda Yoshiyuki (tr. and ed. Anthony H. Angelo) (1976) *Introduction to Japanese Law*, Tokyo: University of Tokyo Press.

Nomura Minoru and Nakazora Toshimasa (1988) Comment in *Waseda Bulletin of Comparative Law*, vol. 7, p. 91.

Novick, Albert (1989) 'Work, Work: Long Vacations Get Short Shrift', *Intersect: Where Japan Meets Asia and the World*, August, pp. 28–39.

Nozick, Robert (1974) *Anarchy, State and Utopia*, New York: Basic Books.

Ōba Shigema (1923) *Keihō kakuron* (Theories on Criminal Law), *jōkan* (vol. 1), 11th edn., Tōkyō.

Ōhashi Yukako (1986) 'My Body Belongs to Me: Women Fight Against a Retrogressive Revision of the Eugenic Law', *AMPO Japan–Asia Quarterly Review*, vol. 18, nos. 2/3, pp. 94–9.

Ohnuki-Tierney, Emiko (1984) *Illness and Culture in Contemporary Japan: An Anthropological View*, Cambridge: Cambridge University Press.

Okamura Chikanobu (1990) *Karōshi to rōsai hoshō* (Compensation for Death and Illness from Overwork, and Accidents at Work), Tōkyō.

Okudaira Yasuhiro (1987) *Some Consideration on the Constitution of Japan*, University of Tokyo Institute of Social Science Occasional Papers in Law and Society, no. 3, Tokyo.

—— (1993) 'Forty Years of the Constitution and Its Various Influences: Japanese, American, and European', in Percy R. Luney, Jr. and Takahashi Kazuyuki (eds), *Japanese Constitutional Law*, Tokyo: University of Tokyo Press, pp. 1–38.

Oliver, M.C. (1981) *Company Law*, London: MacDonald & Evans.

Ōmine Akira (tr. Unno Taitetsu (1992) 'The Genealogy of Sorrow: Japanese View of Life and Death', *The Eastern Buddhist*, vol. 25, no. 2, pp. 14–29.

Onodera Isao (1974) 'Bashoteki ronri to kirisutokyōteki sekai kan: toporogii shingaku e no ishikiron' (Nishida's Logic of *Topos* and the Christian World-View: A Tentative Approach to Topological Theology), *Katorikku kenkyū* (Catholic Studies), vol. 8, no. 25 (June), pp. 48–83.

—— (1984) 'Ai wa ooku no tsumi o oou' (Love Covers Up Many Sins), *Seiki* (The Century), vol. 36, no. 412 (September), pp. 59–69.

Ōno Masayoshi (1966) 'Contradictions in the Functions of Criminal Law', *Osaka University Law Review*, no. 14, pp. 25–34.

—— (1975) 'Capital Punishment and Penal Reform', *Osaka University Law Review*, no. 22, pp. 1–18.

Ono Seiichiro (1950) *Shintei keihō kōgi kakuron* (New Revised Lectures on the Theories of Criminal Law), 3rd edn, Tōkyō.

Oppler, Alfred (1970) 'The Judicial and Legal System', in Supreme Commander of the Allied Powers, *Political Reorientation of Japan, September 1945 to September 1948*, vol. 1, Westport, Conn.: Greenwood Press, pp. 186–245.

—— (1976) *Legal Reform in Occupied Japan: A Participant Looks Back*, Princeton, N.J.: Princeton University Press.

Orlin, Theodore S. (1990) 'The Prohibition of the Death Penalty: An Emerging International Norm?', in Allan Rosas and Jan Helgesen (eds), *Human Rights in a Changing East–West Perspective*, London: Pinter Publishers, pp. 136–73.

Ōsuka Akira (1988) 'Constitutional Protection and Guarantee of Rights and Freedoms: The Case of Japan', *Waseda Bulletin of Comparative Law*, vol. 7, pp. 1–14.

—— (1993) 'Welfare Rights', in Percy R. Luney, Jr. and Takahashi Kazuyuki (eds), *Japanese Constitutional Law*, Tokyo: University of Tokyo Press, pp. 269–87.

Ōtani Hiroshi (1983) *Keihō kōgi kakuron* (Lectures on the Theories on Criminal Law), Tōkyō.

Ōta Tenrei (1967) *Datai kinshi to yūsei hogohō* (Abortion Prohibition and the Eugenic Protection Law), Tōkyō.

—— (1976) *Nihon sanji chōsetsu hyakunen shi* (A Hundred-Year History of Birth Control in Japan), Tōkyō.

Ōtsuka Hitoshi (1987) *Keihō gaisetsu* (An Outline of Criminal Law), Tōkyō.

Philippi, Donald L. (1959) *Norito: A New Translation of the Ancient Japanese Ritual Prayers*, Tokyo.

Pinguet, Maurice (tr. Rosemary Morris) (1993) *Voluntary Death in Japan*, Cambridge: Cambridge University Press.

Pohlman, Edward H. (1969) *Psychology of Birth Planning*, Cambridge, Mass.: Schenkman.

Prall, Susan (1988) 'Privacy II: State Attempts to Regulate Abortion', *Annual Survey of American Law*, pp. 385–427.

Prime Minister (1970) *Sanji seigen ni kansuru seron chosa: shōwa 45 nen sangatsu* (Opinion Survey on Birth Control: March 1970), Tōkyō.

Pyle, Kenneth B. (1989) 'Meiji Conservatism', in Marius B. Jansen (ed.), *The Nineteenth Century* (vol. 5 of *The Cambridge History of Japan*), Cambridge: Cambridge University Press, pp. 674–720.

Ramcharan, B.G. (1985) 'The Concept and Dimensions of the Right to Life', in B.G. Ramcharan (ed.), *The Right to Life in International Law*, Dordrecht: Martinus Nijhoff Publishers, pp. 1–32.

—— (1985) 'The Drafting History of Article 6 of the International Covenant on Civil and Political Rights', in B.G. Ramcharan (ed.), *The Right to Life in International Law*, Dordrecht: Martinus Nijhoff Publishers, pp. 42–56

Ramseyer, Robert L. (1965) 'The *Sōka Gakkai*', in Richard K. Beardsley (ed.), *Studies in Japanese Culture: I*, The University of Michigan Centre for Japanese Studies Occasional Paper, no. 9, Ann Arbor, Mich.: University of Michigan, pp. 141–92.

Reich, Michael R. (1982) 'Public and Private Responses to a Chemical Disaster in Japan: The Case of Kanemi Yushō', *Law in Japan*, vol. 15, pp. 102–29.

Repeta, Lawrence (1987) 'The International Convention on Civil and Political Rights and Human Rights Law in Japan: Introduction to the First Five Issues of "Citizens' Human Rights Reports" by the Japan Civil Liberties Union', *Law in Japan*, vol. 20, pp. 1–28.

Saeki Hitoshi (1984) 'Puraibashii to meiyo no hogo' (The Protection of Privacy and Individual Dignity), *Hōgaku kyōkai zasshi*, vol. 101, no. 7, pp. 1–66; vol. 101, no. 8, pp. 22–63; vol. 101, no. 9, pp. 88–155; vol. 101, no. 11, pp. 1–83.

Saitō Seiichirō (1976) 'Goraku to supōtsu' (Amusements and Sports), in Umesao Tadao, *Nihonjin no seikatsu* (The Daily Life of the Japanese), Tōkyō, pp. 127–56.

Saitō Seiji (1979) *Keihō kōgi kakuron I* (Lectures on the Theories on Criminal Law I), rev. edn, Tōkyō.

—— (1987) *Keihō ni okeru seimei no hogo: nōshi, songenshi, zōki ishoku, taiji no shōgai* (The Protection of Life in Criminal Law: Brain Death, Death with Dignity, Internal Organ Transplants and Damage to Foetuses), Tōkyō.

Saitō Shigeo (1982) *Tsumatachi no shishūki* (Housewives' Autumn), Tōkyō.

Sakamoto Tarō *et al.* (eds) (1967) *Nihon shoki* (The Chronicles of Japan), vols. 67 and 68 of *Nihon koten bungaku taikei* (Japanese Classics Series), Tōkyō.

Sano Yōko (1988) 'Seven Mysteries of Long Working Hours', *Japan Quarterly*, vol. 35 (July–September), pp. 248–52.

Savage, Nigel (1980) *The Companies Act 1980*, London: McGraw-Hill.

Schlichtmann, Klaus (1995) 'The Ethics of Peace: Shidehara Kijūrō and Article 9 of the Constitution', *Japan Forum*, vol. 7, no. 1, pp. 43–67.

Sengoku Tamotsu (1985) *Willing Workers: The Work Ethics in Japan, England and the United States* (tr. Ezaki Kōichi and Ezaki Yūko), Westport, Conn.: Quorum Books.

Shigetomo Ki *et al.* (eds) (1958) *Chikamatsu jōrurishū* (A Collection of Chikamatsu's Ballad-Dramas), *jō* (vol. 1) and *ge* (vol. 2), in *Nihon koten bungaku taikei* (Japanese Classics Series), vols 49 and 50, Tōkyō.

Shimada Haruo (1991) 'The Desperate Need for New Values in Japanese Corporate Behaviour', *Journal of Japanese Studies*, vol. 17, no. 1, pp. 107–25.

Shimazu Ichirō (1974) 'Cases and Legislation Concerning Artificial Insemination: A Comparative Study of Japanese Law', *Hitotsubashi Journal of Law and Politics*, vol. 7, pp. 8–28.

Sieghart, Paul (1983) *The International Law of Human Rights*, Oxford: Clarendon Press.

—— (1985) *The Lawful Rights of Mankind: An Introduction to the International Legal Code of Human Rights*, Oxford: Oxford University Press.

—— (1989) *Aids and Human Rights: A UK Perspective*, London: British Medical Association Foundation for AIDS.

Siemes, Johannes (1966) *Herman Roesler and the Making of the Meiji State*, Tokyo: Sophia University Press.

Sissons, D.C.S. (1965) 'Human Rights Under the Japanese Constitution', *Papers on Modern Japan*, Canberra: Department of International Relations, Australian National University, pp. 50–69.

Smith, Bardwell (1988) 'Buddhism and Abortion in Contemporary Japan: *Mizuko Kuyō* and the Confrontation with Death', *Japanese Journal of Religious Studies*, vol. 15, no. 1 (March), pp. 3–24.

Smith, J.C. and Brian Hogan (1988) *Criminal Law*, 6th edn., London: Butterworths.

Steiner, Kurt (1956) 'A Japanese Case Célèbre: The Fukuoka Parricide Case', *American Journal of Comparative Law*, vol. 5, pp. 106–11.

Stockwin, J.A.A. (1982) *Japan: Divided Politics in a Growth Economy*, 2nd edn., London: Weidenfeld and Nicolson.

Supreme Commander for the Allied Powers (1970) *Political Reorientation of Japan, September 1945 to September 1948*, vol. 2, Westport, Conn.: Greenwood Press.

—— (1970) 'First Government Draft of the Constitution, 4 March 1946', in *Political Reorientation of Japan, September 1945 to September 1948*, vol. 2, Westport, Conn.: Greenwood Press, pp. 625–30.

Tabata Hirokuni (1990) 'Japanese Welfare State: Its Structure and Transformation', *Annals of the Institute of Social Science* (Institute of Social Science, University of Tokyo), no. 32, pp. 1–29.

Tachibana Takashi (1992) *Nōshi rinchō hihan* (Criticism on the Report of the Committee on Brain Death), Tōkyō.

Taeuber, Irene B. (1958) *The Population of Japan*, Princeton, N.J.: Princeton University Press.

Takahashi Sachiko (1991) 'Weary Wives: A Glance Into Japanese Homes Through "Wives of a Kingdom" and "Housewives' Autumn" ', *AMPO: Japan–Asia Quarterly Review*, vol. 18, nos. 2/3, pp. 65–9.

Takayanagi Kenzō (1963) 'A Century of Innovation: The Development of Japanese Law, 1861–1961', in Arthur Taylor von Mehren, *Law in Japan: The Legal Order in a Changing Society*, Cambridge, Mass.: Harvard University Press, pp. 5–40.

Takeuchi Akio (tr. Malcolm D.H. Smith) (1978) 'Should There Be a General Provision on the Social Responsibility of Enterprises in the Commercial Code?', *Law in Japan*, vol. 11, pp. 37–56.

Takikawa Haruo and Takeuchi Tadashi (1965) *Keihō kakuron kōgi* (Lectures on the Theories of Criminal Law), Tōkyō.

Takikawa Kōtatsu (1951) *Keihō kakuron* (Theories on Criminal Law), Tōkyō.

Takikawa Masajirō (1964) *Nihon gyōkei shi* (A History of Japanese Penology), Tōkyō.

—— (1985) *Nihon hōseishi* (A History of the Japanese Legal System), *jō* (vol. 1) and *ge* (vol. 2), Tōkyō.

Tanaka Hideo (ed.) (1976) *The Japanese Legal System: Introductory Cases and Materials*, Tokyo.

Taniguchi Seichō (1975) *Nani ga taisetsu ka?* (What's Important?), Akarui Nihon o tsukuru shirizu kankōkai (Association for Publishing Series on the Making of a Cheerful Japan), Tōkyō.

Tawaragi Kotarō (1992) 'Nihonjin no hōishiki ni okeru "kenri" to "kengi" ' (Concerning '*Kenri*' and '*Kengi*' in the Japanese Sense of Law), *Hōgaku Kenkyū* (Legal Studies) (Faculty of Law, Keiō University), vol. 65, no. 12, pp. 271–88.

Thomson, William A.R. (1977) *A Dictionary of Medical Ethics and Practice*, Bristol.

Tietze, Christopher (1979) *Induced Abortion*, 3rd edn, New York: Population Council.

'Tokushū: nōshi o meguru shomondai' (Special Issue: Various Problems Concerning Brain Death), *Hōritsu no hiroba*, vol. 38, no. 8, pp. 4–45.

Tomatsu Hidenori (1993) 'Equal Protection of the Law', in Percy R. Luney, Jr. and Takahashi Kazuyuki (eds), *Japanese Constitutional Law*, Tokyo: University of Tokyo Press, pp. 187–204.

Treggiari, Susan (1991) *Roman Marriage: Iusti Coniuges from the Time of Cicero to the Time of Ulpian*, Oxford: Oxford University Press.

Tsuda Mamichi (1976) 'On the Death Penalty', in William Reynolds

Braisted (tr. with introduction), *Meiroku Zasshi: Journal of the Japanese Enlightenment*, Tokyo: Tokyo University Press, pp. 498–500.

Tsugita Masaki (tr. and notes) (1984) *Kojiki* (Records of Ancient Matters), vol. 3, (*ge*), Tōkyō.

Uchida Fumiaki (1984) *Keihō kakuron* (Theories on Criminal Law), 2nd edn, Tōkyō.

Uchida Fumiaki *et al.* (1990) *Chikujō hanrei keihō* (Cases and Notes on Criminal Law), Tōkyō.

Uehata Tetsunojō (1988) 'Shokugyōsei sutoresu ni yoru karōshi' (Death from Overwork Due to Occupational Stress), in Hosokawa Migiwa (ed.), *Shinrōdō kagaku hen* (New Work Science: A Selection), May, p. 683.

Uematsu Tadashi (1975) *Keihō gairon II kakuron* (An Outline of Theories of Criminal Law II), rev. edn, Tōkyō.

Uesugi Shinkichi (1935) *Teikoku kenpō chikujō kōgi* (A Lecture on Items of the Imperial Constitution), Tōkyō.

—— (1943 [1913]) (ed.) *Hozumi Yatsuka hakase ronbunshū* (Collected Essays of Dr Hozumi Yatsuka), rev. edn, Hozumi Shigetaka (ed.), Tōkyō.

Ukai Nobushige and Nathaniel L. Nathanson (1968) 'Protection of Property Rights and Due Process of Law in the Japanese Constitution', in Dan Fenno Henderson (ed.), *The Constitution of Japan: Its First Twenty Years, 1947–67*, Seattle: University of Washington Press, pp. 239–55.

Umeda Toshirō (1989) 'Transplants Forbidden', *Japan Quarterly*, vol. 36, no. 2 (April–June), pp. 146–54.

Umehara Takeshi (1982) *Bukkyō no shisō I* (Buddhist Thought, I), vol. 5 of *Umehara Takeshi chosakushū* (Collected Works of Umehara Takeshi), Tōkyō.

—— (ed.) (1992) *Nōshi wa shi de nai* (Brain Death is Not Death), Kyōto.

Urabe Noriho (1993) 'Rule of Law and Due Process: A Comparative View of the United States and Japan', in Percy R. Luney Jr. and Takahashi Kazuyuki (eds), *Japanese Constitutional Law*, Tokyo: University of Tokyo Press, pp. 173–86.

von Gierke, Otto (1883) 'Labands Staatsrecht und die Deutsche Rechtswissenschaft' (The State Rights of Laband and German Studies on Law), in *Schmollers Jahrbuch für Gesetzgebung, Verwaltung und Volkswirtschaft im Deutschen Reich*, vol. 7, no. 4, pp. 1097–1195.

von Mehren, Arthur Taylor (ed.) (1963) *Law in Japan: The Legal Order in a Changing Society*, Cambridge, Mass.: Harvard University Press.

von Stein, J. (1914) *Thibaut und Savigny: zum 100 jährigen Gedächtnis des Kampfes um ein einheitliches bürgerliches Recht für Deutschland, 1814–1914* (Thibaut and Savigny: On the Centenary of the Struggle for a Uniform Civil Law for Germany, 1814–1914), Berlin: Berlag von Franz Bahlen.

Wakabayashi, Judy (1994) 'The Death Penalty in Japan', *Japan Forum*, vol. 6, no. 2, pp. 189–205.

Walker, Nigel (1968) *Crime and Punishment in Britain*, 2nd rev. edn, Edinburgh: Edinburgh University Press.

Watsuji Tetsurō (1971 [1935]) *Fūdo: ningengakuteki na kōsatsu* (Tōkyō 1935). Tr. by G. Bownas under the title, *Climate and Culture: A Philosophical Study* (Tokyo 1971).

Wheaton, Henry (1863) *Elements of International Law, With a Sketch of the History of the Science*, Boston: Little, Brown & Co.

Williams, Noel (1991) 'The Right to Life Under the Japanese Constitution', A paper delivered at a Nissan Institute Seminar, the University of Oxford, on 17 May.

—— (1995) 'Corporate Social Responsibility and the Community', *Kenkyū hōkoku* (Bulletin), Minami Kyūshū University, no. 25(B), (Cultural and Social Science), pp. 121–201.

—— (1996) 'Taiji no seimei wa dare no mono ka? –Igirisu dewa dō kangaerarete iru ka?' (The Foetus's Life is Whose? How is this Matter Viewed in Britain?), A paper presented at a public lecture delivered at Daitō Bunka University, Tokyo, 28 September.

Williams, Yōko (1990) 'The Concept of *Tsumi*', A paper delivered at the Japan Anthropology Workshop's International Symposium on 'Ceremony and Ritual' held at Leiden University, the Netherlands, 26–30 March.

—— (1991) 'The Resolution of *Tsumi*', A paper delivered at the Japan Anthropology Workshop's International Symposium on 'Rethinking Japanese Religion' held at Newnham College, the University of Cambridge, 3–5 April.

Wise, Edward (ed. and tr.) (1978) *Italian Penal Code*, London: Sweet & Maxwell.

Wolfe, Alan (1990) *Suicidal Narrative in Modern Japan: The Case of Dazai Osamu*, Princeton, N.J.: Princeton University Press.

Woodard, William P. (1972) *The Allied Occupation of Japan 1945–1952 and Japanese Religion*, Leiden: E.J. Brill.

Yamaori Tetsuo (1983) *Kami to hotoke* (Gods and Buddha), Tōkyō.

Yano Yūko (1993) 'Boasonādo no shikei haishiron ni kansuru ichi kōsatsu' (An Essay on Boissonade's Theory on the Abolition of the Death Penalty), *Hōgaku Seijigaku Ronkyū* (Journal of Law and Political Studies), Graduate School of Law, Keiō University, no. 17 (Summer), pp. 71–105.

Yasuhira Masakichi (1960) *Kaisei keihō kakuron* (Revised Theories on Criminal Law), Tōkyō.

Yatome Fumimaro (1990) 'Iwayuru anrakushi ni tsuite no ichi kōsatsu: Mori Ōgai "Takasebune" o tōshite' (Euthanasia in Mori Ōgai's *'Takasebune'*), *Dōhō Daigaku Kiyō* (Bulletin of Dōhō University, Institute of Liberal and General Education), no. 4, pp. 131–46.

Yoshikawa Tsuneo (1982) *Keihō kakuron* (Theories on Criminal Law), Tōkyō.

Yuasa Yasuo (1987) *The Body: Toward an Eastern Mind–Body Theory* (tr. Nagatomo Shigenori and Thomas P. Kasulis), New York: State University of New York Press.

Index

abortion 17–23; consent to in English law 27; consent to in Japanese law 18–19, 27–8; consent to in Roman law 27; crimes of 17–19, 27; numbers of 20; opposition to 21–2
absenteeism 76
actus reus 30
akugyaku 56–7
amatsutsumi 6
American Convention on Human Rights 1978 86
American Declaration on the Rights and Duties of Man 1948 86
amnesty *see onsha*
Amnesty Law 1947 39
anrakushi 27, 94, 118 n54
apology suicide 78–83, 95–7; *see also* suicide
appeals system 31, 36–40
Aquinas, Thomas 3
artificial insemination 28
Ashibe Nobuyoshi 14
assisted suicide 25; *see also* suicide
Augustine, St 3
Austin, John 67–8

ba 95
baby boom 19
Bay, Christian 93–4
Bentham, Jeremy 49
birth 16–23, 25
brain death *see nōshi*
British Association for the Advancement of Science 23

British School of Law *see Hōgakushi kai*
Buddhism 45, 93
Bull, Hedley 52

capital punishment 27, 29–50, 86, 89; abolition of 42–8; and age 29–30, 43; appropriate procedures established by law 29–41; Buddhism 45–6; character of *jus cogens* 46; Confucianism 46; constitutionality of 41–4, 47; as cruel 41–4; death penalty order 40–1; and insanity 29–30; and pregnancy 29–30, 43; and treason in English Law 54
Chikamatsu Monzaemon 26
chokkei sonzoku 60; and right to life 55–70
Chūō Kōsei hogo shinsakai 39
Cicero, Marcus Tullius 3
Civil Aviation Law 1952 33
Civil Code 1898, Japanese 16, 60, 99–100
Clark, Rodney 72
Code of Criminal Procedure 1948, Japanese 35, 37, 40
Commercial Code, Japanese 72
Commission on the Constitution 12, 48, 67
company; arrangements after death 80–1; as artificial person 73–4, 90; corporate form and structure 4, 72, 83–4; corporate social responsibility 81–4; *daihyō*